rvic.

MEN AND THE EMERGENCE
OF POLITE SOCIETY, BRITAIN
1660–1800

WOMEN AND MEN IN HISTORY

This series, published for students, scholars and interested general readers, will tackle themes in gender history from the early medieval period through to the present day. Gender issues are now an integral part of all history courses and yet many traditional texts do not reflect this change. Much exciting work is now being done to redress the gender imbalances of the past, and we hope that these books will make their own substantial contribution to that process. We hope that these will both synthesise and shape future developments in gender studies.

The General Editors of the series are *Patricia Skinner* (University of Southampton) for the medieval period; *Pamela Sharpe* (University of Bristol) for the early modern period; and *Penny Summerfield* (University of Lancaster) for the modern period. *Margaret Walsh* (University of Nottingham) was the Founding Editor of the series.

Published books:

Imperial Women in Byzantium, 1025–1204: Power, Patronage and Ideology
Barbara Hill

Masculinity in Medieval Europe
D.M. Hadley (ed.)

Gender and Society in Renaissance Italy
Judith C. Brown and Robert C. Davis (eds)

Widowhood in Medieval and Early Modern Europe
Sandra Cavallo and Lyndan Warner (eds)

Gender, Church and State in Early Modern Germany: Essays by Merry E. Wiesner
Merry E. Wiesner

Manhood in Early Modern England: Honour, Sex and Marriage
Elizabeth W. Foyster

English Masculinities, 1600–1800
Tim Hitchcock and Michele Cohen (eds)

Disorderly Women in Eighteenth-Century London: Prostitution in the Metropolis, 1730–1830
Tony Henderson

Gender, Power and the Unitarians in England, 1760–1860
Ruth Watts

Practical Visionaries Women, Education and Social Progress, 1790–1930
Mary Hilton and Pam Hirsch (eds)

Women and Work in Russia, 1880–1930: A Study in Continuity through Change
Jane McDermid and Anna Hillyar

More than Munitions: Women, Work and the Engineering Industries, 1900–1950
Clare Wightman

Women in British Public Life, 1914–1950: Gender, Power and Social Policy
Helen Jones

The Family Story: Blood, Contract and Intimacy, 1830–1960
Leonore Davidoff, Megan Doolittle, Janet Fink and Katherine Holden

Women and the Second World War in France, 1939–1948: Choices and Constraints
Hanna Diamond

MEN AND THE EMERGENCE OF POLITE SOCIETY, BRITAIN 1660–1800

PHILIP CARTER

Longman

An imprint of **Pearson Education**

Harlow, England · London · New York · Reading, Massachusetts · San Francisco
Toronto · Don Mills, Ontario · Sydney · Tokyo · Singapore · Hong Kong · Seoul
Taipei · Cape Town · Madrid · Mexico City · Amsterdam · Munich · Paris · Milan

Pearson Education Limited
Edinburgh Gate
Harlow
Essex CM20 2JE
England

and Associated Companies throughout the world

Visit us on the World Wide Web at:
http://www.pearsoneduc.com

First published 2001

© Pearson Education Limited 2001

ISBN 0 582 31986 2 (hbk)   0 582 31987 0 (pbk)

British Library Cataloguing-in-Publication Data
A catalogue record for this book is available from the British Library

Library of Congress Cataloging-in-Publication Data
Carter, Philip.
    Men and the emergence of polite society, Britain 1660–1800 / Philip Carter.
        p. cm. — (Women and men in history)
    Includes bibliographical references and index.
    ISBN 0-582-31986-2 — ISBN 0-582-31987-0 (pbk.)
    1. Men—Europe—History. 2. Masculinity—Europe—History. 3. Courtesy—
Europe—History. 4. Etiquette—Europe—History. 5. Europe—Social life and
customs. I. Title. II. Series.

HQ1090.7.E85 C37 2000
305.31′094—dc21   00–041640

Transferred to digital print on demand, 2006

Typeset by 35 in 11/13pt Baskerville MT
Produced by Pearson Education Asia Pte Ltd.
Printed and bound by CPI Antony Rowe, Eastbourne

CONTENTS

LIST OF FIGURES

ACKNOWLEDGEMENTS

I have benefited greatly from the comments and support of many people during the writing of this book. My biggest academic debt is to Joanna Innes, who has consistently and generously offered encouragement, guidance and criticism since this project's origin as a D.Phil thesis: it has been a pleasure to study with her over the last decade. I am also grateful to Donna Andrew, Hannah Barker, Laurence Brockliss, Elaine Chalus, Michèle Cohen, Elizabeth Foyster, Tim Hitchcock, Martin Ingram, Mary Catherine Moran, Roy Porter, Guy Rowlands, Pamela Sharpe and Alex Shepard for their advice at various stages of research and writing.

Konstantin Dierks, Susan Skedd and David Taylor read earlier drafts of the book and their suggestions have considerably improved what follows. I am especially grateful to Sarah Knott, both for her detailed reading of the manuscript and her stimulating conversation and friendship. I would also like to thank my colleagues at the *New DNB*, in particular Michael Bevan, Robert Brown and Annette Peach, for their help and advice. Anne-Pascale Bruneau, Lacy Rumsey and Glenn Timmermans have also been extremely supportive throughout.

Lastly, four people offered reassurance and a sense of perspective when writing made me more blackguard than polite gentleman. This book is for Meg, my brother Tim and my parents Joan and John, with thanks.

We are grateful to the following for permission to reproduce copyright material:

Figure 4.1 and Figure 4.2 © copyright the British Museum; cover: 'The bow' from François Nivelon, *The Rudiments* of *Genteel Behaviour* (1737), by permission of the British Library (British Library Shelfmark 1812.a.28).

INTRODUCTION

Gentlemen, manliness and polite society

On 25 October 1773 Samuel Johnson and James Boswell visited Inveraray Castle in Scotland as the guests of the duke and duchess of Argyll. 'When I went into Dr Johnson's room', wrote Boswell two days later, 'I observed to him how wonderfully courteous he had been at Inveraray, and said, "You were quite a fine gentleman, when with the duchess." He answered, in good humour, "Sir I look upon myself as a very polite man": and he was right, in a proper manly sense of the word.'[1]

This book examines conceptions of, and the interaction between, Johnson's twin attributes – politeness and manliness – over the course of the late seventeenth and eighteenth centuries. It argues that the period saw the emergence of an explicitly innovative concept of social refinement – politeness – practised by and within 'polite society', by which is meant the personnel who sought politeness and the locations, broadly defined as the nation or the city, or as specific venues including coffee-houses, public gardens and the home, where refined conduct was expected and encouraged. My focus here is on the impact of polite society for eighteenth-century definitions of the refined 'gentleman', and also, given polite society's broad application and appeal, its implication for definitions of manliness, here understood as desirable and emulative male behaviour. To its proponents, the emergence of polite society was a consequence of significant, and welcome, late-seventeenth-century social and economic change, consolidated and further stimulated by the political settlement following the Glorious Revolution (1688–9). Through these events the nation was, it was argued, becoming more powerful, prosperous, tolerant and civilised. To these writers, politeness was the means to acquire a suitably refined, yet virtuous, personality that proved superior to many existing forms of manly virtue which, on account of their association with elitism, violence or boorishness, were judged detrimental to truly polite sociability.

1

The precise nature of this improvement in gentlemanly conduct pro-voked debate among writers advocating a reform of male manners. Of these debates, the most significant was that between polite theorists and mid- to late-eighteenth-century proponents of an alternative discourse of refinement: sensibility. Sponsors of this latter culture claimed that existing forms of polite conduct had lost their moral integrity and had become a source of duplicity and snobbery, not sociability. In its place, sentimental writers encouraged more spontaneous, and hence more genuine, displays of social interaction.[2] This debate over modes of refinement also had consequences for mid- to late-eighteenth-century discussions of gentlemanly conduct, as well as the meaning of manliness in an age now seemingly given over to a degree of emotion traditionally associated with women.

At the same time, numerous social commentators remained unconvinced by the association of desirable male conduct with polite society, not least because of men's closer integration with female company. These sceptics, often alarmed by what they saw as the debilitating effects of socio-economic change, sought to defend manhood from what, in their opinion, were un-welcome modes of refinement destructive of existing moral and physical standards. For many of these critics, polite society encouraged 'effeminacy', not improved standards of manliness.

To an extent, this important and vigorous eighteenth-century debate was conducted over matters of nuance rather than basic substance. Like its critics, promoters of refined manhood appreciated the merits of traditional manly attributes which they too considered as central to a new gender identity. Whereas critics saw traditional values, such as sense, self-control and courage, under threat, reformers encouraged gentlemen to adapt these skills into new standards of polite or sentimental manhood. To appreciate the enduring appeal of more traditional male values helps us to see late-seventeenth- and eighteenth-century conceptions of the gentleman less as a dramatic break with the past than as a complex blend of contemporary and more established qualities reconfigured according to the preferences of individual conduct writers and their readers. Important for understanding the debate over manhood during the emergence and consolidation of polite society, this theme of continuity also goes some way to explain the contours of nineteenth-century manliness on its decline.

Aims and context

We might start our investigation by looking at how one of these real-life polite gentlemen, Samuel Johnson, earned his companion's (and his own) praise. Boswell's journal entry for 25 October 1773 provided a detailed description of the evening's events. At one point, Johnson spoke in defence of luxury, and challenged his fellow diners to refute his thesis. The duke then proposed a counter-argument; in turn, Johnson responded, but in doing so 'politely refrained from opposing directly an observation which the duke himself had made'. After dinner Johnson sat with the duke's daughter, Lady Betty Hamilton, and with the duchess, to whom he was 'all attention'. 'I never saw him so gentle and complaisant as this day', wrote Boswell, reflecting on the scene. As they were leaving, the duke also showed himself 'exceedingly polite' by offering Johnson a horse on which to continue his journey; Johnson's decision to thank the duke by letter on the following day provided Boswell with further 'immediate proof' of the politeness shown during the previous evening.[3]

Boswell recalls an encounter that certainly appears to have been extremely civilised. His description brims over with the language and actions of polite living – the duke's kindness and generosity, Johnson's gentleness, deference, considered and considerate conversation, and careful listening – all of which, as we shall see, featured prominently in eighteenth-century guides to idealised sociability. These refinements were perhaps not surprising in such elite and educated company. However, Johnson and the duke were not the only polite men whom Boswell encountered in the autumn of 1773. In early September on the Isle of Skye he and Johnson had enjoyed the company of the Laird of Rasay, 'a sensible, polite and most hospitable gentleman'. There he also met Malcolm Macleod, 'hale . . . tanned by the weather . . . the perfect representation of a Highland Gentleman', whom Boswell found '*polite*, in the true sense of the word'. Later that month he and Johnson were received 'with much kindness' by Martin M'Pherson, a minister from southern Skye, whose 'manners and address pleased us much'. In just over two weeks they reached the island of Mull, where they met with Mr Campbell, a 'genteel, agreeable man' and 'so polite'. Finally, as bad weather slowed their return to the mainland, the pair were forced to shelter in a 'mean' house but 'were agreeably surprised with the appearance of the master [Lachlan MacQuarrie], whom we found to be intelligent, polite, and much a man of the world'.[4]

From these observations several points are worthy of note: the apparent readiness and ability of these men to act politely; the breadth of a gentlemanly ideal comprising dukes, churchmen and small-holders; and, finally, the regularity with which Boswell chose to comment on men's politeness, and the importance he attached to refinement in discussions of admirable male characters. Of course, we should exercise caution when seeking to draw conclusions from this analysis. Boswell provides a personal account based on interpretative evidence, written at a time when many Scottish authors were promoting Highland society as a location of innate sociability and refinement, ranking it alongside, if not above, Lowland and English urban culture.[5]

This said, the following study shows that the views and interests of a commentator like Boswell were widely shared during a period in which, as Anthony Fletcher argues, the 'crucial ingredient in masculinity . . . seems to be the notion of civility'.[6] It is not my proposal that the years 1660–1800 witnessed the 'invention' of the relationship between social refinement and desirable male conduct. Even self-consciously progressive eighteenth-century authors looked to ancient and more recent history for instances and exemplars of aspects of refined behaviour. Likewise, twentieth-century historians have long viewed the eighteenth-century interest in social refinement as a manifestation of a much longer 'civilising process' traceable to the dissemination of sixteenth-century Italian and Dutch humanist thought.[7] A key aspect of this research has been an appreciation of the significance of the civilised male – enshrined in the figure of the Italian courtier, the French *honnête homme* and their English amalgam, the gentleman – as an agent and symbol of this process.

Through translations of Italian and French texts, as well as via original studies, sixteenth- and seventeenth-century English courtesy literature provided predominantly elite men with training in the refined accomplishments necessary for success in court and country life. This tradition was not only influential but apparently enduring. According to several recent studies of eighteenth-century behavioural literature, the courtesy genre remained the principal 'literary expression of gentlemanly qualities . . . until the 1770s', when it finally dwindled following criticism of its last manifestation, Lord Chesterfield's controversial *Letters to His Son* (1774).[8]

James Boswell's experience in Scotland certainly appears to go some way to substantiate these claims. His praise for the duke of Argyll's refinement, for example, depended in part on the latter's status as the all-round gentleman – politician, businessman, social host and man of letters – as had been proposed in numerous guides over the previous two centuries. Likewise, Boswell's admiration for Lachlan MacQuarrie's refinement may have owed something to his being a presumably learned and well-travelled 'man of the world' unexpectedly discovered in a remote Scottish community. Yet it is equally evident that Boswell's understanding of gentlemanly conduct did not depend on such credentials alone. It is significant that he reserved most praise for two men, the plain Malcolm Macleod and the often bluff Dr Johnson, who in their different ways fell short of the early modern ideal of the complete gentlemen, but whose genuine, if not always polished, sociability came closest to the requirements of what Boswell, like many throughout the eighteenth century, specifically valorised as the novel and superior quality of 'politeness'.[9]

As Chapter One shows, this identification of politeness as a distinct phase within a longer tradition is helpful in highlighting some of the distinguishing features of, and shifts in, late-seventeenth- and eighteenth-century concepts of polite society. Against the backdrop of the development and dissemination of this society, Chapters Two to Five explore the relationship of men and social refinement through an examination of three areas: first, discussions of suitable and unsuitable gentlemanly behaviour, as detailed in theoretical statements on the concept of politeness and in prescriptive advice literature; second, the effects of refinement on eighteenth-century notions of manliness, as discussed again in advice manuals as well as in writings on the subject of politeness, and academic analyses of social change; and, finally, the impact of these debates on real social actors (including Boswell) as told through diaries, correspondence and journals.

The theme of manliness has to date merited relatively little attention in historical studies of prescriptive advice literature. Historians of the early modern courtesy book, for example, have tended to treat the subjects of this explicitly male-centred genre as without gender; the courtesy book's aim being the cultivation of individuals whose identity was principally determined by their superior social status.[10] By contrast, historians of eighteenth-century politeness have long been aware of the interrelationship of social refinement and gender but have predominantly discussed this link with reference to women, often associating the emergence of a self-consciously polite culture with the 'feminisation' of society, in which women were now identified as agents of refinement, and were encouraged to participate in certain venues where polite sociability occurred.[11]

Of course the lack of an equivalent investigation into constructions of manliness may partly reflect the absence of explicit discussions within eighteenth-century behavioural literature. Many later seventeenth- and eighteenth-century accounts of male behaviour at first sight do indeed appear little concerned with questions of gender identity. As in an earlier courtesy tradition, identities were fashioned first and foremost with reference to men's performance in relation to issues such as profession, religion and nationality. For men to fall short of these standards was unacceptable, yet the penalties were seemingly ungendered on account of these being goals which men alone were expected to attain – to fail was therefore not 'unmanly' but, to use the language of the time, dishonourable, popish or 'Frenchified'.

However, it would be wrong to claim that such labels were free from connotations of gender. A major feature of recent histories of masculinity has been the realisation that male gender identity was (and is) constructed in relation not just to women, but also, crucially, in relation to other men. In assessing the quality of alternative male lifestyles or personalities it was common, as recent studies show, to identify differences in social practice, religion or national identity in terms of men's competence compared to other more, or less, 'manly' individuals.[12]

It was precisely this competition between male identities that ensured the importance of gender issues in eighteenth-century discussions on the nature of the gentleman. The tone of these discussions was conditioned by the widespread attraction and availability of aspects of polite society. This scope ushered in what Paul Langford describes as an eighteenth-century 'debasement of gentility'; that is, the redeployment of social titles – 'Mr' and 'Mrs'/'gentleman' and 'lady' – from individuals who traditionally occupied specific positions and performed specific social duties to anyone, regardless of profession or social background, laying 'claim to a degree of rank and respectability'.[13] An end to the traditional association of gentlemen with members of a social elite engaged in responsible and traditionally male roles such as politics, law, landholding or warriorship meant the conferring of gentlemanly status on the many rather than the few.

Langford's focus is the changing scope of politeness for eighteenth-century notions of the *gentle*man; but these changes also had implications for contemporary perceptions of gentle*manliness*. Shifting definitions of the gentleman demanded a careful restatement of the reasons why, especially given women's prominence, male participation in polite society underpinned rather than undermined manliness. This restatement took a variety of forms. Thus, eighteenth-century academic analysts offered a history of human social relations which revealed that maleness was not a fixed quality defined by an attachment to a particular social role. As Mary Catherine Moran shows, mid- to late-eighteenth-century Scottish conjectural historians highlighted the malleability of male gender identity compared to the relative stasis of women's nature in the course of human history. Men's personalities, and hence the meaning of manhood, were believed to have changed – according to these commentators for the better – as they became increasingly appreciative of and keen to impress in respectable female company.[14] More practical accounts of male conduct also highlighted the potential for and the benefits of change. In these guides modern gentlemen were shown to draw much of their gender identity from the superiority of their speech, conduct and moral personality compared to other, less refined, and less manly, individuals.

However, an equally large number of commentators were convinced not only that polite society failed to guarantee manliness but that its popularity now threatened traditional male values. To expand on Anthony Fletcher's earlier comment, it would appear that refined behaviour was seen as not only a principal means to acquire manliness, but also one of the surest ways to lose that identity. Both outcomes are certainly implicit in the reported exchange with which I began. Boswell's identification of Johnson as polite 'in the proper manly sense of the word' commended a refined performance that he deemed befitting and productive of manliness. At the same time, Boswell's gendering of a man's polite actions also implied the possibility for certain forms of polite conduct, and those displaying such traits, to be judged as unmanly.

Both critics and proponents of polite society assessed modern gentle-manliness in terms of its proximity to the nebulous yet always troubling state of 'effeminacy'. Detractors anticipated the substitution of traditionally manly qualities such as physical vigour, civic-mindedness and independence, for effeminate conduct defined in terms of delicacy, triviality and debilitating self-indulgence. Modernisers refuted these claims, although throughout our period (and increasingly towards its end) they too appreciated that, without strict regulations, a proficiency for social polish risked reducing men to this unacceptable condition.

Eighteenth-century commentators were not the first to identify a potentially problematic relationship between refinement and normative standards of male conduct. Susan Shapiro's study of medieval and Anna Bryson's survey of early modern civility, for example, both trace the motif of the effeminate courtier as far back as the twelfth century.[15] Yet to appreciate the durability of a concept like effeminacy is not to define the characteristics of that concept at any given historical moment. Michèle Cohen argues precisely this point when she warns against making assumptions about the meaning of effeminacy in past societies. Instead she calls for the historicisation of this once seemingly ahistorical subject, as has recently occurred with early modern concepts of luxury, sexuality and femininity.[16] In doing so, Cohen suggests that understanding the meaning of effeminacy at the time allows us to appreciate the specific factors by which seventeenth- and eighteenth-century commentators defined and evaluated failed, as well as more successful, styles of refined manhood.

Current historiographical debates on eighteenth-century concepts of effeminacy owe much to historians of sexuality, especially male homosexuality. Scholars like Randolph Trumbach have argued for a shift in representations of the homosexual from a seventeenth-century image of the bisexual, rakish libertine to, by the early eighteenth century, a new exclusively homosexual type, the 'molly', identified by his misogyny, transvestism and effeminacy. This equation with effeminacy prompts Trumbach to identify sexual orientation as the key factor in establishing eighteenth-century boundaries between failed and unacceptable manliness, defined as the consequence of deviant (homosexual) and acceptable (heterosexual) sexual activity.[17]

This focus on sexuality as a determinant of manliness is also followed in several more recent studies of early modern manhood, though in these subtler analyses sexuality exists as one aspect within a broader spectrum of male gender identity. As Elizabeth Foyster shows, a reputation for sexual activity, and the avoidance of the stigma of cuckoldry, were central to seventeenth-century notions of male honour. Yet her survey of church court records and popular balladry demonstrates that men's acquiring, maintaining or regaining of a manly sexual reputation was also closely connected to their capacity for other, integral aspects of the manly personality, among them moderation, self-discipline and physical aggression.[18] Foyster's study is part of a recent, welcome trend to acknowledge the complexities and multiplicity of male gender identities in the late seventeenth and eighteenth centuries.[19]

In her own work, Michèle Cohen makes a similar contribution to our understanding of eighteenth-century concepts of manhood; first, as a social category and, second, as an identity principally characterised by an on-going debate over the gentleman's relation to polite society. In doing so, she complements G.J. Barker-Benfield's study of an eighteenth-century 'culture of sensibility', which he identifies as the key motive force for a century-long 'reformation of male manners' from former standards of boorishness to new levels of sensitivity and delicacy.[20] Read together these two studies offer distinctive, but in some senses equally static, pictures of what was in fact a highly fluid discourse of social refinement. Thus, Cohen's focus on the influence of late-seventeenth-century French politeness on the English gentleman overlooks the mid- to late-eighteenth-century development of a culture of sensibility whose contributors, many of whom were Scottish not English, were often motivated by a reaction to earlier models of politeness. Equally, Barker-Benfield's description of sensibility as a general process of refinement across our period underplays the distinction between early (polite) and later (sentimental) eighteenth-century accounts of the gentleman, and in turn the shifting concept of manliness between the two.

By contrast, this book examines the impact of both politeness and sensibility onthe debates surrounding the ideal gentleman and notions of manliness. Crucially, however, it also considers the tensions between these discourses and, in addition, the characteristics of a broader debate between proponents of refined manhood and those who viewed polite society as a source of effeminacy. Principally a book about male gender identity within polite society, it is also my aim to suggest some of the complexities of this latter phenomenon. To understand the vibrancy of polite society for eighteenth-century culture, we need to see it not just as a history of ideas and ideals but as a history of competitions played out, for example, between sober fathers and their irresponsibly refined sons; or as a history of aspirations and self-doubt, as witnessed in the men described in Chapter Five, who struggled to gain and maintain a reputation for gentlemanliness.

The findings of this book are drawn from the type of literature – courtesy books, conduct guides, essay periodicals, magazines, sermons, academic papers and treatises – to which these men often turned for advice and insight. Readers of such material were presented with a discussion of manliness defined specifically in terms of social behaviour with other men, and now with women, in which references to sexual activity were invariably deemed inappropriate and indeed impolite. To argue for manliness as a social category is not to deny the existence of alternative definitions promoting sexuality.[21] However, it is equally the case that eighteenth-century literature on polite society produced important developments in the conceptualisation of idealised manliness from the sexual to the social; or, in terms of popular images of failed manhood, from sexually limited seventeenth-century cuckolds to socially inadequate eighteenth-century fops.

In view of the source material on which much of this book is based, the following chapters are predominantly concerned with *representations* of the gentleman. This decision derives from the still underdeveloped state of historical research into late-seventeenth- and eighteenth-century ideals of manliness, which historians too often associate with sexuality, and of polite society, too often identified as a holistic, English/metropolitan phenomenon. Understanding the terms by which commentators debated male behaviour provides us with a better understanding of eighteenth-century definitions of the qualities determining acceptable and unacceptable gentlemanly conduct, and how these qualities changed over the period 1660–1800.

Chapter outline

Chapter One looks at some of the principal characteristics of late-seventeenth- and eighteenth-century polite society. It examines the different ways in which eighteenth-century commentators envisaged the personnel and location of a concept ranging from the select few, to 'purpose built' centres such as Bath, to the notion of a broader nationwide 'civil society'. This chapter also assesses current historiography on the rise of the polite and sentimental discourses central to polite society, and the means by which these ideas were widely disseminated and practised in a series of new urban venues where gentlemen could expect to find and nurture their reputation for refinement. It has been an implicit assumption of much recent scholarship that men's participation in these public arenas of coffee-house, park and pleasure garden was an unproblematic means of confirming gender identity when contrasted with the restrictions placed on women's involvement. However, by examining debates on manliness as defined principally in relation to other men, not women, we see a more difficult relationship between manhood and public activity which late-seventeenth- and eighteenth-century polite theorists and conduct writers sought to address in accounts of suitably gentlemanly conduct.

Chapter Two examines how these writers encouraged new styles of refined manhood distinguishable from existing images of the early modern courtier and the country gentleman. In place of these figures, reformers proposed the 'polite town gentleman' as the embodiment of more relaxed and genuine forms of sociability located in a series of professional and leisured urban venues. Central to the refined gentleman's genuine sociability was his synthesis of external manners with an inner virtue based on a Christian morality which theorists considered a necessary requirement for participation in polite society. However, despite efforts to characterise politeness as the social expression of good character, it remained a persistent fear that politeness, detached from its moral obligations, would become a tool for selfish deception, not sociability. Such concerns became more pronounced from mid-century, and were fuelled by publications such as Lord Chesterfield's *Letters to His Son* (1774) that were widely condemned for advocating a duplicitous code of social refinement for personal advancement.

Chapter Three argues that the response to Chesterfield's correspondence owed much of its momentum to an already well-established discourse of sensibility. It had been the reaction of early-eighteenth-century theorists against what they saw as the artificiality and stiff formality of early modern courtiers that gave politeness its credibility and appeal. Now, sentimental commentators called for a similar refom to counteract what they believed to be the inherent hypocrisy and corruption of out-dated and formal styles of politeness. The culture of sensibility also required that men revise their understanding of refined and sociable conduct. Whereas accounts of politeness stressed the need for sincere sociability tempered by control, discussions of the later eighteenth-century 'man of feeling' placed greater emphasis on instinctive displays of emotion as an indication of a new style of refined and virtuous manliness. Less dependent on polite conversation, the man of feeling expressed his refinement through a wordless language of actions including weeping, trembling or displays of nervous illness. The apparent similarity of these actions to those expected of refined women did not go unnoticed. Chapters Two and Three also consider the strategies by which advocates of reform underwrote the manliness of refined men. These asserted, on the one hand, the durability of refined styles based on self-control, while, on the other, simultaneously redefining these responsibilities to encompass new qualities as characteristic of an improved gentlemanly ideal.

Chapter Four examines the comments of those who looked less favourably on polite society and its implications for the gentleman. It considers the ways in which false or excessive refinement was characterised, and the perceived implications of this behaviour on standards of manliness through the period's fascination with effeminacy. Our readiness to identify this interest as part of a longer historical continuum should not obscure the particular eighteenth-century significance of a quality relevant to more than discussions of gender relations. The revival of a late-seventeenth-century interest in civic humanist philosophy provided critics of polite society with a potent intellectual framework with which to challenge the supposed progress of the modern world. Much of the power of the civic idiom rested on the emotive language employed to describe personal and societal ruin. Central to this language was the idea of effeminacy – the condition which civic critics traced to the loss of traditional values, such as independence, intelligence and courage, formerly deployed in the fulfilment of public responsibilities and the defeat of political tyranny. In seeking to modify this civic humanist picture of the ideal man, polite theorists were equally conscious of the unacceptability of effeminacy, although for them effeminacy existed as an indication of excessive social polish, not of refinement *per se*. Particular attention is paid in this chapter to literary representations of the popular fop type in this debate. A staple feature of satirical and conduct literature, the fop was a quintessential eighteenth-century character embodying current discussions over the impact of polite society on standards of manhood. Like the broader concept of effeminacy, the fop served either, as civic critics proposed, as a manifestation of the inevitable effects of refinement on men or, to polite reformers, as a timely reminder of the worst excesses of unregulated and corrupted forms of civilised manliness.

Chapter Five shifts the focus from didactic to personal testimonies to examine the relationship between ideal conduct and lived-out practice – or at least the discussion of these practices as told through the diary, correspondence and journal of three men: the legal student, Dudley Ryder (1691–1756); an Anglican clergyman, John Penrose (1713–76); and the writer James Boswell (1740–95). This study develops out of the preceding chapters for, as Anna Bryson puts it, 'there can be no coherent approach to practice without an understanding of ideals and norms'.[22] The personal testimonies examined here go some way to confirm the importance of social refinement for daily life, the strategies by which individuals thought of themselves as men, and the place of politeness and sensibility in the construction of these identities. However, an equally significant theme is the lack of harmony between social ideals and the reports of action by men whose conduct, if often emulative of prescribed norms, was also contingent on a variety of competing factors including company, purpose for social contact, location and time of encounter, amount of alcohol consumed and frame of mind.

11

The restricted number of cases on which this chapter is based inevitably limits the conclusions that might be drawn from an approach used to good effect in recent histories of eighteenth-century women and class formation. An important justification for work in these areas lies in the opportunity to empower historical subjects formerly simplified or 'victimised' within gender-blind models of historical change.[23] Similar incentives are clearly less pressing in an equivalent study of male testimonies written in what remained a highly patriarchal society. By contrast, the value of the approach adopted in Chapter Five is that it allows us, first, to appreciate more fully the day-to-day complexities and pitfalls of achieving (and retaining) a gentlemanly identity and, second, to recognise the need for an ever more sophisticated understanding of the question of gender identity in past societies. Ultimately the findings of this book suggest the need to eschew a holistic history of polite manliness in favour of a methodology which encompasses, like histories of polite society, the messiness and complexity of sometimes consonant, sometimes competing images at a given historical moment. The fact that men could and did resist modern ideas of polite living, coupled with the durability of traditional ideals of manliness within conduct literature, confirms our need to acknowledge the existence of continuation as well as change within histories of male conduct and manliness located somewhere between ideology and practice, intention and action.

Notes and references

1. James Boswell, *A Journal of a Tour to the Hebrides* (1786), ed. Peter Levi (1984), p. 384. Unless otherwise stated place of publication is London.

2. Given its often pejorative twentieth-century connotation, 'sentimental' is used here and throughout this book as the non-judgemental adjectival form of sensibility. This application draws on Erik Erämetsä's survey which traces the convergence of the terms 'sentiment' and 'sensibility': Erämetsä demonstrates how definitions of the former shifted from 'thought' to 'refined and moral feeling' during the second half of the eighteenth century. *A Study of the Word 'Sentimental' and of Other Linguistic Characteristics of Eighteenth-Century Sentimentalism in England* (Helsinki, 1951), p. 59.

3. Boswell, *Journal of a Tour to the Hebrides*, pp. 381–2.

4. *Ibid.*, pp. 251–3, 320–2, 351, 369, 356.

5. According to John Ramsay of Ochtertyre (1736–1814), 'men in The Highlands have always been more courteous and intelligent, more gallant in their manners ... than persons of that humble status in other countries', *Scotland and Scotsmen in the Eighteenth Century*, ed. David J. Brown, 2 vols. (Bristol, 1996), II, p. 396.

6. Anthony Fletcher, *Gender, Sex and Subordination in England, 1500–1800* (New Haven CT and London, 1995), p. 323.

7. The classic, if now substantively modified, statement on this subject remains Norbert Elias, *The Civilizing Process* (1939), trans. E. Jephcott (rpt Oxford, 1994). Recent, often critical, re-examinations include Marvin B. Becker, *Civility and Society in Western Europe, 1300–1600* (Bloomington IN, 1988) and Anna Bryson, *From Courtesy to Civility. Changing Codes of Conduct in Early Modern England* (Oxford, 1998).

8. Marjorie Morgan, *Manners, Morals and Class in England, 1774–1858* (Basingstoke, 1994), p. 10.

9. In addition to his capacity for 'manly' politeness, Johnson was known to many for his lack of external polish. On their first meeting in 1763, for example, Boswell had been struck by Johnson's 'dreadful appearance', 'very slovenly' dress, 'uncouth voice' and 'dogmatical roughness of manners', *Boswell's London Journal, 1762–1763*, ed. Frederick A. Pottle (1950), p. 260.

10. See, for example, John E. Mason, *Gentlefolk in the Making: Studies in the History of English Courtesy Literature and Related Topics from 1531 to 1774* (Philadelphia PA, 1935); George C. Brauer, *The Education of a Gentleman: Theories of Gentlemanly Education in England, 1660–1775* (New York, 1959); Philip Mason, *The English Gentleman: The Rise and Fall of an Ideal* (1982).

11. This elevation of female authority was initially a subject for scholars of eighteenth-century fiction. Historians to consider this subject include Sylvana Tomaselli, 'The enlightenment debate on women', *History Workshop*, 20 (1985), pp. 101–24, and Lawrence E. Klein, 'Gender, conversation and the public sphere in early eighteenth-century England', in Judith Still and Michael Worton eds., *Textuality and Sexuality: Reading Theories and Practices* (Manchester, 1993). The consequences of 'feminisation' and the relationship between models of femininity and women's actual lives remains a much contested historiographical field. Hannah Barker and Elaine Chalus, 'Introduction', in *idem*, eds. *Gender in Eighteenth-Century England: Roles, Representations and Responsibilities* (1997) survey aspects of this literature.

12. On the relationship between Catholicism, nationalism and manliness see Paul Hammond, 'Titus Oates and "sodomy"', in Jeremy Black ed., *Culture and Society in Britain, 1660–1800* (Manchester, 1997); Gerald Newman, *The Rise of English Nationalism: A Cultural History, 1740–1830* (New York, 1987); Michèle Cohen, 'Manliness, effeminacy and the French: gender and the construction of national character in eighteenth-century England', in Tim Hitchcock and *idem* eds., *English Masculinities, 1660–1800* (1999).

13. Paul Langford, *A Polite and Commercial People. England, 1727–1783* (Oxford, 1989), p. 66. See also Penelope Corfield, 'The rivals: landed and other gentlemen', in Negley Harte and Roland Quinault eds., *Land and Society in Britain, 1700–1900* (Manchester, 1996).

14. Mary Catherine Moran, '"The commerce of the sexes": civil society and polite society in Scottish enlightenment historiography' (unpublished paper, April 1999).

15. Susan C. Shapiro, '"Yon plumed dandeprat": male "effeminacy" in English satire and criticism', *Review of English Studies*, 39 (1988), pp. 400–12; Bryson, *From Courtesy to Civility*, p. 125.

16. Michèle Cohen, *Fashioning Masculinity: National Identity and Language in the Eighteenth Century* (1996), p. 5.

17. Randolph Trumbach, 'The birth of the queen: sodomy and the emergence of gender equality in modern culture, 1660–1750', in Martin B. Duberman *et al.* eds., *Hidden from History: Reclaiming the Gay and Lesbian Past* (1991); 'Sex, gender and sexual identity in modern culture: male sodomy and female prostitution in enlightenment England', in John C. Fout ed., *Forbidden History: The State, Society and the Regulation of Sexuality in Modern Europe* (Chicago IL and London, 1992); *Sex and the Gender Revolution*, vol. one: *Heterosexuality and the Third Gender in Enlightenment London* (Chicago IL and London, 1998).

18. Elizabeth A. Foyster, *Manhood in Early Modern England: Honour, Sex and Marriage* (1999).

19. See Hitchcock and Cohen eds., *English Masculinities*; these essays propose a complexity long appreciated in nineteenth- and twentieth-century historiography; Michael Roper and John Tosh eds., *Manful Assertions: Masculinities in Britain since 1800* (1991); James Mangan and James Walvin eds., *Manliness and Morality: Middle-Class Masculinity in Britain and America, 1800–1940* (Manchester, 1987).

20. G.J. Barker-Benfield, *The Culture of Sensibility: Sex and Society in Eighteenth-Century Britain* (Chicago IL and London, 1992), esp. chs. 2–3.

21. Tim Hitchcock, *English Sexualities, 1700–1800* (Basingstoke, 1997).

22. Bryson, *From Courtesy to Civility*, p. 6.

23. For example, Amanda Vickery, *The Gentleman's Daughter: Women's Lives in Georgian England* (New Haven CT and London, 1998), and Margaret R. Hunt, *The Middling Sort: Commerce, Gender and the Family in England, 1680–1780* (Berkeley CA, 1996).

CHAPTER ONE

Exploring polite society

Polite society has recently become an important subject for historians of late-seventeenth- and eighteenth-century Britain. This, to an extent, is a case of scholars now taking seriously a theme that has long been central to popular literary and cinematographic images of an era synonymous with a 'measured code of manners' as practised at the tea-table, the London pleasure garden or at polite resorts such as Bath.[1] Scholarly interest in politeness has prompted renewed scrutiny of these and other areas as a valid and useful subject of historical research. Early findings reveal polite society's importance as a significant, far-reaching and much considered aspect of eighteenth-century culture. As we might expect, its impact has featured prominently in recent studies of eighteenth-century art and design, concepts of taste, and the production and appreciation of high culture.[2] But its reach also guarantees its relevance in other initially less obvious subject areas including scientific exploration, civic consciousness, politics and religion.[3] Finally, the origins and dissemination of polite society has become a vibrant subject in its own right, encompassing histories of ideas, advice literature, publishing and reading.[4]

This chapter offers a closer look at aspects of eighteenth-century polite society as a prelude to my subsequent discussion of gentlemanliness. It begins by considering the ways in which the term has been applied by historians and eighteenth-century commentators and, with these in mind, how I intend to use it for the purposes of this book. A section on 'Polite and sentimental ideologies' examines the rise of early-eighteenth-century theories of politeness and how, in turn, these gave way to an alternative idea of refinement: sensibility. The significance of these intellectual debates was ensured by their communication to a wide-ranging audience of would-be gentlemen and women actively engaged in practising new forms of polite reading and sociability. That many discussions of social refinement came from churchmen and theologians draws attention to an interesting reciprocal relationship between Christian morality and social refinement examined as part of a final section, 'Problematising polite society'. As later chapters show, this stress on morality was crucial for eighteenth-century advocates of new forms of gentlemanliness within a polite society that was constantly regarded as both a source and a potential threat to manhood.

Applications and definitions

How do historians apply, and what do they mean by, 'polite society'? To offer a few examples: J.G.A. Pocock interprets the post-medieval drive towards 'more polished and humane modes of conduct' and the 'increased circulation of goods' as 'a major step in the direction of a commercial and polite society.' Paul Langford suggests that by the mid-eighteenth century 'the unity of polite society', composed of a professional class, had coalesced 'into a largely consistent mass'. Amanda Vickery's survey of community relations in eighteenth-century East Lancashire provides us with a study of a 'local polite society' of 'minor gentry, professional and mercantile families'. Finally, Richard Sher notes both the appeal of Moderate Church of Scotland ministers to a 'polite society' of 'well-bred people of taste and refinement', and the criticisms from other members of the kirk against what they saw as the Moderates' pandering to 'the impious affectations and amusements' of that society.[5]

Even from this modest selection it is apparent that the concept of 'polite society' can be used in a variety of ways to characterise different themes and distinct social groups. Thus Pocock applies the term in its broadest sense as a synonym for that section of the population, unspecified as to class or geographical location, which benefited from developments in a late-seventeenth-century consumer economy. Paul Langford's 'polite society' similarly encompasses a wide-ranging professional group whose aspiration for social improvement helped to erase regional variations and establish a shared culture. Amanda Vickery's study does much to confirm Langford's picture of a mobile and fashion-sensitive population eager to draw upon the latest offerings of an intra-regional commercial economy. However, Vickery's local focus also allows her to explore the tensions between named families for whom catalogue shopping or attendance at a nearby polite resort was intended less as conformity than as a bid to establish status over neighbouring social equivalents. Within the confines of a regional study, therefore, the concept of 'polite society' exists as a more geographically and demographically restricted category wherein the potential for social rivalry produced a less holistic, more competitive community composed of individuals thought to have attained politeness, and defined in opposition to those who had not. Lastly, Richard Sher's identification of 'polite society' as a negative descriptor reveals the ambivalence of eighteenth-century observers to the effects of social change both on national society and on local communities seemingly given over to pursuing trivial metropolitan culture or, as in the case of the Moderate Church of Scotland, to promoting an immoral and profane theology.

In contrast to its frequent use in recent scholarship, the precise term 'polite society' appears to have been seldom applied in eighteenth-century commentaries. One of the few exceptions occurs in the preface to Bernard Mandeville's *The Fable of the Bees* (1714). It was here that Mandeville proposed his soon infamous thesis linking public benefits not to acts of civic pride, but to innate private self-interest. Communities 'cured of the Failings they are Naturally guilty of' would, he believed, 'cease to be capable of being rais'd into such vast, potent and polite Societies, as they have been under the several great Commonwealths and Monarchies that have flourished since the Creation'.[6] Mandeville's application in certain ways prefigures Pocock's; that is, as an identification of an advanced level of societal development measured in terms including new standards of refined conduct.

These ideas, purged of what critics identified as Mandeville's unpalatable cynicism, proved especially popular among a later generation of enlightened social observers for whom daily standards of affluence and interpersonal behaviour were evidence of Britain's successful evolution into a sophisticated and civilised society. If the precise language of 'polite society' was absent from these discussions, the idea certainly was not. Writing in the 1740s, the Scottish moral philosopher and historian David Hume (1711–96) contrasted the incivilities of former 'barbarous nations' with those of a modern 'polite people'. The legal scholar William Blackstone in turn rooted Hume's work in the England of the 1760s when he declared it a nation of 'polite and commercial people'.[7] A decade on, John Millar (1735–1801), professor of civil law at Glasgow University, detected an 'advancement of society in civilization, opulence and refinement'.[8] Millar's fellow countryman, James Boswell, who had of course been impressed by behavioural standards in Highland Scotland, likewise spoke several years later of the 'advantage of civilised society' in a 'nation [with] all the symptoms of a great and flourishing state'.[9]

Certain eighteenth-century commentators also applied the language of polite society to descriptions of more restricted communities. Thus, in the subtitle to his *Reflexions Upon the Politeness of Manners* (translated 1707), the French conduct writer Jean-Baptiste Bellegarde offered to teach readers the 'maxims for polite society'. Bellegarde's subsequent comments suggest this to have been a limited category, since "'Tis not common to find so great a confederacy of Perfections, and therefore 'tis no wonder if the numbers of the *Polite* be so small.'[10] In an essay from *The Spectator* periodical (1711–14), Richard Steele bemoaned how, on leaving university, few students entered the 'polite World' of fashionable London.[11] The anonymous guide to *The Man of Manners* (1733) warned the reader to avoid behaviour that would be 'a prejudice to him in polite Company'.[12] Samuel Johnson chose to address only 'the politer part of mankind' in an essay from his periodical, *The Rambler* (1750–2), while in 1769 James Boswell explained Johnson's potential for boorishness in terms of his having 'not . . . lived more in polished society' – by which Boswell, given his frequent bouts of snobbery, presumably meant the elegant parts of London rather than the provincial Lichfield of Johnson's birth.[13]

In these applications, as in those by recent scholars, we are presented with a diverse range of people and locations claiming or being granted polite status. At its broadest and most inclusive when describing the inhabitants of a nation or civil state, the concept of polite society was also applied more specifically to the cities of that nation, like London, or to fashionable new resorts, notably Bath, described in 1762 as 'the most polite and agreeable Place in England'.[14] More precisely still, polite society could exist as locations within the city in the form of Steele's 'polite world' and Boswell's 'polished society'. Finally, we see an inclusive concept of civil society reworked to designate yet more distinctive sets of people – Johnson's 'politer parts' or 'the polite Company' – limited to those with whom 'men of manners' thought it wise to be associated.

Clear tensions exist within these examples. James Boswell, for instance, applied the concept of polite society both as a descriptor of the national condition and as a select group within that nation. Boswell's example alerts us to the snobbery and competition that infused many eighteenth-century discussions of polite status in advice guides or in private diaries and correspondence. Moreover, it is evident that the large majority of people who were included in national surveys of civil society had neither the money nor the time to break into more restricted communities of polite living. Thus Bath – a resort whose promoters boasted its accessibility, informality and lack of snobbery – was claimed, even when 'rank' was 'laid aside', to be the chosen resort of 'private gentleman upwards'.[15]

From such evidence it is apparent that eighteenth-century concepts of 'polite society' defy simple categorisation; indeed, its range of applications arguably makes it a meaningless term if used to describe a single social group or location. However, if we recognise these variations, contradictions and tensions as an integral feature of eighteenth-century debates over, and the implementation of, social refinement, then the concept of 'polite society' becomes a useful means to understand the breadth and importance of a subject that, as we shall see, many commentators understood, discussed and exploited in all of its ideological and practical complexity.

Conceived of in this way, polite society can be said to consist broadly – as it will be applied in this book – of those who sought a reputation for refinement, whether this reputation be politeness or sensibility, sociability or snobbishness; and of those activities and locations within which individuals, conduct writers or social analysts claimed to detect and pursue refined behaviour, whether this be the nation at large, the city or more intimate venues within these spheres. Thus, participation in this polite society could, as Boswell shows, be understood both as a statement of national progress and as a symbol of competition facilitating personal advancement. Equally, Bath's polite society could exist as a venue conducive to egalitarian mixing of social ranks while excluding those lacking the financial status of a 'private gentleman'.

Yet at the same time, the importance of polite society to eighteenth-century culture owed much to the aspirational tone evident in each of these commentaries, regardless of their specific focus. To its promoters, polite society (however conceived) remained a source of self- or societal improvement, though to its critics these aspirations brought social disharmony and, as we shall see, declining gender standards. What gave this debate added vitality was the range of people who thought or were told to think of themselves as actual or potential members of polite society. While it is true that the 'private gentleman' may have been an individual of some means, crucially he remained (like the 'polite Company' from the distinctly aspirational *Man of Manners; or Plebian Polished*) a loosely defined character to whom a wide range of readers, eager for self-improvement, might aspire within the context of their own lives. Central to the attraction of eighteenth-century discourses of social refinement was an emphasis on good character, not just on means. Moreover, as many eighteenth-century definitions of politeness and sensibility made clear, the character of the modern 'private gentleman' was such that it might well be acquired by every careful reader.

Definitions

In December 1733 the *Gentleman's Magazine* printed a satirical letter from 'Martha Meanwell', a young woman new to London, who asked the editor to 'explain the Word polite', and to give advice on 'how I am to understand it in order to my Improvement'. 'Meanwell' described how during recent visits to church she had watched men and women parade in the aisles before entering a pew, talk during the service, and ogle members of the opposite sex through spying glasses: was this, she speculated, what was meant by being 'polite'?[16]

Her question was presumably not prompted by an unfamiliarity with the word itself, first identifed by the *Oxford English Dictionary* (*OED*) in the mid-fifteenth century to describe things 'smoothed, polished, neat or orderly'. Eighteenth-century dictionary references suggest the durability of this meaning throughout the early modern period: *Dictionarium Britannicum* (1730) defined 'polite' as that which was 'well-polished; neat or exact'; Samuel Johnson interpreted it as 'glossy, smooth' (1755); and Nathan Bailey as 'well polished, accurate, neat, genteel, accomplished' (1773).[17] Bailey's mention of gentility and accomplishment draws attention to a second, and more common, association with civilised social behaviour. It seems equally likely that 'Martha Meanwell' would have known this second definition, which developed from an alternative early modern use signifying elevated taste and academic learning. Eighteenth-century dictionaries commonly drew attention to an associated quality which *Dictionarium Britannicum*, for example, also defined as 'well bred, accomplished, genteel'.

Rather, it would appear that 'Meanwell's', and others', primary concern was to explore more closely the characteristics of, and ways to achieve, what she described as the '*Politenesses*' – the gentility, good breeding and accomplishment – 'by which I am to improve myself'.[18] Several months later, the *Gentleman's Magazine* published a reply to her inquiry which provided a more substantive definition of 'politeness' and of being 'polite'. The conduct of her fellow church-goers was not to be emulated since 'nothing that is indecent or disagreeable can be polite'. To behave in such a way impinged on others' enjoyment and thus contravened a definition of true politeness comprising 'an agreeable and delicate manner . . . a certain Decency in Words and gestures in order to please [which] by shewing the Regard we have for others [by] an Assemblage of Discretion, and Complaisance . . . renders to every one the Dues he has a Right to require'.[19]

The protean nature of polite society should prepare us for the variations and inconsistencies in meanings attached to the important and much debated eighteenth-century ideal of politeness. None the less, many definitions do throw up common themes. For example, the 1734 account in the *Gentleman's Magazine* developed ideas present both in Abel Boyer's 1702 definition 'as dextrous management of our Words and Actions, whereby we make other people have better Opinion of us and of themselves', and in Jean-Baptiste Bellegarde's description of 'a combination of Discretion, Civility, Complaisance and Circumspection, to pay every one the Respects they have a right to demand of us . . . dress'd and set off with an agreeable and insinuating Air, diffus'd thro' all our Words and Actions'.[20] What applied to the early part of the century endured in successive generations. 'Politeness', noted the anonymous author of *Farrago* (1792), 'is the assimulation of our behaviour to the practice of all those qualities that form the most refined pleasures of social intercourse, the appearance of universal benevolence, generosity, modesty, and of making our own happiness spring from the accommodation of others'.[21]

From these discussions, we can identify three of the essential principles on which, broadly speaking, eighteenth-century commentators focused when defining 'politeness'. The first may be characterised as a propriety or decorum – present, for example, in the *Gentleman's Magazine*'s call for a 'certain Decency'; in Bellegarde's emphasis on 'discretion' and 'circumspection'; and in the 'modesty' that *Farrago* expected to accompany a politeness of 'quiet unassuming conduct, that is intended to give no offence'. Such characteristics were, according to *Farrago*, a distinctly English interpretation of politeness. French practitioners, by contrast, were said to favour a more decorative and assertive style in which politeness consisted of the 'active distribution of civility' through displays of fine manners. French men, it was claimed, began their education in politeness when still children so that by adulthood they were fully schooled in the intricacies of dress, wit and deportment. This, *Farrago* suggested, had also been the lot of Englishmen until the 1760s, when changing fashions had seen a declining interest in Parisian education and the parallel formation of a distinct, national style.[22]

Such claims were only partially borne out in other late-century definitions which, on the whole, proved rather more appreciative of what can be identified as the second requirement of politeness defined by lexicographers like Nathan Bailey as 'accomplishment', 'elegance of manners' or 'the quality of behaving with elegant complaisance'.[23] In their association of politeness with manners, Bailey and others also drew on a longer tradition which, if it did not encourage the levels of French elegance described in *Farrago*, certainly highlighted the importance of what Boyer identified as a 'dextrous Management of Words and Actions'; Bellegarde viewed as the 'agreeable and insinuating Air, diffus'd thro' all our Words and Actions', and *Gentleman's Magazine* welcomed as 'an agreeable and delicate Manner of speaking, acting, and writing'.

While polish and elegance proved a standard feature of conduct literature throughout the century, polite commentators were anxious not to overplay the importance of manners to the detriment of a third, and perhaps the most frequently considered, element of politeness: the display of generosity and accommodation to one's companions. It was the increasing importance of this final component that led *Farrago*'s author to consider late-century English politeness as superior to the continental models practised by previous generations. In fact such views had also proved popular

21

with earlier writers who, in stressing the generosity and sociability of modern politeness, sought to distinguish it from what they saw as overly rule-based models of civilised behaviour. Writing in 1702, Abel Boyer claimed politeness 'not to be stated or determined by Rules', being rather wholly dependent 'upon Usage and Custom, and varies according to the difference of Place, Time, Persons, Sex and Condition'.[24] In the *Rambler* periodical (1751), Samuel Johnson likewise declared that manners, though desirable, were not an essential part of 'genuine politeness', the principal purpose of which was 'rather ease than pleasure'; that is, accommodation rather than diverting elegance.[25] Key themes in eighteenth-century definitions of politeness, 'ease' and 'easiness' were what one specialist title described simply as the 'pleasure of knowing ourselves'; actions 'naturally free and unconfined' to be set against less suitable behaviour consisting more of 'outward Address, than Sincerity and Affection'.[26] Johnson elsewhere defined easiness as 'freedom from harshness, formality, forced behaviour or conceits', and in *Rambler* No. 98 labelled it conduct requiring that 'no man should give preference to himself'. In turn, he criticised those who misconstrued politeness and seldom 'extend their care beyond the exterior and unessential parts of civility' and 'variations of fashionable courtesy'.[27]

Johnson's comparison of desirably 'polite' or 'easy' behaviour with 'civility' and 'courtesy' raises an intriguing point of convergence for histories of 'politeness' as both a linguistic codifier and a concept of idealised social behaviour. From the late seventeenth century, 'polite' and 'politeness' rapidly emerged as key terms for those seeking a social reputation and, as numerous book titles reveal, for those who professed to understand the secrets of modern modes of genteel living.[28] It is tempting therefore to speculate how closely the popularisation of the term 'politeness' paralleled this equivalent late-seventeenth- and eighteenth-century emphasis on the easiness, freedom and generosity of desirable social conduct. Johnson's decision to contrast 'politeness' favourably with two established concepts of good behaviour, 'courtesy' and 'civility', appears to bear out this suggestion.[29] Nor was Johnson alone in equating civility with inferior or incomplete forms of social behaviour. 'Politeness', wrote the anonymous author of *The Polite Academy* (1771), 'is the Influence of natural Refinement . . . the happy Mixture of Greatness with Benignty.' Civility, 'though often falsely thought the same', was clearly distinct. Certainly of some value in curbing poor conduct, codes of civility were said to lack the morality of politeness, and remained 'mostly a Surface without Depth', spreading 'a Gloss over the Outside even of Vice and Meanspiritedness'.[30]

Though they are worthy of note, we should perhaps not read too much into these or similar statements. In her study of early modern conduct literature, Anna Bryson traces the appearance of a vocabulary and concept of 'civility' to the late sixteenth and early seventeenth centuries but reminds us that it remained 'only one of a shifting set of keywords, constantly described and justified in terms of each other'.[31] Much the same can be said for the eighteenth-century treatment of 'politeness'. In one sense applications of 'civility' persisted on account of the continuing importance of one of its core components, decorum, for eighteenth-century concepts of good behaviour. Equally, the term endured because of its often loose and inconsistent application even within the pages of a single guide. Thus, in *The Polite Academy*, civility was elsewhere more positively described as the ability to 'sacrifice one's self-love', and as behaviour characterised by 'ease, propriety, and Grace'. These variations leave open the possibility that this second definition may have been more the product of carelessness than considered thought. Yet the prevalence of equivalent explanations by other highly regarded commentators is also noteworthy. The Methodist leader John Wesley identified 'courtesy' as 'behaviour that naturally springs from the heart', while it was Samuel Johnson's 'courtesy' at Inveraray Castle that Boswell praised in October 1773.[32] Likewise, the philosopher John Locke's definition of 'civility' as 'care not to shew any slighting, or contempt, of any one' and David Hume's description of a quality that 'leads us to resign our own inclinations to those of our companion' rather suggest the synchronicity of established and more modern vocabularies in eighteenth-century conduct literature.[33]

In view of this blurring of precise terms, it seems wise to adopt Lawrence Klein's application of 'politeness' as a 'master metaphor' for a range of social and cultural practices to which eighteenth-century writers attached a variety of labels: civility, good breeding, manners, easiness, gentility and so on.[34] As with the act of labelling, so individual commentators proposed variations in the blend of the propriety, elegance and easiness required for 'true politeness'. What mattered about politeness, and what distinguished it from earlier modes of seemingly cold and self-interested refinement, was less its name than its innovative synthesis of relaxed outer polish with inner moral values to produce a force for superior sociability.

Polite and sentimental ideologies

This notion of politeness as innovation features prominently in recent scholarly accounts of its rise, traced to the period 1660–1715. According to J.G.A. Pocock, for example, 'the idea of politeness . . . first appeared in the Restoration'. Lawrence Klein likewise describes how 'politeness . . . entered in its significant career only in the mid-seventeenth century', and how its consolidation 'was closely associated with a reorganisation of culture and social life at the beginning of the eighteenth century'. Nicholas Phillipson detects a similar reconceptualisation during 'a major revolution in the language of English politeness' largely carried out by pro-Whig periodical writers such as Joseph Addison (1672–1719) and Richard Steele (1672–1729) between 1709 and 1713.[35]

The rise of politeness

Within this broad chronology (1660–1715), individual surveys point to specific episodes to account for the timing and character of an emerging polite culture. Pocock's focus on the 1660s and 1670s is determined by his identification of politeness as, first, a consequence of increasing commercialisation and, second, an element 'of the latitudinarian campaign to replace prophetic by sociable religiosity' shortly after the end of the Interregnum in 1660.[36] Lawrence Klein points to additional influences, principal of which was a gradual decline in the cultural importance of the court alongside the development of a metropolitan and provincial urban society. Klein also emphasises the impact of the Glorious Revolution (1688–9) and its aftermath: the expansion of the commercial sector following the Bank of England's establishment (1694); the lapse in 1695 of the Licensing Act and with it restrictions on print culture; and the consolidation of a first-generation Whig party which fared better under William and Mary than it had in the later part of the reign of Charles II and in that of James II. As Klein shows, it was from this new political culture that there emerged some of the most influential early eighteenth-century polite theorists, among them Anthony Ashley Cooper, third earl of Shaftesbury, and later the periodical essayists Joseph Addison and Richard Steele.[37]

However, in transforming Whig fortunes, the post-1688 political and cultural order also brought new dilemmas to a party now required to authenticate the Williamite order while maintaining its traditional defence of political and personal liberties. Klein identifies two principal courses adopted by Whig apologists conducive to the 'rise of politeness'. The first involved a reaction against popular but misguided notions of sociability. Modern, debauched lifestyles, commonly seen as the consequence of Restoration court life, were now denounced as morally corrupt and socially offensive. Moral campaigners called for a reformation of manners, here broadly defined, to replace mistaken notions of civilised living with greater spirituality and seemliness.[38] In addition to Klein, historians like G.J. Barker-Benfield attach considerable importance to these moral reform movements, centred on organisations such as the Society for the Propagation of

Christian Knowledge (established 1698), to explain the popularity of an early-eighteenth-century literature calling for improved standards of behaviour, especially in men. The message of moral reform is traced from these societies to the later heyday of Whig journalism in two of the century's most influential and popular essay periodicals, Addison and Steele's *The Tatler* (1709–11) and *The Spectator* (1711–14). Barker-Benfield highlights the distinctly pious and conservative tone adopted by both authors who, sharing the 'reformation goals of the SPCK', declared it their 'general intention [to] . . . recover the age out of its desperate state of folly and vice'.[39]

This emphasis on the importance of tradition is certainly helpful for better understanding the aims of periodicals like the *Spectator*, once regarded simply as a self-help guide for an aspirational, forward-looking bourgeois readership. In truth, as the work of Klein, Pocock and others demonstrates, the *Spectator*'s account of men's relationship to commerce proved a complex blend of traditional values, of which stoicism remained a key component, now relocated in a modern and dynamic city culture. It was in their pursuit of this blend that Addison and Steele proposed a second, more original, response to the post-1688 settlement, defined in harmony with, rather than opposition to, recent developments in commercial and urban living. In doing so, Whig commentators remodelled seventeenth-century civic humanist concepts of virtuous behaviour – characterised by a suspicion towards innovation as detrimental to social order – in favour of a more up-to-date understanding of politeness as the guarantor of political liberty and new moral standards in a commercial society. Participants in this society, freed from the formalities and constraints inherent in earlier definitions of refinement, were able to practise and perfect an important Whig and broader enlightenment maxim, namely mankind's natural propensity for company. With its moral validation of urban sociability and focused discussion of the means for personal interaction, politeness offered the most complete opportunity for individuals to fulfil Addison's understanding of man as a 'Sociable Animal'.[40]

Addison's aphorism was central to his and other Whig commentators' promotion of the merits of modern living as a cogent response to political, social and economic change post-1688. At the same time, we also need to see the efforts of these early-eighteenth-century English writers as one in a series of contributions to, and modifications of, theories of politeness taking place both before and after this significant episode in Whig journalism.

Several recent accounts of seventeenth-century French manners and their influence in England have highlighted the importance of writers such as Jean-Baptiste Bellegarde in challenging established ideas of refined conduct then closely associated with life at court. In place of what he and others considered overly formal court civilities, Bellegarde advocated a republic of letters where conduct was based less on hierarchically defined rules than on the easiness, benevolence and genuine sociability of the individual encounter – independent, though never entirely divorced from, considerations of participants' social status.[41] Historians of French conduct literature argue for an active cross-pollination of ideas between writers like Bellegarde and early-eighteenth-century English authors engaged in the translation or imitation of French works.[42] French ideas were subsequently reinterpreted in England to suit a less elite, more city-based readership than was found in the still predominantly exclusive Parisian salon. A later generation of French periodical writers (at work in the 1720s) would in turn embrace these interpretations as markers of urbanity, and reapplied Whig forms of journalism to extend the range of places and opportunities wherein polite behaviour might be expected beyond the salon society.

Having looked back to the antecedents of Whig polite theory, we also need to ask how these ideas fared later in the century. Within current historiography there is a strong suggestion that, once established, the Whig project maintained its intellectual dominance over subsequent generations. For Lawrence Klein, for example, this 'new kind of culture' became the prevailing feature of 'an era of English cultural history corresponding to a "long" eighteenth century . . . defined by its politeness'.[43] There is certainly something to be said for this long view. As Chapter Five shows, for example, would-be polite men continued to consult seminal guides to polite conduct like the *Spectator* throughout the century.

Yet equally we must not over-play either the durability or acceptability of Whig models within later accounts of refined society. As Chapters Four and Five also indicate, eighteenth-century discussions of politeness 'in action' reveal a robust and often contradictory debate over the condition and scope of polite society at any point in our period. To propose a positive and uncomplicated history of politeness also ignores the existence of a vigorous civic tradition whose contributors remained unconvinced by, and defined themselves against, Whiggish claims of social and moral progress. Finally, to focus on the early exponents of politeness as the dominant model of refinement also overlooks the specific contribution of subsequent progressive authors to a mid- to late-century picture characterised as much by the development as it is the consolidation of earlier ideals.

In contrast to Klein's somewhat hegemonic model of politeness, other historians interpret the later story of eighteenth-century polite society as one of enhanced intellectual sophistication centred less on London than on the universities and debating societies of Lowland Scotland. This is not to deny the impact of earlier metropolitan concepts of politeness on Scottish thought. Publications like the *Tatler* and *Spectator* enjoyed considerable success in Scotland, not least, as Nicholas Phillipson has argued, for the new sense of civic purpose they gave to a social elite deprived of political identity by the Act of Union (1707).[44] However, Scottish commentators also viewed the relationship between northern and southern Britons with ambivalence. Elsewhere, Phillipson reveals how David Hume, while acknowledging his debt to earlier Whig writers, considered the *Spectator*'s application of politeness to be somewhat limited in scope. Hume's achievement was to 'transform the language of Addisonian politeness by showing that it could be turned into a vehicle of science and used to derive an entirely new account of the principles of human nature and of the principles of commerce'.[45] Whereas English Whig thought characterised politeness as a guarantor of liberty and social order (principally, as Pocock suggests, by taming passions in a commercial society), Hume and his fellow Scottish social analysts – notably Adam Smith (1723–90), Glasgow professor of moral philosophy – saw participation in a modern commercial economy as stimulating interpersonal refinement by encouraging greater levels of knowledge and skills, and by making people keener and more able to socialise.

Central to this thesis was the idea that changes in personal conduct were determined by one's socio-economic environment. As the fourth and final sequence in an evolutionary model of societal development, commerce inevitably gave modern populations the best opportunity yet to achieve refinement: the laws determining societal evolution quite simply prevented the existence of equivalent levels of refinement in earlier cultures. Hume, for example, detected the superiority of modern manners in a declining level of gluttony and drunkenness among men who now eschewed the traditional pleasures of quantity for the refinements of quality. Significantly, Scottish theorists perceived the presence of these and other improvements beyond the locations and personnel of the *Spectator*'s metropolitan haunts. This breadth of application was especially important to promoters of a vibrant, post-Union Scottish culture. Keen to discover the laws of human conduct and to create a 'science of man', mid-century Scottish enlightenment thinkers proposed the emergence of a much broader polite society – variously identified as 'Man', 'mankind' or 'the people' – whose members, sharing universal principles of human nature, experienced the benefits of a particular (here the most advanced) economic and cultural state at a specific historical moment: the present.

From politeness to sensibility

There was little especially original in this idea of people being drawn by irresistible social and economic forces to share common experiences. From the late seventeenth century it was typical for civic critics of social change to explain what they saw as moral and physical ruin in terms of the destructive effects of an unregulated commercial economy. Where eighteenth-century Scottish moral philosophers differed was in their interpretation of the consequences of economic change. Thus, while civic critics saw the erosion of traditional social bonds, David Hume identified the means to embellish an essentially sociable and benevolent instinct as common not only to man but to every sentient being. 'Nature', he wrote in a 1742 essay, 'has implanted in all living creatures an affection between the sexes, which . . . is not merely confined to the satisfaction of the bodily appetite, but begets a friendship and mutual sympathy, which runs through the whole tenor of their lives'.[46]

Sympathy was central to Hume's understanding of sociability and may be broadly defined as the quality by which one person reproduced and came to experience the feelings of another by observation.[47] Increased opportunities to fulfil naturally sociable urges in the modern world necessarily stimulated the flow of sympathy between its members. At the same time, it was claimed that an on-going refinement of manners enabled individuals to appreciate more fully the quality of these feelings. As Hume commented elsewhere, improvement in the liberal arts and sciences 'softens and humanises the temper', giving rise to a society that 'cherishes those fine emotions, in which true virtue and honour consist'. This increased fineness or delicacy of emotion in turn enhanced the quality of sociability by tempering self-interest and by providing 'a greater sensibility of all the decencies and duties of life'.[48]

For Hume, as for other academic analysts and later popularisers, sensibility indicated not just quickness of perception or feeling but the application of this perceptiveness for moral ends. In the context of social conduct, moral purpose derived from the beneficial effects gained from the binding of individuals in webs of sympathetic exchange. As a discourse of social refinement based on inner virtue, sensibility therefore bore close similarities to politeness. These proximities, moreover, are well worth highlighting in view of my suggestion of a mid- to late-eighteenth-century shift from politeness to sensibility. Certainly 'sensibility' was a much discussed idea by the third quarter of the eighteenth century. But at no point during the rise of the fashion for sensibility did it fully replace interest in things and people 'polite'. 'For all the tensions between them', writes John Brewer, 'sentiment and politeness coexisted, not least in the breast of many a refined person. Even between the 1760s and 1790s, at the height of the rage for sensibility, the language of politeness was never abandoned.'[49]

This image of politeness and sensibility in tandem is certainly apparent from the regularity with which commentators applied the terms interchangeably. In addition, descriptions of sensibility often referred to qualities already familiar to practitioners of an early-eighteenth-century model of politeness. The definition, by the Church of Scotland theologian Hugh Blair (1718–

1800), of sensibility as 'native feeling heightened and improved by principle', for example, echoed Joseph Addison's or Samuel Johnson's understanding of politeness as moderated and civilised complaisance.[50] Late-eighteenth-century accounts of 'politeness' likewise drew on some of the ideological themes and linguistic forms that were then commonly used by what might be described as archetypal sentimental authors. John Harris, author of *An Essay on Politeness* (1775), appeared at first to reassert early-eighteenth-century ideas of social refinement when he defined his subject as the means of moderating and 'giving polish' to a generous virtue. Yet Harris went on to modify his interpretation. The polish of one's performance was identified as 'compliment', a lesser quality to 'true politeness' which he believed 'more easily felt than understood' and which, based on 'sympathetic and generous feelings', seldom appeared but when 'it springs from the heart'.[51] Harris's contemporary Hestor Chapone likewise considered theirs the first generation to appreciate what she and others regarded, literally and metaphorically, to be the heart of social refinement. It was, she argued, the 'boast of the age to have discovered that true politeness consists, not in modes and ceremonies, but in entering with delicacy into the feelings of our companions'.[52]

Harris and Chapone's statements warn us against seeking an overly rigid definition of competitive polite and sentimental discourses founded on simplistic comparisons of reason and emotion. Nevertheless, both of these examples also indicate a clear shift in tone in eighteenth-century definitions of the requirements of idealised social conduct. As John Brewer puts it, as a 'new type of refinement', sensibility's merits lay in its prioritisation of benevolent spontaneity over what many sentimental authors now saw as the potential artifice of polite living: 'while politeness emphasised forms of public presentation in the creation of refinement, sentiment stressed inner feeling'.[53]

The roots of this culture of feeling are deep and much contested. Certainly many of the linguistic and conceptual components of a mid- to late-eighteenth-century definition of sensibility – benevolence, tenderness, generosity, moral sense and fellow feeling – can be found in the work of late-seventeenth- and early-eighteenth-century moral reformers and theologians.[54] The late seventeenth century also saw significant advances in theories of human anatomy and the perceived association between the physical body and the mind. These developments followed the construction of a physiology in which, in contrast to early modern ideas surrounding static humours, fluids were thought to move continuously around the body. This mechanistic interpretation in addition emphasised the movement of sensations which passed or flowed as resonances along a wire-like system of nerves. Physicians set out to show how differences in the composition of nerves, or changes in their form through lifestyle, were central for explaining variations in the quality of a sensibility dependent on the transmission of sensory perceptions that flowed in to the brain and then returned to the body.[55]

The rise of a mid- to late-eighteenth-century culture of sensibility owed much to the transition of this research to non-scientific literature produced both by academic analysts, like David Hume, and by less intellectual social observers in a range of established genres including essay periodicals and sermons. Here complex medical theories were made accessible by comparisons of the body with finely tuned musical instruments, with sympathy described as the activation of a nervous physiology through sensory perceptions of daily life and conveyed via readily identifiable social signs. The results included displays of fellow feeling through bodily actions – among them weeping, blushing and trembling – or, more constructively, acts of charity ultimately stimulated by nervous activity. Alternatively, sensibility was manifest as a type of physical and psychological self-injury variously categorised as hypochondria, melancholy or the spleen. These ailments indicated high levels of nervous sensitivity and became stock-in-trade features of the admirable man or woman of feeling as sketched in sentimental novels and magazines, two additional and newer literary genres that were particularly significant in popularising sensibility.[56]

In part, sensibility's power rested on its development of already well-established concepts of desirable social behaviour. Yet its impact also owed much to its image as a modern corrective to what proponents identified as the recent corruption of a supposedly advanced and refined society. This idea of sensibility as a response to established notions of refinement gone awry prompts us to consider the relationship between feeling and politeness. Eighteenth-century advocates regularly stressed sensibility's value as a force for moral good, inspired by sensation and channelled towards beneficial ends in a sober and responsible fashion. Moral feeling, it was argued, could not and should not necessarily be restrained by the level of decorum and self-control deemed appropriate by earlier behavioural writers. The result was a body of advice literature which saw less need for the niceties of older definitions of refined behaviour, either because of their incompatibility with displays of feelings, or because of their association with the artifice which sensibility's advocates saw as inherent to earlier forms of polite society.

While dismissing politeness for its potential shallowness, sentimental writers worked to establish their own equation between sensibility and social refinement. Here it is worth restating the importance attached to sympathy as a means of binding individuals into a community based on the sharing or imagining of other people's feelings. Aptitude for sympathy was also thought to determine the quality of that community by guaranteeing and preserving refined sociability. In this instance 'refinement' proves a particularly apposite term to describe the process by which individuals were expected to conduct themselves. Accounts of sensibility identified its origins in the fineness of an individual's physiology, in the sensitivity or perceptiveness of his or her observations, and in the resultant delicacy of tastes and actions. Thus David Hume's understanding of a modern civilised society was characterised by men who ate and drank less voraciously, not just because such actions were deemed unbecoming by an external code of conduct, but because such appetites were now more difficult to feel and sustain among a refined people.

Sentimental authors identified a variety of processes as contributing to this shift from an uncivilised past to a civilised present. For the poet William Cowper (1731–1800), contemporary manners were directly attributable to the evolution of a physiology capable of sympathetic exchange. Modern men and women, argued Cowper in 1788, were cosseted and protected from the severities of the British climate with the effect that any comparative hardship – easily endured by their forefathers – now induced distress. By 'bodily feelings', he wrote, 'we are so well admonished of every change in the atmosphere . . . as to have hardly any need of a weather-glass to mark them'. Cowper believed the benefits of this development to be clear: enhanced sensitivity stimulated higher levels of feeling, and feeling prompted a sensibility that, as 'the sine qua non of real happiness', allowed for more tasteful, intricate and gratifying social encounters.[57]

Cowper's determinism recalls that of mid-century Scottish moral philosophers who also viewed sensibility as a consequence of socio-economic conditions only present in a modern civilised community. Adam Smith thought that men in less developed, non-European societies were characterised by a physical and mental hardiness 'most suitable to the circumstances of a savage'. In a hunting or subsistence economy there was neither the time nor the incentive to sympathise with rivals in possession of limited resources. Conversely, in advanced communities whose population experienced 'general security', people were able to practise and respect a culture of 'sensibility' that befitted 'one who lives in a very civilized society'.[58] Later popularisers of sensibility modified this stark comparison between boorish/ unfeeling and civilised/sentimental society in their attempts to provide readers with more attainable models of ideal and unacceptable conduct. In these accounts, the alternative to refined feeling was less often a brutal, but conceptually distant, savagery than more recent masculine cultures of once respectable yet now hard-hearted, unfeeling stoicism.

This section began by examining the recent historiographical trend to view politeness as an attempt to validate and sustain political, cultural and economic changes post-1660, accelerated in the wake of the Glorious Revolution. The success of these attempts was considerable and, as Lawrence

Klein suggests, long lasting. There is much to be said for this thesis. However, we have also seen how later discussions of refinement – encapsulated in the mid- to late-eighteenth-century concept of sensibility – also developed and challenged elements of the polite code. To its proponents, sensibility emerged as an alternative, and superior, discourse in which genuine fellow feeling prevented the artifice and duplicity that was now thought an inherent feature of politeness. This discussion has focused principally on politeness and sensibility as considered by polite theorists and academic social analysts. However, both discourses were more than ideas. Rather, they were lifestyles to be acquired, displayed and enjoyed. It is to the communication and implementation of polite society that we come next.

Communicating and practising

In the preface to his 1660 behavioural guide, *The Gentile Sinner*, Clement Ellis advised readers first to consult two other studies, *The Whole Duty of Man* and *The Gentleman's Calling* (both published in 1660 by Richard Allestree), modestly considered by Ellis as superior manuals for anyone seeking to become 'a Man, a Gentleman, and a Christian'. Ellis's statement demonstrates a generosity and benevolence which all three texts identified as the principal characteristics of the modern gentleman. Such recommendations are arguably not surprising coming from two Anglican clergymen; nor perhaps was the success of all three works, given the enduring piety of many late-seventeenth- and eighteenth-century readers of behavioural literature.[59]

Literature for refinement

As Anthony Fletcher suggests, the popularity of these particular guides also had much to do with their topicality and appeal to a readership previously raised on a diet of advice literature comprised largely of sixteenth- and seventeenth-century continental sources in translation. Allestree, Ellis and other Restoration writers provided a 'new genre of male conduct books' written specifically for the English gentleman, for whom a complex, moral definition of refinement now became a defining feature both of social and gender identity.[60] Fletcher's claim accords with that of recent French scholars who detect an equivalent development in innovative works like Antoine de Courtin's 1671 *Nouveau Traité de la Civilité* – which, in contrast to earlier models of courtly instruction, addressed readers from a range of backgrounds on inner character and outer refinements necessary to socialise in a consciously pluralistic community.[61]

In seeking to explain the rise of an eighteenth-century concept of politeness, historians attach considerable importance to the role of print in reflecting and influencing changing perceptions of desirable social relations. The period witnessed the development of a literary culture in which the possession of borrowed or bought reading matter became an increasingly important symbol of and means for personal improvement. Few would now question the contribution especially of purpose-written behavioural guides in developing a series of eighteenth-century discourses on individual and societal refinement.

However, there is less consensus on how to characterise these developments. Marjorie Morgan, for example, categorises the majority of seventeenth- and eighteenth-century discussions on social behaviour as part of a well-established courtesy literature. Originating in the Italian and Dutch Renaissance, the courtesy book provided elite male readers with information on a complete education in personal and professional affairs, a significant part of which remained the value and means to cultivate breeding equivalent to their natural position in society. Only in the third quarter of the eighteenth century, argues Morgan, did the courtesy tradition give way to a new form of 'conduct' literature, defined by its promotion of the merits of morality over the specifics of refined manners.[62] Others, like Nancy Armstrong, apply the conduct label both to sixteenth- and seventeenth-century guides for the male elite and, subsequently, to a new genre of texts setting exacting standards of prescription for female readers in the period 1760–1820 – an era elsewhere confusingly described as the 'age of courtesy books for women'.[63]

Variations in nomenclature are ultimately less significant than the types of works included within these categories and their role in cultivating eighteenth-century discourses of refinement. To treat, like Morgan, the majority of eighteenth-century studies as the tail-end of an early modern courtesy tradition presents a rather static picture of what in fact proved to be a dynamic and innovative prescriptive literary scene. Certainly it remains the case that guides for 'complete gentlemen', among them such classic early modern texts as Baldassare Castiglione's *Il libro del Cortegiano* (1528) and Giovanni della Casa's *Il Galateo* (1558), continued to be reprinted during the seventeenth and eighteenth centuries in English translation. Yet new editions of these works were also regularly updated to appeal to a modern audience; the 1774 edition of *Galateo*, for example, included a section on the relationship between refinement and sensibility.[64]

An attachment to the 'courtesy' label also overlooks the breadth of those new literary formats by which the ideals of polite society were often disseminated. Of these, the early-eighteenth-century development of the three- to five-page essay periodical has been the subject of much scholarly interest.

Instructive and diverting, tri-weekly or daily papers like the *Tatler*, *Spectator* and another of Richard Steele's titles, *The Guardian* (1713), combined advice on suitable behaviour with a readable, entertaining format that did much to exemplify the relaxed and sociable tone of advice within each series. Though merely the inheritors rather than the originators of an essay format traceable to Michel de Montaigne and Francis Bacon, early-eighteenth-century periodicalists firmly established the place of what later became a widely imitated medium among polite authors. Mid-century imitations often copied the periodical format, prominent examples of which included Eliza Haywood's *The Female Spectator* (1744–6), Samuel Johnson's *The Rambler* (1750–2), Edward Moore's *The World* (1753–6) and Henry Mackenzie's *The Mirror* (1779–80) and *Lounger* (1785–7). Later one-off compilations – among them *The Polite Companion* (Birmingham, 1749), *The Polite Miscellany* (Manchester, 1764) and *The Polite Preceptor* (1776) – also reprinted earlier periodical essays.[65] That such collections were published not just in London but also in Birmingham, Manchester and (in the case of the 1792 *Farrago*) Tewkesbury suggests a demand for polite literature that, in John Brewer's assessment, went far beyond an elite metropolitan audience and 'may have embraced almost everyone who was literate'.[66] Many imitators or compilers of polite anthologies were undoubtedly encouraged by the commercial success of early-eighteenth-century periodicals – the *Spectator's* circulation, for example, regularly reached between 3000 and 4000 copies per edition in the wake of the 1712 Stamp Tax, and peaked at 12,000 for specific issues. The periodical's blend of entertaining anecdote, moral guidance and scholarship also convinced intellectual commentators, including David Hume, that the merits of refinement might best be communicated through readable volumes such as his *Essays, Moral, Political and Literary* (1742/52). Later popularisers of sensibility likewise used essays, sermons and addresses to instruct readers, and in particular the young, on the pleasures and pitfalls of refined society. Such themes were also especially prominent in a distinct magazine genre which, originating in the 1730s, came into its own with a new series of titles in the late 1760s and 1770s. More eclectic than the periodical, the magazine quickly emerged as an ideal vehicle for short commentaries on contemporary manners, humorous satires on social stereotypes and serialisations of often overtly didactic fiction which also appeared in the single- or multi-volume 'novel' format.

Any study of advice literature, however categorised, can only provide us with a selective insight into how a particular society conceptualised, debated and refashioned standards of good (and bad) social conduct. As Anna Bryson points out, discussions of manners 'are concerned with ideals, and may themselves give little indication of the distance between these ideals and real behaviour'.[67] Between printed word and deed lies the subjective

process of reading and interpretation which, claims Roger Chartier, trans-
forms texts into 'the product of a reading and . . . a construction on the
part of its reading'.[68] In defending her own study as more than a history of
a literary genre, Bryson recommends that written accounts of conduct be
assessed not as 'accurate' or 'inaccurate' commentaries upon real behaviour
but as a 'significant cultural fact', illustrating the broad preoccupations of a
society characterised by a series of social, cultural and political influences
at a particular historical moment.[69] The value of studying attitudes towards
social behaviour rests on the fact that historians still know relatively little
about how previous societies defined good social conduct and its implications
for early modern concepts of personal, communal and national identity.

Bryson's comments are timely for my own purposes, given the explicit
focus in subsequent chapters on representations of idealised and failed
gentlemanliness within polite society. An examination of these debates provides insights into the ways in which published eighteenth-century authors
evaluated the relationship between refinement and gender construction,
and allows us – by noting this literature's inconsistencies as well as its
shared values – to gain a more accurate picture of the complexities and
possibilities of gender identity in that society. Understanding how modes
of good and bad behaviour were accomplished is also useful if we are to
address the basic but often ignored issue of how and to what extent literary
accounts of social behaviour were reproduced in readers' actions. We should
be cautious not to identify this relationship simply as the comparison of
prescription and practice, for the sources typically used in historians' search
for an eighteenth-century 'reality' offer not the 'truth' about individuals'
actions but an alternative, though still important, representation of social
actions. The diary, letters and journal examined in Chapter Five, for
example, provide personal interpretations of (refined and unrefined) daily
conduct in which experiences were recorded for the benefit of personal or,
on occasions, public consumption. Whatever their limitations, such representations provide opportunities to explore the congruence or tension between an
individual's understanding and experience of refined sociability. Taking the
study beyond prescriptive literature to a world where ideals were variously
followed, ignored, striven for or found elusive presents us with new ways
to think about polite society as a living experience continually complicated
by competing class-based, racial, geographical, generational and national
forms of social identity.

This sense of the potential distance between polite words and deeds can
also be discerned from the comments of eighteenth-century conduct writers
themselves. Though still promoting the merits of their own advice in a
competitive literary field, authors regularly advocated actual social engagement as, ultimately, the only means of achieving true refinement. The

image of the well-read but socially inept scholar remained a commonplace of eighteenth-century satire, and it was in an attempt to avoid similar faults that readers of guides like *The Polite Academy* (1771) were encouraged to 'betray no Air of Study' in company; 'for such will very ill suit the Ease that charms to so great a Degree in the polite Gentleman'.[70] This need to disguise bookish origins can be seen as one of two responses to conduct within polite society, however conceived. For aspiring members of a particular social circle, evidence of scholarship exposed the artificiality of an attribute preferably seen as the effortless achievement of a select minority. In a broader, possibly more generous concept of society, where politeness was characterised by its sincerity and potential omnipresence, the benefits of actions over words were perceived as a necessary means of achieving and further perfecting a desired level of sociability. As the *Guardian* declared in 1713, the 'virtues of men' could 'only really be learned in the company of the polite', an idea reiterated in later compendia restating the themes of early-century Whig periodical literature.[71]

Locations for refinement

Where was polite company to be found? As befits Richard Steele's and Joseph Addison's emphasis on the link between politeness and a developing commercial economy, it was natural for these writers to locate polite society at the heart of the consumer revolution: the town. As Addison put it in one of the *Spectator*'s many comparisons of urban and rural living, life in the early-eighteenth-century town encouraged 'an unconstrained Carriage, and a certain Openness of Behaviour', superior to the 'Manners of the last Age' still practised by 'People of Mode in the Country'.[72] The benefits of urban living were also appreciated by later reformers. According to David Hume, men and women who 'flock to the cities' were better able to display 'their wit or their breeding', and experienced 'an encrease of humanity, from the very habit of conversing together, and contributing to each other's pleasure and entertainment'.[73]

Of course, sponsors of city life also remained alert to its dangers and corruptions and worked hard to direct readers to venues where the opportunities for polite sociability were at their greatest. A number of these locations were new (or reworked) spaces developed as part of a late-seventeenth- and eighteenth-century 'urban renaissance' stimulated by an expanding town-based population; reconstruction after fire damage (London post-1666); and commercial expansion prompting the development of distinct resort towns such as Bath and the rise of new, popular social centres to rival existing but now increasingly marginal sites such as the court.[74]

This idea of a shift from court to city is central to many theoretical models of urban development, and to subsequent empirical historical analyses which chart the early-eighteenth-century relocation of social refinement, as 'politeness', within a reinvigorated urban environment. Several of these changes feature prominently in the development of what the German sociologist Jürgen Habermas describes as 'an emerging public sphere of civil society'; that is, the physical and ideological phenomenon by which, post-1660, private individuals came together via the interaction of print media and social spaces to create an anonymous public distinct from, and often critical of, state authority.[75] The power of this public rested, argues Habermas, in its self-perception as a homogeneous and inclusive entity, whose members, once strangers, were required to meet to overcome personal differences for the fulfilment of a wider social ideal. It was a principal function of politeness to effect this inclusiveness among previously isolated individuals, to moderate subsequent debates, and to validate the morality of activity within commercial society. At the same time, the gradual relocation of cultural and artistic activity towards these new social spaces further imbued them with the patina of polite taste.

Of the various locations in which this polite public formed, it is the coffee-house which has most interested historians, not least because of its prominence in Habermas's original thesis. Writing in 1650, the Oxford antiquary Anthony à Wood recorded the establishment of what may well have been the country's original venue when 'this yeare Jacob a Jew opened a coffey house at the Angel in the parish of S. Peter, in the East, Oxford'.[76] London's first site appeared in the following year in St Michael's Alley, Cornhill, providing typically, but not exclusively, male patrons with locations in which to drink and converse. The story of the coffee-house during the later seventeenth century is one of rapid growth coupled with criticism centred on its association with enervating beverages, pompous disputation and the substitution of natural social distinctions for an apparent republic of tongues. In the wake of the Interregnum this association with free speech was interpreted by critics as both potentially seditious and corrosive of true standards of refinement. In place of civilities predicated on social distinction, coffee-houses were seen to promote false notions of refinement based simply on one's presence in these self-consciously fashionable venues.

According to one Restoration critic:

> *Now being entered, there's no needing*
> *Of complement or gentile breeding,*
> *For you may seat you any where,*
> *There's no respect of persons there.*[77]

What changed over the next half-century was less the style than the perception of coffee-house conduct. To their promoters, such venues offered unparalleled opportunities for the informal, thoughtful and genuine sociability central to achieving new standards of 'polite' conduct. Historians have in turn employed changing perceptions of the coffee-house as a synecdoche for the early-eighteenth-century success of a polite, metropolitan Whig culture. In time, as was the case with other sociable spaces, the coffee-house phenomenon spread to provincial towns where, as in London, its presence was validated as contributing to the increasingly refined sociability of its patrons. As a venue where 'the social virtues reign triumphant', by mid-century the coffee-house offered what non-metropolitan commentators like Thomas Burr described as the 'easy freedom, and cheerful gaiety' which, 'arising from the nature of a public place, extends its influence over them'.[78]

Similar stimulation was provided by alternative venues, many of which enjoyed a new lease of life with the emergence of polite society. Of these, Habermas pays particular attention to the late-seventeenth-century playhouse. This revival in theatrical fortunes was due partly to the identification of the playhouse, like the coffee-house, as a popular social space and as a site for occasionally tasteful and instructive cultural activity. 'Theatrical performances', wrote one Bath resident in the 1740s, 'when conducted with decency and regularity, have always been esteemed the most rational amusements by the polite and thinking part of mankind.' The opening of Liverpool's first theatre in 1772 likewise brought players with 'graceful ease and polish to impart,/Refine the taste and humanize the heart.'[79] However sincere these opinions, developers remained alert to the competitiveness of polite society and catered for this snobbery in sites that denied indiscriminate social mixing. As Peter Borsay points out, for example, calls for a new theatre in Bath during the 1740s were motivated by a desire to construct a venue which, if open to a diverse range of people, none the less preserved what were described as the 'politer part's' gradations through tiered seating.

Such distinctions were not restricted to indoor venues. In good weather, eighteenth-century Londoners did much of their socialising along the public walks situated at the Inns of Court and Moorfields or in St James's and Hyde Park. As discreet locations removed from the bustle of the street, such venues were associated with higher standards of social behaviour. A man who 'may *waddle* into a Church, or Coffee-House', wrote one mid-century satirist, 'towards St James's . . . won't pass muster'. Such carelessness was to be ironed out by dancing-masters such as Pierre Rameau who, while agreeing that street greetings 'may be made more carelessly', urged that those executed in 'publick walks, where Persons of the best fashion resort . . . must be made with more Care and Regard'.[80] At the time that Rameau's advice became available to English speakers, royal parks like St James's had been prime locations for outdoor sociability for well over half a century. By this date, however, moves were also afoot to create a new type of social space, promoted partly by the public's desire for fresh, modish entertainments and for at least a sense of the exclusivity which no open park could fully guarantee.

There had been a pleasure garden at Vauxhall on the south bank of the Thames since the 1660s, though for much of the late seventeenth and early eighteenth century it carried a reputation for sexual lasciviousness and immorality. Demand for more sophisticated and genteel facilities induced the entrepreneur Jonathan Tyers to remodel the garden as a controlled environment offering paying visitors the quintessence of polite living. The success of the new Vauxhall, which opened in 1732, prompted the establishment of rival venues, the principal ones being Marylebone (1738) and Chelsea's Ranelagh (1742); over the next few decades similar gardens opened across the country. Competition between sites focused on the promotion of refined credentials: Ranelagh's reputation as a place ideally suited to what one promoter described as 'genteel and polite company' was matched by a rival who identified the 'darling Resort' of 'Persons of Reputation and Taste' as Vauxhall. Achieving a reputation for exclusivity did not necessarily require a draconian admissions policy. Vauxhall's promoters were at the same time eager to report that, on payment of a shilling, 'Multitudes from this vast City' entered its gates in search of a haven from an otherwise boorish urban environment. Patrons, it was claimed, were distinguished by their complicit understanding that certain forms of unattractive behaviour – in this case drunkenness – would not be tolerated 'in a place free and open to Thousands' who were able to 'polish without corrupting the Mind'.[81] Alongside these pretensions to morality, would-be visitors were no doubt equally motivated by their desire to patronise specific venues at times when the chances of being identified as genteel were at their greatest. Later consumers searching for polite reputations were assisted by manuals such as John Trusler's *London Adviser and Guide* (1786), which provided details of the daily and seasonal patterns of the capital's main venues, including pleasure gardens and the recently opened Pantheon in Oxford Street. Such advice offered the uninitiated information on how best to use their time and money in pursuit of and integration within a series of locations, the success of which, like polite society at large, depended on their dual reputation for accessibility and exclusivity.

Problematising polite society

John Trusler's guide is a timely reminder of the readiness of perhaps all eighteenth-century polite individuals to perceive refinement less as a high-minded moral issue than as personal presentation with a more limited community of friends and new or potential acquaintances. Acknowledging this individualism should make us cautious of viewing polite society as an overly homogeneous entity. Polite society, its purpose and locations varied from person to person at any given moment and, across time, within the work of individual commentators. Historians must relate broader discussions of refinement as 'change over time' with the myriad, apparently contradictory, statements from eighteenth-century writers addressing the 'who, when and where' of politeness at a particular historical moment. Later chapters raise similar issues from the perspective of eighteenth-century attitudes to manliness, a conundrum further complicated by the inevitable dissonance between advice read and actions performed. It is not my intention here, or elsewhere, to attempt to cover up the ambiguities that reveal a society no less complex than our own. By contrast, it seems prudent to accept and draw attention to these tensions between the particular and the general as an inevitable and important feature of what eighteenth-century writers fully understood to be the protean quality of their subject.

Indeed, to explore its often contradictory nature helps in understanding the vibrancy of debates over polite society. Seen from the perspective of individuals across our period, politeness comes alive as part of a wider evaluation of social conditions both between contemporaries and between the generations. These debates took various directions. Some, like Jonathan Swift, remained unconvinced that theirs was indeed the politest age. Writing in the first decade of the eighteenth century, Swift looked back to the late 1620s and 1630s as the country's 'highest Period of Politeness'. Since then a negligence of manners during the Interregnum and the false courtliness of the Restoration had reduced modern standards of conduct to what Swift considered its now parlous state.[82] Later commentators suggested a similar trajectory across different timescales. Nostalgic conversation with a friend in 1775 led James Boswell to reminisce on the 1730s when 'there was more politeness and gentility'; while in 1783 the Edinburgh publisher William Creech contrasted the 'decency, dignity, and delicacy' of manners in his home town in 1763 with those of 'looseness, dissipation, and licentiousness' twenty years on.[83]

For others, however, the same period was one of progress and improvement; a claim that appeared not only in wide-ranging theories of social evolution, but also as part of more specific observations, often on the development of city manners. Typically, successive generations judged themselves practitioners of ever more genuine and relaxed forms of sociability. Writing in the early 1790s, the author of *Farrago* detected a 'wonderful change in national manners' in the three decades since men had abandoned the constraints of continental refinement for their now 'familiar intercourse with

mankind in general'.[84] However, for the early nineteenth-century memoirist, Nathaniel Wraxall, the London of the late 1770s and 1780s had been
a society 'subjected . . . to fetters from which we have since emancipated
ourselves – those of dress, etiquette and form. The lapse of two centuries
could scarcely have produced a greater alteration in these particulars than
have been made by about forty years.'[85]

Discussions on the course of polite society paid particular attention to the
behaviour of young men, who were seen as most receptive to current trends
in conduct. Thus, it was common for those who detected falling standards
to attribute these errors to the youth of the day. By contrast, more optimistic
social observers were keener to praise the younger generation for a com-
monsense that liberated individuals from established strictures of over-
formality. Yet even here there remained the potential for inter-generational
contest. As Richard Steele suggested in 1713, 'few young people please in
Conversation' because of their 'want of Experience'.[86] The need for successive generations to instil or refashion this experience goes some way to
explain the enduring topicality, and controversy, of eighteenth-century discourses on refinement. It is this vibrancy that much existing historiography
remains reluctant to analyse and problematise through the incorporation of
micro-histories of quotidian social conduct within existing macro-historical
models of change.

Of these models it is that of an emerging public sphere which continues
most strongly to influence the parameters of research into the evolution
and character of eighteenth-century polite society, the picture of which is
inevitably coloured by the preoccupations of Habermas's original thesis. To
conclude this chapter, I wish to consider recent discussions of the public
sphere and polite society with regard to two further subject areas – the first
pertinent to the ways historians understand early-eighteenth-century definitions of politeness, the second to the study of attitudes towards manliness
within this polite environment – which, though important to eighteenth-
century polite commentators, have featured less prominently in modern
scholarship. Both, as we shall see in subsequent chapters, are significant
modifications necessary if we are to understand the nature of eighteenth-
century debates over gentlemanliness in polite society.

Religion and polite society

It is a central tenet of the Habermasian model that the public sphere's
rise was partly precipitated by a long-term deterioration in two established
centres of early modern cultural activity: the royal court and the Anglican
Church, on the latter of which I intend to focus here. The consequences of

this suggested decline are apparent in a number of recent histories. J.G.A. Pocock, for example, charts the rise of a 'secular culture' during the opening decade of the 1700s; David Shields for the same period identifies the transmission of 'a secularized, cosmopolitan, genteel culture' between Britain and America; while Anthony Fletcher describes a late-seventeenth-century shift from a behavioural literature offering 'religious and moral advice' to one 'firmly secular in its ideological tone'.[87] Elsewhere, the rise of politeness, if not replacing religious faith, is depicted as dominating and controlling the excesses of an until recently highly factional church. Thus the later seventeenth century did not, in Lawrence Klein's opinion, 'see a decline of the religious spirit but instead witnessed rigorous attempts at submitting it to social and civil discipline'; the resultant 'polite religion' evaded the bitterness of former doctrinal debates by 'operating within society according to principles of sociability and politeness'.[88]

It is certainly possible to find evidence of sharp tensions between religious and polite society, especially in the pronouncements of mid-eighteenth-century evangelicals who criticised current modes of social refinement as a facet of corrupt modern living. Calvinistic Methodist leaders such as George Whitefield characterised 'the polite and fashionable diversions of the age' as 'destructive to the soul and body', while the more moderate John Wesley condemned as 'miserably defective' late-seventeenth- and eighteenth-century translations of several influential conduct guides.[89] Meanwhile, Church of England critics of evangelicalism, and of what they saw as the pusillanimity of current practices within mainstream Anglicanism, identified this opposition to politeness as a factor in Methodism's growing popularity. The mid-century theologian Samuel Angiers claimed that Anglican ministers who used 'polite, genteel words . . . preached away their Congregations' to men like Whitefield, whose plain talking attracted what Angiers thought the majority of sober, God-fearing church-goers.[90] Critics of Angiers's hard line also addressed their comments to a readership whom they evidently thought shared his hostility. Numerous efforts to challenge this notion of antagonism between refinement and religion suggest its durability in the popular mind: 'the religion of Christ', as John Harris felt it necessary to state in the 1770s, 'does not discourage but rather promotes good manners'.[91] Finally, the tensions between refinement and religion are further evident in the work of a select group of writers, the most notorious being David Hume, who went far beyond statements on secularisation. In developing his science of human nature, Hume's scepticism led him to attack Christianity's preoccupation with salvation, as a result of which men and women were alienated from what Hume called an earthly 'common life' of natural sociability central to the foundation of superior forms of morality and civilisation.

From the tone of these statements (aside from Hume's) it is clear that the discrepancies identified between religion and refinement were contingent on a critical equation of politeness with triviality and moral corruption. Tensions between polite living and religious worship were repeatedly explained in terms of the deterioration of the contemporary understanding of a quality that, in its 'untainted' form, was actually closely related to benevolent Christianity. This emphasis on benevolence is important in that it adds a new dimension to Lawrence Klein's idea of 'polite religion' as worship simply contained and controlled by the proprieties of genteel daily conduct. Good Christians were certainly expected to behave with decorum. Adam Petrie's 1720 guide to deportment, for example, provided details on suitable dress and conduct within church, or, as Petrie described it, 'an Academy of Piety, prudence and good Breeding', presided over by ministers adept in 'Politeness and Complaisance'.[92]

At the same time, many sponsors recognised that Christianity also contributed to the further development of politeness, fostering a generosity of spirit central to eighteenth-century notions of idealised refinement. William Howdell, vicar of East Hardwick, near Pontefract, spoke in 1744 of the 'Christian Religion [as] . . . productive of Politeness and Good-breeding'. If, he continued, 'the End of Good-breeding is to exalt and refine the Nature of Man, what can exalt and refine it more than the religion of Christ?' Howdell identified a dual role for religion as both a means of moderating unruly conduct and a source of the 'warmest affection' and 'unbounded Benevolence' required for true politeness. The sermon's hero was St Paul, whose display of these qualities in the presence of King Agrippa earned him respect in numerous accounts of desirable behaviour. Howdell's villains were the Methodists who, like Samuel Angiers, he considered blunt and unduly censorious but against whose challenge, in keeping with his particular interpretation of Christian worship, Howdell advocated not a rival spirit of sobriety but greater gentility.[93]

Later in the century, the increasing attraction of sensibility enhanced this relationship between ideal behaviour and revealed religion. The commensurability of Christianity and refinement, and the added lustre each brought to the other, proves a striking feature of work by the likes of John Harris and the Tonbridge School master and popular essayist, Vicesimus Knox (1752–1821). Harris, for example, repeatedly identified religion as the basis for refined behaviour – common links being charity, feeling, friendship, humility and affection. Knox proposed a similar synthesis. Nothing, he wrote in 1782, 'can be more conducive to it [true politeness] than a religion which every where recommends brotherly love, meekness and humility'. 'True politeness' in turn allowed individuals to act with Christian compassion in abnegating personal interests for companions who were treated with 'a gentleness of sentiment and conduct'. Knox explored this relationship from another angle when he attributed modern criticisms of religion to writers incapable of refined sympathy, the majority of whom he identified as academics whose cloistered lifestyles had deprived them of the 'tender charities of husband, father, brother, friend'.[94] Nor was this simply the opinion of mainstream Anglicans. Any identification of Methodism, and especially Whitefield's Calvinistic theology, as a critique of politeness needs to be balanced by John Wesley's later discussions of the compatibility of virtuous refinement with an ideal Methodist lifestyle.[95] Moreover, as the work of Richard Sher and others shows, polite self-control and later benevolent sensibility were similarly important to the teaching of prominent Moderate Church of Scotland theologians, notably Hugh Blair. The considerable popularity of Blair's five volumes of *Sermons* (1777–1801) clearly demonstrates a market for the cleric as social instructor at the end of a century which, we should remember, also saw the enduring popularity of the works of Restoration clergymen like Richard Allestree.[96]

The contribution of religious writers to the debates over good and bad social conduct confirms the proximity between refined sociability and morality that proved essential for early-eighteenth-century lay writers keen to portray politeness and its embodiment, the polite gentleman, as superior to early modern forms of refinement. In turn, a growing concern that displays of politeness could be faked for personal gain gave an added urgency to sentimental writers' reassertion of this equation through a selection of male role models, principal of which, as we shall see in Chapter Three, was the generous, refined and manly Christ.

Masculinity and polite society

My second addendum to Habermas's thesis, and its subsequent treatment in histories of polite society, concerns the place of gender in an eighteenth-century public sphere. Feminist historiography has questioned what is seen as Habermas's implicit identification of the public sphere as an area of predominantly male activity. Scholars influenced by Habermas's thesis, it is argued, have since developed this gender distinction between public and private spheres, paying particularly close attention to the development of an eighteenth-century understanding of bourgeois femininity too closely bound up with the responsibilities of a restricted domestic 'private sphere'. Challenges to the completeness of this model have taken two directions. The first sees a re-examination of the meaning of the public/private distinction and, based on empirical research, the experience of eighteenth-century women relative to these often interconnected environments.[97] Second, scholars have examined the relationship of men and attitudes to male conduct to this model of separate spheres. To date, a key aim of this research has been to develop existing pictures of eighteenth-century manliness as a blend of private and public actions, and to see the success of the latter as increasingly dependent on men's involvement in this supposedly female-orientated, domestic sphere. Thus for Leonore Davidoff and Catherine Hall, two pioneers in this field, the late eighteenth century saw the emergence of a middle-class ideal of manliness in which men's 'power to command or to influence people, [was] . . . embedded in networks of familial and female support which underpinned their rise to public prominence'.[98]

This blurring of the traditional (implicit) equation of manliness with the public sphere has implications for the arguments developed in the rest of this book. Chapter Three explores how conduct writers approached the question of male refinement in the home or with family members. Within sentimental discourse the domestic environment was often seen as a prime location in which refined men were expected to operate and where the true quality and extent of their personal refinement was ascertained. Much of the advice literature discussed elsewhere in the book considered behaviour within public spaces such as the coffee-house, park, public garden or church. On the face of it, this focus on attitudes to men's conduct at these locations, coupled with the absence of a full discussion of expected female behaviour in what to some extent were all mixed social spaces, runs the risk of reproducing a Habermasian image of an unproblematic male-dominated public sphere.

This, however, is not my intention. Rather, I aim to show, first, how eighteenth-century discussions of men in the public sphere were concerned with constructing and establishing, rather than simply confirming, ideas of male gender. In addition, while viewing the public sphere as a series of locations where masculine (and polite) reputations were made, I also examine the potential pitfalls to which men were in danger of succumbing to the detriment of gentle and manly identity. Representations of the effeminate fop considered in Chapter Four remind us that men's participation in polite social spaces provided opportunities for exposing oneself to ridicule as well as establishing a reputation for manliness. That men should make these mistakes while pursuing a responsible image was a much rehearsed concern; commentators realised that notions of acceptable masculinity depended not only on participation but also on suitable conduct within these areas. It was the claim of many behavioural writers, and the hope of their readers, to be able to navigate these dangers and to delineate forms of male conduct compatible with both politeness and manliness. It is to these attempts that we now turn.

Notes and references

1. Langford, *Polite and Commercial People*, p. 1.

2. See John Brewer, *The Pleasures of the Imagination: English Culture in the Eighteenth Century* (1997); Tom Williamson, *Polite Landscapes: Gardens and Society in Eighteenth-Century England* (Stroud, 1995).

3. Steven Shapin, *A History of Truth: Civility and Science in Seventeenth-Century England* (Chicago IL and London, 1994); Peter Borsay, *The English Urban Renaissance: Culture and Society in the Provincial Town, 1660–1770* (Oxford, 1989); Paul Langford, 'Politics and manners from Sir Robert Walpole to Sir Robert Peel', *Proceedings of the British Academy*, 94 (1996), pp. 103–25; Lawrence E. Klein, 'Shaftesbury, politeness and the politics of religion', in Nicholas Phillipson and Quentin Skinner eds., *Political Discourse in Early Modern Britain* (Cambridge, 1993); Richard B. Sher, *Church and University in the Scottish Enlightenment: The Moderate Literati of Edinburgh* (Edinburgh, 1985).

4. Lawrence E. Klein, *Shaftesbury and the Culture of Politeness: Moral Discourse and Cultural Politics in Early Eighteenth-Century England* (Cambridge, 1994); Nicholas Phillipson, *Hume* (1989), ch. 2; Stephen Copley, 'Commerce, conversation and politeness in the early eighteenth-century periodical', *British Journal of Eighteenth-Century Studies*, 18 (1995), pp. 63–77; Bryson, *From Courtesy to Civility*.

5. J.G.A. Pocock, *Virtue, Commerce and History* (Cambridge, 1985), p. 198; Langford, *Polite and Commercial People*, pp. 116, 120–1; Vickery, *Gentleman's Daughter*, p. 17; Sher, *Church and University*, p. 57.

6. Bernard Mandeville, *The Fable of the Bees* (1714, 1732 edn) ed. F.B. Kaye, 2 vols. (1924, rpt Indianapolis IN, 1985), I, pp. 7–8.

7. David Hume, 'Of the rise and progress of the arts and sciences' (1742), in *Essays, Moral, Political and Literary* (1742/52), ed. Eugene F. Miller (Indianapolis IN, 1985), p. 133; Blackstone quoted by Langford, *Polite and Commercial People*, p. 1.

8. John Millar, *Observations Concerning the Distinction of Ranks in Society* (1771), p. 37.

9. *Boswell: The Ominous Years, 1774–1776*, eds. Charles Ryskamp and Frederick A. Pottle (1963), p. 140.

10. Jean-Baptiste Bellegarde, *Reflexions Upon the Politeness of Manners* (Paris, 1698; trans. 1707), p. 3.

11. No. 54 (2 May 1711), in the *Spectator* (1711–12, 1714), ed. Donald F. Bond, 5 vols. (Oxford, 1965), I, p. 232.

12. *The Man of Manners; or Plebian Polished* (1733), p. 3.

13. No. 100 (2 Mar 1751) in *The Rambler* (1750–2), eds. W.J. Bate and Albrecht B. Strauss in *The Yale Edition of the Works of Samuel Johnson*, 16 vols. (New

Haven CT and London, 1958–90), IV, p. 169; Boswell, *Life of Johnson* (1791), ed. Pat Rogers (Oxford, 1980), p. 400.

14. Cornelius Pope, *The New Bath Guide* (1762, 1764 edn), p. 36.

15. John Wood, *An Essay towards a Description of Bath*, 2 vols. (2nd edn, 1747), II, p. 411.

16. *Gentleman's Magazine*, 3 (1733), p. 641.

17. Samuel Johnson, *Dictionary of the English Language* (1755, repr. 1979); Nathan Bailey, *A Universal Etymological Dictionary* (23rd edn, 1773).

18. *Gentleman's Magazine*, 3 (1733), p. 641.

19. 'Of true politeness', *Gentleman's Magazine*, 4 (1734), p. 191.

20. Abel Boyer, 'On conversation, society, civility, and politeness', *The English Theophrastus; or, Manners of the Age* (1702), p. 108; Bellegarde, *Reflexions Upon Politeness*, p. 1.

21. 'Of politeness', *Farrago. Consisting of Essays, Moral, Philosophical, Political, and Historical*, 2 vols. (Tewkesbury, 1792), I, p. 96.

22. *Ibid.*, I, pp. 96–7.

23. Bailey, *New Universal Dictionary* (1755); *Universal Etymological Dictionary* (25th edn, 1790); James Barclay, *Complete and Universal English Dictionary* (1774).

24. Boyer, *English Theophrastus*, p. 108.

25. 'The necessity of cultivating politeness', *Rambler*, No. 98 (23 Feb 1751), in Johnson, *Works*, IV, p. 161.

26. *The Art of Being Easy* (1724), pp. 6, 77, 46.

27. Johnson, *Dictionary*; *Rambler*, No. 98, in *Works*, IV, p. 162.

28. Titles, among many others, include, *The Polite Gentleman* (1700); James Forrester's *Polite Philosopher* (1738); *The Polite Miscellany* (Manchester, 1764); *The New Polite Instructor* (1771); John Trusler's *Principles of Politeness* (York, 1775); and William Bews's *The Polite Entertainment* (1791).

29. The *OED* dates 'courtesy' to the early thirteenth century, and 'civility' to the mid-sixteenth century.

30. *The Polite Academy; or, School of Behaviour for Young Gentlemen and Ladies* (5th edn, 1771), p. 1.

31. Bryson, *From Courtesy to Civility*, p. 48.

32. John Wesley, 'On pleasing all men' (1787), in *Sermons*, ed. Albert C. Outler, in *The Works of John Wesley*, ed. Frank Baker, 26 vols. (Nashville TN, 1982–95), III, p. 424.

33. John Locke, *Some Thoughts Concerning Education* (1693), in *The Educational Writings of John Locke*, ed. James L. Axtell (Cambridge, 1968), pp. 250, 169; Hume, 'Rise and progress', in *Essays*, p. 126.

34. Klein, *Shaftesbury and the Culture of Politeness*, p. 8

35. Pocock, *Virtue*, p. 236; Lawrence E. Klein, 'Liberty, manners, and politeness in early eighteenth-century England', *Historical Journal*, 32 (1989), p. 583; *Shaftesbury and the Culture of Politeness*, p. 13; Nicholas Phillipson, 'Politics, politeness and the Anglicisation of early eighteenth-century Scottish culture', in Roger Mason ed., *Scotland and England, 1286–1815* (Edinburgh, 1987), pp. 226–46; Phillipson's distinction between English and Scottish models of refinement is an important one, considered below.

36. Pocock, *Virtue*, p. 236.

37. Lawrence E. Klein, 'Coffee-house civility, 1660–1714: an aspect of post-courtly culture in England', *Huntington Library Quarterly*, 59 (1997), esp. pp. 44–51; *Shaftesbury and the Culture of Politeness*, pp. 8–14, 125–31.

38. The subtitle of an anonymous pamphlet, *The Reformed Gentleman* (1693) – 'the old English morals rescued from the immoralities of the present age. Shewing how inconsistent those *pretended genteel accomplishments* of swearing, drinking, whoring and sabbath-breaking, are with the true generosity of an English man' (my italics) – provides a flavour of this campaign.

39. Barker-Benfield, *Culture of Sensibility*, p. 61. See also Hunt, *Middling Sort*, ch. 4.

40. *Spectator*, No. 9 (10 Mar 1711), I, p. 39.

41. Daniel Gordon, for example, refers to the 'egalitarianism' of Bellegarde's advice centred on the communal salon; *Citizens Without Sovereignty: Equality and Sociability in French Thought, 1670–1789* (Princeton NJ, 1994), p. 96. See also Dena Goodman, *The Republic of Letters. A Cultural History of the French Revolution* (Ithaca NY, 1994), pp. 111–19.

42. In addition to the *Reflexions*, prominent French contributions to the debate on politeness include Antoine de Courtin's *Nouveau Traité de la Civilité* (1671), translated in the same year as *The Rules of Civility*. Bellegarde's *Modèles des Conversations pour les Personnes Polies* (3rd edn, The Hague, 1699) was translated as *Models of Conversation for Persons of Polite Education* in 1765. For the influence of French writing on Abel Boyer's *English Theophrastus* see Goodman, *Republic of Letters*, p. 120.

43. Klein, 'Coffee-house civility', p. 51.

44. Nicholas Phillipson, 'The Scottish enlightenment', in Roy Porter and Mikulás Teich eds., *The Enlightenment in National Context* (Cambridge, 1981).

45. Phillipson, 'Politics, politeness and Anglicisation', p. 235.

46. Hume, 'Rise and progress', in *Essays*, p. 131.

47. The precise nature of this experience aroused debate among Scottish thinkers. Adam Smith, for example, rejected Hume's belief in an observer's ability to recreate another's feelings and to experience them as if at first hand.

48. Hume, 'Rise and progress', in *Essays*, p. 131; 'Of national characters', *ibid.*, p. 202.

49. Brewer, *Pleasures of the Imagination*, p. 115.

50. Hugh Blair, 'On gentleness', *Sermons*, 5 vols. (Edinburgh, 1777–1801), I, p. 150.

51. John Harris, *An Essay on Politeness* (1775, 3rd edn 1820), pp. 19, 24, 33.

52. Hester Chapone, 'On conversation', in *Miscellanies in Prose and Verse* (1775), p. 29.

53. Brewer, *Pleasures of the Imagination*, pp. 100, 117.

54. R.S. Crane, 'Suggestions toward a genealogy of the "man of feeling"', *Journal of English Literary History*, 1 (1934), 205–30. Crane and his critics are discussed in John Sheriff, *The Good-Natured Man: the Evolution of a Moral Ideal, 1660–1800* (Tuscaloosa AL, 1982).

55. For late-seventeenth- and eighteenth-century medical theories of the nervous system see Barker-Benfield, *Culture of Sensibility*, ch. 1; G.S. Rousseau, 'Towards a semiotics of the nerve: the social history of language in a new key', in Peter Burke and Roy Porter eds., *Language, Self, and Society. A Social History of Language* (Cambridge, 1991).

56. The modes and implications of this popularisation are discussed in John Mullan, *Sentiment and Sociability: The Language of Feeling in the Eighteenth Century* (Oxford, 1988), ch. 5. This, in addition to Markman Ellis, *The Politics of Sensibility: Race, Gender and Commerce in the Sentimental Novel* (Cambridge, 1996), ch. 1, and Langford, *Polite and Commercial People*, ch. 10, provides an excellent survey of sensibility as both an intellectual and a popular phenomenon.

57. William Cowper to Margaret King, 19 June 1788, in *Letters and Prose of William Cowper*, eds. James King and Charles Ryskamp, 5 vols. (Oxford, 1979–86), III, pp. 179–80.

58. Adam Smith, *The Theory of Moral Sentiments* (1759), ed. D.D. Raphael and A.L. Macfie (Oxford, 1976), pp. 205–7.

59. Clement Ellis, *The Gentile Sinner: or England's Brave Gentleman both as he is and should be* (Oxford, 1660), iv. Allestree's most successful work, *The Whole Duty of Man*, reached its sixty-fourth edition in 1842.

60. Fletcher, *Gender, Sex and Subordination*, p. 331.

61. Goodman, *Republic of Letters*, pp. 111–19.

62. Morgan, *Manners, Morals and Class*, ch. 1.

63. Nancy Armstrong, 'The rise of the domestic woman', in Armstrong and Leonard Tennenhouse eds., *The Ideology of Conduct* (1987); Joyce Hemlow, 'Fanny Burney and the courtesy book', *Proceedings of the Modern Language Association (PMLA)*, 65 (1950), pp. 732–61.

64. *Galateo: or a Treatise on Politeness and Delicacy of Manners*, trans. Richard Graves (1774). Earlier variations in title are similarly suggestive of changing concepts of social conduct: the 1774 study of 'politeness' and 'delicacy' had been preceded by a *Galateo of Manners; or Instructions to a Young Gentleman* (trans. 1703) and *The Refin'd Courtier; or A Correction of Several Indecencies crept into Civil Conversation* (trans. 1663).

65. *Spectator* No. 631 on politeness and appearance, and issue nos. 24 and 162 from the *Guardian* (1713) on conversation and complaisance appeared in, for example, *The Polite Preceptor* (1776).

66. Brewer, *Pleasures of the Imagination*, p. 102. Amanda Vickery also reveals a rich regional culture in which the tensions and aspirations of refinement closely reflected those of the metropolis but to which many members of the northern middle class remained happily impervious: for one it was Pontefract, not London, that merited the title of the 'capital of politeness', *Gentleman's Daughter*, p. 172. Lawrence Klein notes the appeal of polite guides further down the social scale in 'Politeness for plebes: consumption and social identity in early eighteenth-century England', in John Brewer and Ann Bermingham eds., *The Culture of Consumption. Image, Object, Text* (1995).

67. Bryson, *From Courtesy to Civility*, p. 6.

68. Roger Chartier, *Cultural History. Between Practices and Representations*, trans. Lydia G. Cochrane (Cambridge, 1988), p. 42. On the implications of subjectivity for women readers see Vivien Jones, 'The seductions of conduct: pleasure and conduct literature', in Roy Porter and Marie Mulvey Roberts eds., *Pleasure in the Eighteenth Century* (1996). The reception of advice literature in a broader debate on the historical meaning of reading is discussed in James Raven, Helen Small and Naomi Tadmor eds., *The Practice and Representation of Reading in England* (Cambridge, 1996).

69. Bryson, *From Courtesy to Civility*, p. 279.

70. *Polite Academy*, p. 114.

71. No. 24 (8 Apr 1713), in *The Guardian* (1713), ed. John Calhoun Stephens (Lexington KY, 1982), p. 113; later reprints of this issue include the *Polite Preceptor*, p. 224.

72. No. 119 (17 July 1711), I, p. 487.

73. Hume, 'Of refinement in the arts and sciences' (1752), in *Essays*, p. 271.

74. Borsay, *English Urban Renaissance*; Mark Girouard, *The English Town* (New Haven CT and London, 1990); Roy Porter, *London. A Social History* (1994).

75. Jürgen Habermas, *The Structural Transformation of the Public Sphere* (1962, Engl. trans. Cambridge MA, 1989), pp. 25–6.

76. Anthony à Wood, *The Life and Times of Anthony à Wood*, eds. Andrew Clark and Llewelyn Powys (1932), p. 40.

77. *The Character of a Coffee-House* (1665), p. 2.

78. T.B. Burr, *A History of Tunbridge-Wells* (1766), quoted in Borsay, *English Urban Renaissance*, p. 280. See also Aytoun Ellis, *The Penny Universities: A History of the Coffee Houses* (1956) and Steven Pincus, '"Coffee politicians does create": coffee-houses and Restoration political culture', *Journal of Modern History*, 67 (1995), pp. 807–34.

79. Quoted in Borsay, *English Urban Renaissance*, pp. 259–60.

80. *A Trip from St James's to the Royal Exchange* (1744), p. 5; Pierre Rameau, *The Dancing Master* (trans. 1728), pp. 18–19. On walks see Girouard, *English Town*, ch. 8.

81. *Description of Ranelagh Rotundo Gardens* (1762), p. 5; *A Sketch of Spring Gardens, Vauxhall* (1750), pp. 27–9.

82. Jonathan Swift, 'Hints towards an essay on conversation' (*c.* 1710), in *Works of Jonathan Swift*, ed. Herbert Davis, 14 vols. (1939–68), IV (1957), p. 94.

83. Boswell, *Ominous Years, 1774–76*, p. 174; William Creech, *Letters . . . Reflecting the Mode of Living* (Edinburgh, 1791), p. 34.

84. 'Of politeness', *Farrago*, I, pp. 97–8.

85. Nathaniel Wraxall, *Historical and Posthumous Memoirs, 1772–1784*, ed. Henry Wheatley, 5 vols. (1884), I, p. 98.

86. *Guardian*, No. 24 (8 Apr 1713), p. 112.

87. Pocock, *Virtue*, p. 237; David S. Shields, *Civil Tongues and Polite Letters in British America* (Chapel Hill NC and London, 1995), p. 12; Fletcher, *Gender, Sex and Subordination*, p. 335.

88. Klein, *Shaftesbury and the Culture of Politeness*, p. 10; 'Shaftesbury, politeness and the politics of religion', p. 284. For a reappraisal of this trend see Jeremy Gregory, '*Homo-religiosus*: masculinity and religion in the long eighteenth century', in Hitchcock and Cohen eds., *English Masculinities*.

89. Whitefield's interpretation is taken from the title of a sermon delivered in 1740. Wesley's selected titles included *The Refined Courtier*, Nathaniel Walker's 1663 translation of *Il Galateo*, and Pierre d'Ortige de Vaumorière's *The Art of Pleasing* (1691, trans. 1707), 'On pleasing all men', in *Sermons*, III, p. 417.

90. Samuel Angiers, *The Polite Modern Divine* (1756), p. 46.

91. Harris, *Essay on Politeness*, p. 35; similar efforts were made in Vicesimus Knox's 1782 essay 'Religion and moral principles not only consistent with, but

promotive of, true politeness', in *Works*, 7 vols. (1824), I, pp. 471–5. Knox's popular essays originally appeared in the first or second edition of his *Essays Moral and Literary* (1778, 1782).

92. Adam Petrie, *The Rules of Good Deportment* (1720), in *Works* (Edinburgh, 1877), pp. 130, 132. Petrie followed this with his more specific guide to *Rules of Good Deportment for Church-Officers* (1730).

93. William Howdell, *Religion Productive of Joy and Consistent with Politeness. A Sermon* (York, 1744), pp. 23–4. Richard Steele had previously described St Paul as a 'Gentleman' of 'good Breeding' in his influential *The Christian Hero* (1701), ed. Rae Blanchard (Oxford, 1932), pp. 57, 59. John Harris thought Paul a 'man of fine address', *Essay on Politeness*, p. 35.

94. Knox, 'Religion and . . . true politeness', in *Works*, I, p. 473; 'The want of piety arises from the want of sensibility' (1782), in *ibid.*, p. 448.

95. On the relationship between Methodism and sensibility see Barker-Benfield, *Culture of Sensibility*, pp. 71–7.

96. Attitudes to politeness in the Church of Scotland are considered in Sher, *Church and University*, esp. ch. 2. John Dwyer notes the importance of sensibility to the Moderate clergy in 'Clio and ethics: practical morality in enlightened Scotland', *The Eighteenth Century: Theory and Interpretation*, 30 (1989), pp. 45–72.

97. Lawrence E. Klein, 'Gender and the public/private distinction in the eighteenth century: some questions about evidence and analytic procedure', *Eighteenth-Century Studies*, 29 (1995), pp. 97–109. Much of the work on women and publicity is based on an increasingly sophisticated reading of essentially permeable public and private realms. The result, writes John Brewer, has seen historians direct their research 'not to those spaces at the polar ends of public and private but to the spaces in between', 'This, that and the other: public, social and private in the seventeenth and eighteenth centuries', in Dario Castiglione and Lesley Sharpe eds., *Shifting the Boundaries: Transformations of the Languages of Public and Private in the Eighteenth Century* (Exeter, 1995), p. 10.

98. Leonore Davidoff and Catherine Hall, *Family Fortunes: Men and Women of the English Middle Class, 1780–1850* (1987), p. 13.

CHAPTER TWO

Men and the rise of politeness

In 1684 a Somerset landowner, Edward Clarke, asked his friend John Locke for guidance on the education of his son. In response, Locke produced the first of what became a series of letters later published as *Some Thoughts Concerning Education* (1693). Written for a young man from a specific social milieu, and with advice on subjects including an education in the classics, estate management and the continental tour, Locke's *Thoughts* was clearly of particular interest to those upper-class readers whom its author readily admitted required 'different ways of Breeding' to other, less privileged men. In this sense, Locke's guide had much in common with an established tradition of courtesy literature offering professional and recreational instruction for the complete gentleman of good birth. But in other ways Locke's advice was more original and, as a result, of greater relevance to a broader eighteenth-century readership. At the heart of Locke's thinking was the idea that advice on conduct was more than a list of dos and don'ts to be acquired before entering society. Rather, education was intended to fashion a moral character well versed in Christian and humanist thought, and to provide young men with a deep-seated wisdom, ensuring appropriate behaviour in the myriad social engagements that even the most nuanced conduct guide could not hope to cover.

Locke's grounding of good behaviour in moral character is especially evident in his consideration of refined social conduct for boys. Central to this discussion was the need for congruence between thought and action. Of the two, Locke believed good thoughts, or what he termed 'inward Civility', the more important. With inner refinement as a base it was more than likely that an individual's external actions would be pleasing: 'genuine Marks' of 'such a well-formed Mind . . . cannot but be easy and unconstrain'd'.[1] In these circumstances there was, in Locke's opinion, little

53

need to trouble the young with an unnecessary list of rules or 'manners' which did nothing but cause confusion and promote excessive awkwardness.

For older children and young men, Locke proposed a more sophisticated relationship between inner civility and outer gesture. Again, 'civil' men were identified by their moral qualities evident in 'a disposition not to offend others', and a 'general Good will and Regard for all People'. But it was equally true that men became 'Well-fashion'd' when they embellished these virtues with a series of graceful movements and phrases, through which company was drawn to the virtuous individual and made 'easy and well pleased'. Aware that with maturity it became increasingly important to abide by established social conventions, Locke encouraged young men to show respect for others according to the 'Fashion and Way of that Country'. Certainly, these specifics had to be learned; though Locke again emphasised the importance of not over-burdening readers with a particular set of rules. Put together, 'inward civility' and the art of being 'well-fashion'd' equipped young men with a sufficient blend of adaptability and social awareness to please, regardless of social environment. Locke identified this combination as 'good breeding', the purpose of which was to 'soften Men's Tempers that they may bend in compliance and accommodate themselves to those they have to do with'.[2]

Originating as advice for a single reader, Locke's *Thoughts* became a classic eighteenth-century guide, regularly reprinted and imitated by later educational theorists. Certainly its success did not rest solely on Locke's account of good breeding. Yet the tone of this particular discussion, in which idealised behaviour was based on inner virtues of which all men were capable, and from which others were able to benefit, gave his account an authority and relevance beyond the confines of a social elite. If in some ways a restatement of traditional courtesy literature, Locke's definition of refinement also located his book within the late-seventeenth- and eighteenth-century culture of politeness outlined in Chapter One. With its emphasis on breeding as a virtue engendering benevolence, consideration and thoughtfulness, polished through a relaxed and pleasing deportment, Locke's *Thoughts* had much to contribute to this new culture and, more specifically, to men's understanding of themselves as 'polite' gentlemen.

This chapter examines in more detail the relationship between men and politeness. As befitted the originality of 'politeness', early-eighteenth-century discussions of male manners regularly highlighted the differences between existing images of male refinement, notably the courtier and the country gentleman, and newer, town-based gentlemen who socialised freely in male and now also in female company. This proximity to women was a significant feature of the new ideal, and was thought an important stimulus to further refinement on the part of polite gentlemen and polite society at large. However, such proximity also demanded justification. A discussion of 'Manliness and politeness' examines how conduct writers demonstrated the 'manly' content of these new forms of conduct. This validation of gender identity was also taken up by Scottish enlightenment thinkers, who characterised modern styles of manhood as not only compatible with traditional values such as industry and courage, but as superior expressions of qualities now embellished by refinement. In doing so, enlightened social analysts employed an overt discourse of manliness to illustrate what they saw as the personal and societal benefits of a modern commercial economy. The emphasis that Locke and later polite theorists attached to 'inner civilities' did not prevent certain conduct writers, often dancing-masters turned author, from giving extremely detailed advice on matters of external posture and deportment. A final section examines aspects of this advice, and looks at the controversy surrounding the publication of Lord Chesterfield's *Letters to His Son* (1774) which, with its apparent advocacy of external manners independent of inner virtue, was accused of exploiting the Lockeian synthesis and bringing politeness into disrepute.

Men of court and town politeness

In her recent study of early modern English conduct literature, Anna Bryson charts the rise of a concept of civility which, over the course of the sixteenth and seventeenth centuries, replaced an existing medieval concept of courtesy. This transformation, which Bryson shows to be gradual and uneven, took the form of a shift from traditional styles of lordship and service, located in the noble household, to new forms of mannered self-presentation required for successful participation in an orderly but less familiar 'civil' society. Original concepts of civility also found expression in new locations, such as the royal and ducal courts of Renaissance Italy. One of the sources most influential in developing the concept of civility, Baldassare Castiglione's *Il libro del Cortegiano* (1528), was drawn directly from the author's experience at the ducal court of Urbino. Castiglione provided an original treatise setting out a 'comprehensive ideal of the nobleman or gentleman as courtier' based on an 'exposition of courtly grace and ease expressed . . . in a variety of aesthetic, intellectual, and physical accomplishments'.[3] What was striking about this ideal was its attention to the presentation of personality by means of an accepted code of elegant or civilised conduct; a key purpose of the social graces being to charm and influence holders of power within a competitive court environment. In England, as in other European countries, Castiglione's concept of courtliness became available to elite male readers either via Bartholomew Clerke's Latin edition or Thomas Hoby's English translation, *The Book of the Courtyer* (1561). Castiglione's text also inspired several close imitations including Eustache du Refuge's *Le Traité de la Cour* (1616) and Nicholas Faret's *L'honnête homme; ou l'art de plaire à la cour* (1630) which, respectively translated as *A Treatise of the Court* (1622) and *The Honest Man; or, the Art to Please in Court* (1632), achieved a particular authority with English readers.

Translations and re-editions of these accounts suggest an audience that extended beyond the immediate personnel of the Tudor or early Stuart court. In its search for guidance this wider, less elite readership also turned to a second brand of behavioural literature. Again originating in Italy, works like Giovanni della Casa's *Il Galateo* (1558) have been interpreted by some scholars simply as later contributions to an existing Castiglionean model of courtliness.[4] However, while owing a considerable debt to Castiglione, della Casa's equally influential guide differed in that it appealed less to those aiming to polish established principles than to young men seeking the essentials of good breeding for both a courtly and, more commonly, a non-courtly environment. These basic requirements gave rise to a type of guide listing acceptable and unacceptable actions in such categories as table manners, dress, personal hygiene, the discharge of bodily waste, street conduct, and relations with social superiors and inferiors. Within this literature, good behaviour was typically characterised as a display of self-control that enabled individuals to regulate their natural desires or bodily functions for the sake of others.[5]

An alternative to reforming possibly boorish men in adulthood was to instil these elementary standards of civility at an earlier point in the education process. This was the aim of a third category of early modern advice literature for boys, the principal contribution to which was *De Civilitate Morum Puerilium* (1526) by the Dutch humanist, Desiderius Erasmus. First translated as *A Lytell Booke of Good Maners for Chyldren* (1532), Erasmus's *De Civilitate* again produced a series of imitations, among them William Fiston's *The Schoole of Good Manners* (1609) and, slightly later, *Youth's Behaviour; or Decencie in Conversation amongst Men*, itself a translation from an early-seventeenth-century French text. Such studies again gave careful consideration to establishing appropriate levels of social conduct, notably in their detailed cataloguing of the social errors committed by spitting, scratching, belching and poorly or partially dressed young men. Yet however important these practicalities, few sixteenth- and seventeenth-century humanist writers sought to promote a notion of good breeding based on external civilities alone. Rather, Erasmus and his English imitators understood visible civility as the product of a virtuous personality characterised as much by humanist learning as by lineage: 'by the Manners', wrote Fiston, 'are lively represented the habit of the Minde; and disposition of Man'.[6]

The potential here for developing a concept of gentlemanliness based as much on personality as on birth appears to have attracted particular attention in early modern English advice literature. As James Raven suggests, the majority of seventeenth-century English civility guides at least tolerated the idea of merchants and traders appropriating gentility, while several actively promoted themselves as manuals of social advancement for both landed and non-landed readerships.[7] But breadth of application also made apparent the tensions inherent within early modern behavioural literature. It was a common concern that guides providing detailed advice on civil and uncivil behaviour threatened to undermine what Raven calls the 'myth and mystery of gentility', either by eroding traditional hierarchies of deference and respect, or by suggesting that external manners might exist independent of true virtue.[8]

In the light of this debate, John Locke's reassertion of the equation between inner and outer refinement can be seen as a timely reminder to young male readers who, faced with books offering readily imitable lessons on civility, may have been thought likely to adopt inadequate modes of refinement. There exists of course no empirical evidence to suggest a deterioration in standards of manners at the time Locke delivered his instructions. Moreover, the possibility that outer conduct might be separated from inner feeling had been appreciated by Renaissance writers, for whom the ability to ingratiate oneself through calculated self-presentation was thought a necessary element of the courtier's repertoire.

What did give an added edge to late-seventeenth- and early-eighteenth-century discussions were attempts by writers such as Abel Boyer, the third earl of Shaftesbury, Richard Steele and Joseph Addison to encourage a new 'polite' moral order compatible with political, social and cultural developments consolidated by the Glorious Revolution (1688–9). The attention these authors placed on politeness as a modern virtue made it necessary to propose forms of gentlemanly social conduct that fully discounted and discredited the possibility of duplicitous behaviour. Such efforts had clear implications for the ways in which certain eighteenth-century commentators looked back on earlier, seventeenth-century statements on desirable male conduct, and from this fashioned their own, contemporary understanding of refined manhood.

We can get some idea of this historical analysis from later reactions to important mid-seventeenth-century guides like Francis Osborne's *Advice to a Son* (1656). A descendant of a Bedfordshire gentry family, Osborne held several minor governmental positions before he moved to Oxford to supervise the education of his son, for whom he wrote his own della Casian guide for the young; its success (five reprints in two years) led to the publication of an enlarged edition together with a second part shortly before his death in

1659. Osborne's advice is strikingly practical and self-centred in the tone employed to discuss standard topics such as personal conduct and habits, politics, religion and the merits of travel. The result, in effect, was a study in how to avoid making errors (and how to disguise them once made) as a means of maintaining one's standing and reputation in a distinctly competitive and ungrateful society. 'Imagine', he wrote, 'few the more capable of Trust, because you have formerly obliged them . . . [be] little flattered to doe good out of hope of requitall'. Survival within this community required the adoption of a less than generous model of human interaction: '*Court him alwaies, you hope one day to make use of, but at the least expence you can*', it being scarcely an 'act of prudence to *doe more for another, then in reason may be expected from him againe upon in like occasion*'. At all times the successful 'gentleman' was expected to promote his self-image for which, first and foremost, Osborne recommended a dress and appearance 'exceeding rather than cumming short of others of like fortune' as the means to find 'acceptance where ever you come'; sensible men 'spare all other waies, rather than prove defective in this'.[9]

The publishing success of Osborne's *Advice* indicates a popularity borne out by Restoration readers. The diarist Samuel Pepys, for example, recorded how he consulted the book on several occasions, and spoke warmly of 'my father Osborne's rule for a gentleman'.[10] But a later generation judged Osborne's ideal gentleman superficial and callous. In a paper devoted to the subject of men's appearance, the *Spectator* periodical juxtaposed Osborne's thoughts on power dressing with its own more moderate assertion that 'the medium between a Fop and a Sloven is what a Man of Sense would endeavour to keep'.[11] The *Spectator*'s comments developed those of *Tatler* No. 230, in which Jonathan Swift had included Osborne in a list of Restoration authors characterised by a dated literary style once common among 'Men of Court' but now 'perfectly ridiculous' to practitioners of 'Town Politeness'.[12]

Swift's comments can be viewed as one manifestation of an early-eighteenth-century polite culture, whose proponents, in seeking to distance themselves from what they saw as cold and competitive manners, often looked unfavourably on courtiers as embodying the inadequate refinement of former ages. This is not to say that the courtly milieu or its inhabitants were ever straightforward targets during the eighteenth century. To take just two examples: *Tatler* No. 30 acknowledged the court's place as a 'College for the Conduct of Life' producing courtiers who, if uninspiring acquaintances, were seldom embarrassing in their social encounters; likewise Samuel Johnson, a man capable of acting and writing with modern politeness, recommended that James Boswell read Castiglione's *The Courtier* as 'the best book that ever was written upon good breeding'.[13]

Nevertheless, the majority of early-eighteenth-century polite theorists remained distrustful. Courts, according to Abel Boyer, were places of 'false Friendship' and 'affected Gratitude' best suited to courtiers, the 'Apes of a King', who, like marble, were 'well Polished' but 'very hard'.[14] This image of the impeccable but inscrutable courtier occurred frequently in the *Tatler* and *Spectator*. For Richard Steele, these self-proclaimed 'worthies' were distinguished for 'being Servile with an Air' and for their capacity for 'cold and repeated Civilities', what elsewhere he termed 'the meer conformity of Looks and gestures'.[15] Alongside this predominant characteristic there existed several alternative and equally unacceptable images. One was of the courtier as immoral libertine, traditionally associated with Charles II's supposedly hedonistic regime post-1660. Later calls for better standards of male sexual and social conduct extended beyond reformation of manners societies to polite periodicalists, who criticised current levels of licentiousness and boisterousness which – according to Addison's eighteenth-century biographer Robert Bisset – they attributed 'to the corruption of the [Restoration] court'.[16] Court men were further identified as prone to excessively mannered conduct. *Spectator* No. 240 included a letter from one 'Rustick Sprightly' describing 'the unhappy arrival' of a courtier to his village. A subsequent display of stylised and exuberant gestures – including deep bows to each man and the kissing of women on greeting – had thrown impressionable villagers into confusion over correct forms of refined conduct, bringing existing forms of sociability to an end.[17]

In their attempt to move away from an outmoded, if still sometimes beguiling courtliness, it was necessary for eighteenth-century commentators to juxtapose the courtier's faults with more enticing forms of polite male conduct. Swift's promotion of men of 'town politeness' over those of the court provided one such route of particular value for other progressive Whig authors eager to bestow commerce with the moral force of refined sociability. Thus in Richard Steele's comparison of a courtier and a city tradesman's conduct in *Tatler* No. 207, the latter's behaviour was clearly equal to that of his (superficially) more genteel peer. The paper, which described a fictitious meeting between three cousins – courtier, scholar and tradesman – provided a now familiar picture of the showy courtier alongside that of another undesirable archetype, the pedantic academic. The trader, by contrast, was praised, partly on account of his being neither ridiculous nor obnoxious, but also because his professional sociability was said to pertain most closely to the ideals of politeness, those we examined in Chapter One. The 'tradesman who deals with me in a Commodity which I do not understand with Uprightness', wrote Steele, 'has much more right to that Character [of a 'gentleman'], than the Courtier who gives me false Hopes, or the Scholar who laughs at my Ignorance'.[18] The quality of uprightness –

comprising honesty, simplicity and a genuine interest in others – was best served by participation in locations like the market-place where, according to Steele, such skills emerged as a specific requirement for success with customers and, more generally, as the effect of socialising within a pluralistic city culture.

Yet the modern polite male was more than simply the product of a civilising urban environment. In composing their ideal character, early-eighteenth-century writers developed another conduct tradition upon which we have not yet touched, namely the figure of the good Christian. Among studies within this genre, Richard Braithwait's *The English Gentleman* (1630) and Richard Allestree's immensely popular *The Whole Duty of Man* and *The Gentleman's Calling* (both 1660) proved of lasting value for eighteenth-century writers. Echoing medieval concepts of noble courtesy, such guides stressed the desirability of men who valued practical acts of charity and compassion over courtly polish. The legacy of these works surfaces in later accounts of gentlemanliness, the prominence of Christian teaching on benevolence providing early-eighteenth-century writers with important, alternative male role models to those populating the Renaissance court. For Richard Steele, therefore, it was not courtliness but latitudinarian theology which distinguished Archbishop John Tillotson as 'a most polite Man' and an 'authority with all who are such'.[19]

The polite gentleman

Compared with early- to mid-seventeenth-century guides providing precise stipulations on – to name a few – fidgeting, nose-blowing, chewing, walking and sitting, both the *Tatler* and the *Spectator* were notably unspecific in their instructions for day-to-day refined male conduct. The polite man was by definition an exponent of a behavioural style which, in theory at least, placed greater emphasis on explicitly interactive qualities such as benevolence, altruism and accommodation. This said, contributions to both publications were intended to educate readers in correct modes of conduct, even if the method adopted was one of veiled instruction by example as opposed to overt didacticism. Through the comments of each title's fictional narrator, Isaac Bickerstaff and Mr Spectator, and the correspondence sent to the editors, eighteenth-century readers were able to construct a more detailed picture, first, of the personality of the polite male – his appearance, his treatment of others, how and to whom he spoke – and, second, of the ways in which these precise qualities contributed to the wider ideals of polite sociability.

Character, conduct and conversation

An examination of these qualities might best begin with first impressions, and a consideration of the gentleman's appearance. Issues of dress and self-presentation had proved an essential element in the majority of late-sixteenth- and seventeenth-century guides wherein, broadly speaking, good dress had been defined by its appropriateness, allowing wearers to conform with established civilised norms. How was genteel appearance conceived of in early-eighteenth-century periodical literature? To an extent, notions of suitable clothing continued to be determined by issues of conformity and moderation. As *Spectator* No. 150 put it, 'men of sense' avoided both the foppery of over-dress and the slovenliness of neglect. This said, there is also evidence of a shift in the discussion in line with early-eighteenth-century redefinitions of politeness. Thus, although the wider social benefits of (responsibly) modish dressing had not passed unmentioned in earlier sources, there were signs that the *Spectator*'s authors saw themselves supervising a debate within what they considered a now more relaxed and commercially aware society. Whereas Restoration tradesmen had been castigated for fashionable dress, it was now 'the Honour of our present Age' that a respectable merchant or politician might wear a modish wig and so be identified not as a rake or fop but as 'the genteelest Man in the Company'.[20]

Readers hoping to gain insight into the precise styles of genteel wigs would have been disappointed with the *Spectator*. Addison and Steele's interest in the ethos rather than the details of polite conduct meant, when it came to dress, a focus on broader issues such as the condition and the ways in which clothes were worn. According to *Spectator* No. 631, it was of less consequence that garments were fashionable than that they conformed to that basic 'Mark of Politeness': presentability. This equation of neatness with politeness took several forms. To an extent, suggestions that cleanliness was necessary to avoid offence reiterated a theme popular in an early modern advice literature concerned with regulating bodily functions. In other ways, however, the *Spectator*'s was a more topical thesis in which dress contributed to refinement by stimulating the wearer to new heights of sociability. Echoing Lockeian sensationalist psychology, Addison explained how 'our senses . . . only transmit the Impression of such Things as usually surround them'. 'Pure and unsullied thoughts' were the result of contact with 'those Objects that perpetually encompass us, when they are beautiful and elegant', the effect of good dress being to stimulate 'refined Sentiments and Passions' in the wearer.[21] Where provided, more detailed descriptions of dress concentrated on the styles detrimental to rather than productive of modern politeness. *Spectator* No. 631, for example, also included a critical assessment of a 'dirty beau' whose blackened suit, unruly periwig and snuff-coated linens brought misery to the passengers with whom he shared a carriage. Elsewhere, city correspondents to the periodical commented on the elaborate and overly formal dress of rural gentlemen who, like courtiers, were said still to favour a late-Restoration style, consisting of a red coat with brocade cuffs, large laced hat and heavy periwig. In *Spectator* papers comparing town and country conduct, there emerged a clear sense of the superiority of urban styles of comfortable, informal clothing which, by permitting unselfconscious and relaxed movement, served practically and metaphorically as a means to acquire a superior brand of easy and polite sociability.

The importance of 'easiness' in early-eighteenth-century definitions of polite male behaviour was also evident in the ways that men were expected to behave at obviously sociable encounters such as the dinner party. Once again, hints towards correct conduct were often indicated by way of negative example. In *Spectator* No. 119, for example, Addison identified the offending individual as a country gentleman who, at a dinner held for Mr Spectator, made 'as many Bows in half an Hour, as would a Courtier for a Week'. Such protracted displays meant that the meal went cold before his hosts could 'adjust the Ceremonial, and be prevailed to sit down'. Further delay was caused by the country gentlemen's refusal to serve themselves before their neighbour and, afterwards, the formal nature of their departure during which guests and superiors were made to quit the room first.[22] A very different model could be expected in one of London's many coffee-houses, described as places of 'rendezvous to all . . . who are thus turned to relish and ordinary Life'. Here Mr Spectator passed his time in more relaxed company, listening, reading, negotiating or conversing with 'Men formed for Society', too sociable to remain in private and too considerate to worry about the troublesome niceties maintained by their country contemporaries.[23]

Of these recreations it was coffee-house patrons' aptitude for conversation which most exercised *Tatler* and *Spectator* contributors. As the crucial means for uniting and engaging friends, professional associates or strangers, conversation was recognised as central to the polite ideal and a key requirement of the modern gentleman. Certainly its importance has not been overlooked by historians. As Peter Burke and others demonstrate, conversation became a defining feature of late-seventeenth-century polite French salon culture and then, through works produced within this environment, emerged as the 'paradigmatic arena' for eighteenth-century modes of 'English politeness'.[24]

The importance which is rightly attached to conversation as a defining feature of an early-eighteenth-century public sphere should not obscure the frequent references to verbal communication predating the coffee-house or the translation of the late-seventeenth-century French studies by the likes of Antoine de Courtin and Jean-Baptiste Bellegarde. Writing in the early 1620s,

Henry Peacham had demanded that gentlemen's 'discourse be free and affable, giving entertainment in a sweete and liberall manner, and with a chereful courtesie'; jesting without purpose was to be avoided, at the same time as serious speeches were to be lightened by the 'wit and pleasant invention' of epigrams and anecdotes.[25] Peacham's contemporary William Fiston echoed Italian Renaissance authors when he called for well-mannered men to be, at least with their equals, 'amiable . . . familiar and friendly' as well as gentle and deliberate in their tone of voice. When spoken to, gentlemen were expected to look the speaker in the face and to avoid coughing, laughing or the 'unmannerly part', interrupting.[26] Over half a century later, John Locke reiterated Fiston's warning against appearing disputatious or interventionist; that speakers should not be interrupted was the one rule that Locke expected boys, otherwise free from the details of good breeding, to observe.[27]

The efforts taken by early modern authors to improve speech with the common values of levity, intelligence and consideration indicate the need to view Addison and Steele's contribution as part of a much longer European tradition. This said, the eighteenth century also saw more than a restatement of familiar themes. Rather, the promotion of a well-established discourse on good conversation within the particular social and cultural landscape of the early-eighteenth-century town provided a topical and valuable statement on the day-to-day requirements of polite manliness. Having reiterated the equation between polite gentlemen and men of good conversation, both the *Tatler* and the *Spectator* provided clear advice on the means by which city gentlemen were to engage in successful communication. From the many references to the subject, two essential requirements stand out. First, conversation was to be the product of genuine sociability. Richard Steele's 'Gentleman perfectly qualified for Conversation' was therefore a man for whom erudition and wit were subordinate to goodwill or 'complaisance'; a quality later described by Addison as 'generally born within us' – and hence distinct from acquired manners – without which 'there is no Society or Conversation to be kept up in the World'.[28] In highlighting the naturalness of good sociability, Addison distinguished between modern forms of polite and earlier modes of courtly conversation. Seemingly accommodating and relaxed, courtly speech had been conditioned by what Castiglione had described as *sprezzatura* or the acquired art of appearing easy. Courtiers were to learn the appearance of nonchalance and to apply their skills in courtly competition, either to ingratiate or to intimidate with seeming ease.[29] Polite gentlemen, by contrast, were expected to be less concerned with competing than with socialising, and hence were thought in need of just a few general guidelines by which to achieve good speech: namely, interesting, respectable subjects presented in a direct, clear, yet pleasing tone.

The importance attached to complaisance is further apparent in the equal emphasis given to listening when other people spoke. In his discussion of coffee-house society, Richard Steele pointed out that a man would 'be more agreeable to his Company . . . in being only an Hearer', the assumption being that all men enjoyed talking and would look favourably on attentive friends who listened in silence.[30] There was of course a risk that such respectful deference might subject listeners to the formalities of overly mannered country gentlemen or the pedantry of the verbose scholar. Later eighteenth-century commentators certainly viewed this as a potential problem. John Trusler, for example, described how polite men could be trapped with an ignorant or frivolous conversant because 'it is worse than rudeness not to listen to him' just in case – whatever the reality of the situation – the speaker gained the impression that he was 'a blockhead and not worth the being'.[31] Others went further in cautioning male readers against indiscriminate displays of good will. 'Benevolence', admitted the portrait painter and essayist Joseph Highmore, 'is a most amiable natural quality' and 'absolutely necessary, to extend a man's influence in the world'. However, an excess of fellow feeling produced the 'tyranny of unlimited complaisance', an 'evil' which Highmore defined as the 'unreasonable yielding up of ourselves, our inclinations, our time'.[32]

It was in a bid to prevent such encounters that eighteenth-century theorists identified self-discipline as a second requirement of polite male conversation. The value of what Joseph Highmore described as 'firmness and resolution' was particularly evident when it came to extricating oneself from difficult social situations. Yet the majority of polite theorists and conduct writers offered a more altruistic justification for acting with resolve and self-control: namely, that speakers did everything in their powers not to offend their audience. Discussions emphasised the need for gentlemen to control their conversation so as to show respect while avoiding comments that shocked, embarrassed or intruded into others' privacy.

As with the need for good will, calls for self-regulation had also featured in earlier advice literature. The anonymous *Art of Complaisance; or the Means to Oblige in Conversation* (1673) was one of many guides to encourage seventeenth-century gentlemen to practise modesty and brevity followed by silence 'to give the rest of the Company time to speak their thoughts'.[33] Neatly dovetailing the themes of polite sociability and commercial transaction central to early-eighteenth-century Whig cultural politics, James Forrester later equated male conversation to an exchange or a bank. Speakers, like investors, gained 'their respective Shares' by balancing spoken contributions with the amount of time they spent considering the interests of others. Participants maintained their creditworthiness so long as they preserved this equilibrium by regulating the content or frequency of their interjections.[34]

This need for control applied to exchanges between friends as it did with strangers. In the former instance, affection was to be moderated by a proper sense of independence and distance in order to avoid unseemly or embarrassing self-revelation. In his essay 'On conversation, society, civility, and politeness', Abel Boyer thought it 'necessary for a man to avoid too much familiarity in Conversation' since intimate 'communication discovers Imperfections that reservedness concealed'.[35] For Richard Steele, the sociable 'Man of Conversation' needed above all to possess 'good Judgement' and an ability to avoid 'giving Offence'. Through self-control, 'the greatest human Perfection . . . [and] most amiable Quality in the Sight of others', Steele believed that men displayed the 'winning deference to Mankind' necessary for virtuous sociability.[36] Indeed, rational self-control remained central to specific studies of conversation and general accounts of polite conduct, at least until the third quarter of the eighteenth century, when interest in sensibility encouraged less regulated styles of social performance. John Constable's 1738 guide rejected as 'impertinent Protestations' all uncontrolled and immoderate statements, which he viewed as 'a greater weakness of Mind, than Sincerity of Heart'.[37] Readers of *The Polite Companion* (1760) were similarly reminded that good conversation was ultimately dependent on self-control: 'A man must be Master of himself, his Words, his Gestures and Passions, that nothing must escape him, to give others a just occasion to complain of his Demeanour'. Such detachment also benefited those who encountered less disciplined figures, allowing the polite gentleman to endure 'all Kinds of behaviour, while his own Character as a Man, or as a *Christian,* is not thereby debased'.[38]

Attempts to preserve men's aptitude for self-containment and control also prompted commentators to warn against excessive consumption when in company. This emphasis on the importance of the 'golden mean' restated a familiar early modern theme linking excess with an abandonment of the God-given dignities by which humans were distinguished from animals, and of the rational independence that set male citizens apart from women, children and effeminate adult men.[39] None the less, these considerations also maintained their relevance in eighteenth-century discussions of the gentleman. In Chapter One, for example, we saw the importance David Hume attached to modern men's rejection of excessive food consumption as evidence of the distance between civilised society and a former state of boorish gluttony born of want. In terms of day-to-day living, however, the question of immoderate consumption, especially of drink, continued to provoke disputes such as that which took place between Sir Joshua Reynolds and Samuel Johnson in April 1776. For Reynolds, alcohol was a means of improving 'conversation and benevolence' (in his opinion by raising spirits through stimulation of blood circulation). Johnson disagreed and described how the drinking man 'loses that modesty, and grows impudent and vociferous', abandoning edifying conversation for 'clamorous merriment'.[40] James Boswell, who observed the debate, interpreted it as a contest between alcohol's ability to enhance fellow feeling or to reduce self-regulation. Presumably sober when he wrote up his account of the debate, Boswell came down in favour of a balance which, as we shall see in Chapter Five, he was often unable to strike in his own awkward handling of the relationship between drink and polite society.

Polite gentlemen and female society

A notable feature of this chapter so far has been its concentration on men's socialising in male-orientated groups. This focus can be attributed in part to the influence of an early-eighteenth-century periodical tradition which paid particular attention to sociable encounters at, for example, the country gentleman's dinner table, among city tradesmen in the market-place, or at one of the *Spectator*'s favourite London haunts, Child's coffee-house – described by Richard Steele as a place of contact for 'all that live near it' valuing 'calm and ordinary Life'.[41] Much has recently been made of this image of the coffee-house as an affordable and welcoming venue where questions of social distinctions were subordinate to the pleasures of moderate drinking and regulated conversation. In many ways this emphasis is rightly placed: polite theorists, city patrons and foreign visitors did indeed identify coffee-houses as sites where new styles of easy and inclusive politeness were condoned and practised. However, it is again worth recalling the gender bias of Steele's choice. Reading on, we find that the coffee-house provided a particular type of haven for those, like Steele, for whom calmness and regularity involved avoiding the more 'Mirthful meetings of Men, or Assemblies of the fair Sex'.[42]

In this contrast between the politeness of the coffee-house and the mixed-sex assembly there are few occasions when either Steele or Addison's concept of politeness so closely reflected that of their influential Whig predecessor, the third earl of Shaftesbury. For Shaftesbury, politeness was very definitely the consequence of conversation among learned gentlemen rather than between men and women. Indeed, Shaftesbury believed women's company to be not only unnecessary but detrimental to the process of male refinement, replacing masculine sense with what he considered the 'Gothic' horrors of triviality and gallantry.[43] Shaftesbury's fears fit within an early modern tradition of advice literature which, by and large, proved ambivalent to women's role in male refinement. At the very least, a considerable number of late-sixteenth- and seventeenth-century English commentators failed to consider the impact of female society, no doubt because few thought mixed company an important requirement for the cultivation of male civility. To judge from early modern advice literature intended for a female readership, women's merits were principally identified in terms of a moral and practical domesticity more suited to household management than to the courtly, professional world of would-be civilised men. In this light, guides like John Locke's *Thoughts Concerning Education* – notable for its silence on women's role (other than as mothers of the very young) – appear closer to an established courtesy genre when compared to many subsequently more gender-conscious studies. As Shaftesbury would do, other seventeenth-century writers took a more actively hostile line against female society, warning male readers away from company which, compared to hardier male society, threatened to undermine traditional manly qualities. The true gentleman, as Clement Ellis claimed, makes 'more use of the *Vaulter* and the *Fencer*, than the *Dancer*; for his desire was more to be a *Man*, then a *Puppit*, and to be a *servant* to his *Country* rather then his *Lady*'.[44]

Not all early modern conduct writers overlooked the benefits of female company, of course. Drawing on an earlier tradition of chivalry and courtly love, Baldassare Castiglione had noted the merits of the duchess of Urbino's presence at an otherwise male-dominated court. Similar praise for leading ladies can be found in early-seventeenth-century French guides to life at court. Such sources undoubtedly contributed to the further development of the Castiglionean idea of male refinement as a process involving (still restricted) contributions from women, albeit from women drawn in limited numbers from a social elite active within prescribed male arenas of civility.

Later seventeenth- and eighteenth-century discussions can be seen to continue this appreciation, though with several significant shifts of focus. These accounts of female society were distinguished by a growing understanding of women, now often defined with greater attention to gender rather than social status, as the principal agents of male social improvement on account of the very qualities, such as moral superiority, for which they had been excluded from earlier courtesy guides. French influences were again strong in a development closely associated with the mid-seventeenth-century rise of a female-governed Parisian salon culture providing alternative non-courtly venues for refined sociability.[45] French discussions of a new concept of politeness brought fresh vitality to the idea of women's potential in late-seventeenth-century England and produced a number of home-grown statements to this effect. As William Ramesey put it, in terms much repeated throughout our period, women were 'more pitiful, more pious, faithful, merciful, chaste [and] beautiful, than Men', a difference which he ascribed to men's being formed of the 'dust of the Earth' while women, created 'of Man himself', were of 'more Noble Matter, and refined'.[46]

Likewise the *Spectator*, while continuing to praise coffee-houses for cultivating sober male-orientated conversation, also encouraged men to make contact with those respectable women whom, significantly, its authors now included within their intended readership. Joseph Addison set the tone when he identified the virtuous woman, characterised by her softness and modesty, as best equipped 'to temper Mankind and sooth them into Tenderness and Compassion', and who, in so doing, 'polishes and refines [men] out of those Manners which are most natural to them'.[47] What in the previous century had proved a minority view subsequently emerged as a central and enduring component of discussions on polite gentlemanliness. 'It is', wrote James Forrester in 1738, 'the Acquaintance of the *Ladies* only, which can bestow that Easiness of Address, whereby the *fine Gentleman* is distinguished from the Scholar'.[48] Jonathan Swift similarly thought it impossible for 'our sex . . . to support it [politeness] without the company of women', while in a chapter, 'How far converse with the FAIR SEX may advantage a YOUNG MAN', Jean-Baptiste Bellegarde described female society as the means by which 'we arrive at a high degree of politeness'.[49]

It is worth noting how this appreciation of women's role extended from the would-be makers of polite society to its analysts. David Hume, for example, believed that modern men revealed themselves in terms of their capacity for 'gallantry'. Hume defined gallantry – previously rejected by Shaftesbury – as sensitivity, courtesy and gracefulness drawn out through men's involvement with the opposite sex. Thus, 'among a polite people . . . both sexes meet in an easy and sociable manner; and the tempers of men, as well as their behaviour, refine apace'.[50] The Glasgow historian and professor of civil law John Millar later illustrated his belief in the merits of female company with the negative example of ancient Greece where women's exclusion from society had prevented 'the two sexes from improving the arts of conversation', leaving Greek men 'remarkably deficient in delicacy and politeness of manners'. According to Millar, standards had not begun to improve until the medieval period, when a culture of male chivalry had prompted more respectful and civilised conduct by men towards women.[51]

In these and many similar statements it is possible to identify two principal mechanisms by which eighteenth-century commentators understood women's refining role to operate. The basic premise that women, either through nature or upbringing, were more sensitive and less argumentative than men demanded, first, that male speakers further temper their conversation to avoid performances which, though perhaps acceptable in male-only company, would offend in mixed and, hence, polite society. Men were advised to curb what was identified as their naturally aggressive and indelicate temperament, the emphasis being, as Swift put it, to 'lay a Restraint upon those odious Topicks of Immodesty and Indecision into which the Rudeness of our Northern Genius is so apt to fall'.[52] According to Hume, a woman's presence put a man 'on his guard, lest he give offence by any breach of decency', while Bellegarde saw the merits of mixed company in shaming men who spoke in 'a manner that favours libertinism, and puts modesty to the blush'.[53]

Second, in addition to curbing natural excesses, time spent in female company was valued for improving and embellishing what many regarded as an otherwise defective masculine personality. Exposure to women's compassion, sensitivity and eloquence would, it was hoped, stimulate admiring men to adopt equivalent characteristics. James Forrester described as 'Men of *true* Taste' those who through conversation in mixed company appropriated 'every Art of Pleasing, which is the Disposition at once the most grateful to others, and the most satisfactory to ourselves'. Once attained, a continued 'intimate acquaintance with the other *Sex*, fixes this *Complacence* into a *Habit*, and that Habit is the very Essence of *Politeness*'.[54] Descriptions of this process regularly described female society as 'smoothing' or 'polishing' away the rough edges of the male character. Jean-Baptiste Bellegarde spoke for many eighteenth-century commentators when he likened women's company – by which men 'rub off their rust and become agreeable' – to 'the school to complete a man'.[55]

By the mid-eighteenth century, Scottish enlightenment thinkers offered more sophisticated explanations as to why these mutual forces of male restraint and female embellishment proved so effective. Central to their analysis was a new-found, if never absolute, confidence in the benefits of commerce as the fourth and final sequence of a stadial model of societal development from savage to civil society. This was an argument made with particular clarity in 1771 in John Millar's *Observations Concerning the Distinction of Ranks*. Millar believed that commercial society now afforded women greater levels of economic and social responsibility. As a result, women's talents became apparent to men living in a community where dexterity and communication were as important as aggression had once been in less advanced societies. This, according to Millar, was not the first time that women's talents had been realised. During the medieval age the practice of chivalry had brought a 'great respect and veneration for the ladies' which 'has still a considerable influence upon our [men's] behaviour'.[56] But Millar saw the medieval period as only a step in the right direction, not the highpoint of male manners. Further improvement could only be achieved in a more complex commercial society where men became fully appreciative and respectful of virtuous female accomplishments. The result was a less showy but more sincere and practicable display of sensitivity towards women, whose talents Millar and other men now recognised as having 'so much influence upon every species of improvement' and contributing 'in so many ways to multiply the comforts of [a man's] life'.[57] Like Hume and Adam Smith, his own former tutor, Millar intended to convince readers of the improvements which he believed Britons were now privileged to enjoy. The superiority of modern British manners was further apparent when compared with the social and gender failings of the ancients or contemporary non-European peoples: for example, the Greeks whom, like Millar, Hume criticised for failing to treat women 'as part of the polite people' or, as Adam Smith suggested, the native Americans for whom intimate male/female contact 'much indulged in ages of humanity and politeness, is regarded . . . as the most unpardonable effeminacy'.[58] Smith's confidence in social progress ensured, at least in this instance, that the link between refinement and effeminacy remained a feature of historically or geographically distant communities. This, however, was not a view shared by less optimistic social observers when presented with a seemingly more 'feminised' society. In attempting to disprove these fears, conduct writers and academic theorists devoted considerable efforts to establishing the compatibility of manliness and polite society.

Manliness and politeness

Historians of early modern manliness have recently highlighted the importance of qualities such as independence, moderation, courage and self-command to sixteenth- and seventeenth-century definitions of the ideal gentleman. These attributes owed much to the renewed popularity of the Roman stoical philosophers, notably Epictetus, whose work first appeared in English translation in 1567. Epictetus's emphasis on the male virtues of forbearance and self-command became an integral part of the image of dignified and public-spirited nobility. The predominant picture in early modern advice guides and diaries was of men as the physically and mentally stronger sex characterised by rationality, intelligence, discretion and self-control. Virtuous females, by comparison, were depicted as less rigorous in mind and body but capable of a greater capacity for compassion, sensitivity and charity.[59]

At the same time, much recent scholarship also reveals how, away from prescriptive texts, early modern debates were seldom as clear cut as this comparison suggests. Sixteenth- and seventeenth-century preoccupations with hermaphroditism, cross-dressing and female disorder demonstrated an intense insecurity over the apparent rigidity of sex and gender boundaries in a nominally but highly contested patriarchal society. Lately historians have also concentrated on revealing the tensions and weaknesses of a patriarchal system based on the hard-won dominance of a male identity itself characterised by contradictions, limitations and challenges.[60] According to Susan Amussen, one such challenge to traditional male ideals of independence and self-control came with the rise of the late-sixteenth- and early seventeenth-century code of courtly gentility which, in its emphasis on 'civility, proper behaviour, good manners and refinement', engendered tensions between 'being a man and being a gentleman'.[61]

If anything, we might expect these tensions to become increasingly acute with the rise of a more egalitarian polite discourse during the late seventeenth and early eighteenth century. As we have seen, polite theorists now proposed that a broader range of men might become refined in ways seldom countenanced by the majority of earlier court and non-court writers, notably through closer contact with women.

In fact, a similar readiness to rethink traditional standards of manliness, including rational intelligence, courage and honour, can be seen in eighteenth-century reforms proposed for established male professions such as academia or the military. Scholarship may have traditionally demanded heightened powers of reason, intelligence and clarity, but for many polite writers the life of the mind left men in danger of becoming dull and anti-social. As the dancing-master Stephen Philpot put it in the 1740s, young men who paid too much attention to academic learning were 'very apt to degenerate into pedantry; and to cause the person (who might otherwise deserve Esteem) to be despised'.[62] In part a dancing-master's self-advertisement, Philpot's advice highlighted a much discussed eighteenth-century tension between scholarship and sociability. It was, as a rival conduct book claimed, a well-known fact that 'persons of the greatest Knowledge are usually the most unpolite', as their erudition made them both contemptuous of and incomprehensible to their intellectual inferiors.[63] Politeness, as its advocates reiterated, was an ideal achieved through a combination of reading and active social engagement – and this in mixed company – in which it was thought few cloistered scholars were willing to participate. In place of this traditional image, polite reformers, including the dramatist and essayist Oliver Goldsmith (1730–74), proposed that scholars seek improvements in both educational standards *and* manners. Goldsmith's role model was the 'man of taste' who, situated 'between the world and the cell', possessed a degree of 'polite learning' that allowed even the most learned philosopher to gain 'popular applause'.[64]

Criticisms levelled against the pedantic scholar were likewise directed, if not to military men *per se*, then certainly to those whom polite authors judged to be associating manliness with an outdated concept of courage detrimental to their sociable personality. Attention was further drawn throughout the period to the unacceptability of other expressions of male violence, such as duelling and hunting, on which instruction had often been provided in early modern guides to gentlemanly education.

For some, like Bernard Mandeville, duelling remained an important part of masculine identity, especially within the military. Early-eighteenth-century efforts to end the practice by the 'restraining, conquering, and destroying of Pride, Anger, and the Spirit of Revenge' failed, according to Mandeville, to appreciate that duelling was the corollary of the honour by which men gained the courage to fight.[65] It was, as Mandeville's contemporary John Cockburn maintained, impossible for military men to avoid duelling 'for if they did their fellow Soldiers, both Officers and others, would not keep their Company'. However, for Cockburn, a prominent anti-duelling campaigner, this claim was based on what he regarded as an erroneous definition of honour satisfied by a ritual known for its 'inconsiderate and shameful Brutishness'.[66] In attacking the duel, critics like Cockburn concentrated on discrediting an anachronistic concept of honour now deemed incompatible not only with ecclesiastical and temporal law but also with new ideals of polite society. Modern honour, by contrast, was a quality less associated with warriorship than with lawfulness, religious respect and sociability. As a correspondent to the *Gentleman's Magazine* claimed in 1761, 'a people of polished manners and enlightened understanding' identified 'honourable men [as] . . . those who most contribute to the felicity of society, by a courteous and polite beneficence'.[67] Modern notions of polite gallantry were judged equally incompatible with the material trappings of combat. Thus the Bath master of ceremonies, Richard 'Beau' Nash (1674–1761), banned gentlemen from wearing swords in the town's ballroom partly in response to several duels in this supposed centre of polite society. But Nash had a further motive in his attempts to facilitate a gentlemanliness based on intimate male/female contact which had previously proved difficult since swords, when drawn, 'often tore the ladies cloaths, and frighted them'.[68]

In their emphasis on compassion, generosity or closer contact with women, and in their request that men 'smooth' or 'soften' their tempers, polite theorists were clearly seeking to reform male manners and, in the process, to redefine the meaning of manliness. Just what effect this redefinition had for standards of male behaviour remained a subject of heated debate throughout the eighteenth century. To critics of social change, sceptical of women's contribution to men's company and alarmed by increasing levels of what they saw as fashionable and luxurious consumption, polite society threatened to undermine tried and tested male values. In their place would arise 'effeminate' manners, characterised as physical and mental debility resulting in dependence, indulgence, inconstancy and irrationality. For critics of modern manners, effeminacy remained an absolute state into which large sections of the population would inevitably descend in view of their participation in this luxurious and polished commercial society.

Sponsors of polite society dismissed these fears as outdated. For these writers it was important to demonstrate the compatibility of being polite and manly. In doing so, polite theorists drew attention, on the one hand, to the persistence of traditional male virtues in emerging styles of polite manliness and, on the other, to the ways in which being polite demanded a proficiency in new, yet still manly, qualities.

Treatment of a subject like male dancing shows the ways in which behavioural writers promoted newer polite arts as compatible with more established notions of manhood. John Locke, an early advocate of dancing in gentry education, thought it contributed not only to gentility but to 'above all things Manliness', by which he meant hardiness, confidence and physical and mental poise.[69] Later conduct authors followed Locke's lead, defining dancing as a source both of physical and mental rigour as well as gracefulness. Stephen Philpot identified the benefits in terms of 'a decent, but manly Assurance', while the education writer James Nelson thought it produced 'great Firmness'.[70] Lewis Lockee, master of the Chelsea military academy, considered dancing a means to acquire 'a manly confidence which even the best characters require for their deportment in public life', and recommended that young officers took lessons as part of their training.[71]

Similar attention to the practice of traditional manliness is evident in discussions of men's conversation. Though probably lacking the scholar's intellectual rigour, the good conversationist was regularly depicted as thoughtful, well-read and quick thinking; someone who was able to talk constructively on a range of subjects and who knew when a particular subject was unsuited to the polite tastes of his audience. When it came to conversing, the need to temper the style of one's delivery or to prevent oneself from interrupting others also demanded rationality and control. Consequently, many commentators saw modern men's bid to acquire the art of pleasing as grounded first and foremost in an age-old capacity for self-regulation. According to the writer on conversation, John Constable, 'true friendship' was characterised not by 'over-fondness and impertinent Protestations' but 'a more manly temper, and knows the Medium between being kind, and weak'. Moreover, it was through this middle way that men were expected to maintain their independence even within a busy urban community.[72]

At the same time, the centrality of self-control, moderation and independence to notions of polite male conduct should not obscure the innovations within late-seventeenth- and early-eighteenth-century discussions of polite manliness. While continuing to encourage an attachment to traditional virtues, progressive commentators saw themselves promoting a new understanding of suitably male conduct which improved on existing styles as advocated by classical authors, early modern court writers or Restoration country gentlemen. For David Hume, for example, the limitations of classical manliness were clearly attributable to men's exclusion of women from social engagements. Hume realised that many of his contemporaries – those 'more zealous partizans of the ancients' – still considered women's marginalisation as desirable and feared that current fashions for mixed socialising would make men 'foppish and ridiculous'. In response, Hume spoke of the benefits of men's mixing in female society, making it clear that through such company modern men redefined and confirmed, rather than abandoned, their manliness. Thus in less civilised societies men had been expected to establish their innate mental and physical superiority by subordinating, beating and even killing women. Among a 'polite people', by contrast, men were praised for their attempts to minimise or 'alleviate that superiority' and hence 'discover their authority' through acts of generosity, complaisance and gallantry.[73]

Of course, Hume's polite gentleman continued to demonstrate his authority through a display of traditional male qualities – naturally greater physical and mental strength, for example – to which, as we have seen, new standards of gender identity remained indebted. Even the politest man, while narrowing the behavioural gap between the genders, preserved his manliness by being essentially more rational and intelligent than the majority of women with whom he socialised in a relationship invariably characterised as an idealised correspondence between, rather than a synthesis of, the sexes. For men to achieve refinement before sensitive female company presupposed a natural masculine talent for rationality and self-mastery. In this sense, women's contribution to male refinement was confined to stimulating or embellishing established male characteristics – a diminution of responsibility also seen in the belief that women merely polished the delivery of an erudite conversation typically originating first in male-dominated societies such as the academy, coffee-house or club.[74]

In other ways, however, the very need for men to restrain themselves suggested a natural male personality as much characterised by aggression and selfishness as by reason. According to Hume, throughout history men had shown themselves to be figures of pride and unreasonable passion. With an ancestry of this kind, Hume's polite men were a far cry from their unreformed predecessors, now able through 'refined breeding . . . to preserve, in all their behaviour, the natural appearance of sentiments different from those to which they naturally incline'. The effect of refinement turned traditional forms of manliness on their head: thus, while all men were instinctively 'proud and selfish . . . a polite man learns to behave with deference towards his companions'. In the same process of inversion, the polite man revealed his superiority by being respectful of his elders (whom Hume thought naturally fearful of youths), generous to foreigners and strangers (who expected nothing) and, of course, gallant to women who had previously found themselves victims of male boorishness and violence.[75]

It is not difficult to see how such refinements might have been useful to men of certain lifestyles – the leisured connoisseur, the latitudinarian clergyman or the urban tradesman, for example. As one mid-century writer on professions put it, for the mercer who 'traficks most with the ladies', commercial success depended on the ability 'to accommodate himself to their taste and Understanding as much as a rational Creature can'.[76] However, Hume's interpretation of polite manliness was surely unsuitable for other professions, notably soldiers, whose abilities rested, as Bernard Mandeville argued, on the very qualities – pride, self-interest and aggression – which polite theorists aimed to reform. It is therefore an indication of the intended comprehensiveness of politeness and its compatibility with a manliness blended from traditional and more modern virtues that Hume also sought to relocate the successful man of war within polite society.

Nor was Hume's the first attempt to demonstrate what in 1660 Clement Ellis had identified as the congruity of an '*Ingenious, Virile, strong* and *Masculine*' with a '*sweet* and *Winning*' personality.[77] In guides from the late-seventeenth-century *Art of Complaisance* to the translation of Jean-Baptiste Bellegarde's *Models of Conversation* (1765), soldiers were encouraged to polish their manners by now familiar methods such as participation in female company. What is striking about these discussions is the implied inferiority of those who failed to heed this advice. The soldier who refused to engage in polite society remained 'simply a man of War who has never sweeten'd his manners' with a mind 'onely full of Armies and Assaults'.[78] In contrast, added Bellegarde, the modern refined soldier 'soon ceased to be a man of fire and sword, to become sociable', a transformation that 'opened a thousand [mouths] in his commendation'.[79]

But how was it possible to make such a transition and retain a reputation for courage, given what many felt to be the potentially debilitating effect of women's company? Unfortunately, neither of these commentators provided a particularly detailed explanation. The *Art of Complaisance* considered it sufficient that the soldier performed well in company, the implication being that excursions into polite society were of no obvious detriment to courage. Readers of the *Models of Conversation* found the issue tackled a little more directly. Aware of the potential equation between female company and male effeminacy, Bellegarde played down its significance in view of what he believed to be, first, women's natural aversion to cowards and, second, their appreciation of courage as an aspect of modern notions of manliness without which 'all other good qualities vanish at once'. What female society brought about was not therefore a dilution but a redefinition of courage which saw the brutality and inhumanity of traditional models refined, as men tempered their behaviour to appeal to polite women.[80]

Bellegarde's advice may have been intended to reassure but his approach – with its emphasis on female society as the guarantor both of male refinement and courage – remained a highly particular one which, for many, overplayed the importance of women's role in matters of national interest. For a full reconciliation of politeness with courage, and hence the complete validation of new styles of male conduct, we must turn to David Hume's 1752 essay, 'Of refinement in the arts and sciences'. Hume's achievement was to square military life not only with men's involvement in female society but also with the broader phenomenon of an emerging commercial economy. Advances in prosperity and knowledge led inevitably to 'mildness and moderation' as men learned the 'advantages of humane maxims above rigour and severity', the chief distinction of 'a civilized age from times of barbarity'. By this process traditional forms of courage based on anger were replaced through 'politeness and refinement' with a superior 'sense of honour'. Crucially, Hume maintained that in substituting honour for anger men would not 'lose their martial spirit, or become less undaunted and vigorous in defence of their country or their liberty', for which he provided two explanations. First, to be successful in a commercial society required 'industry', a quality which mitigated against physical enervation while providing modern men with new levels of mental and physical stimulation. Second, Hume considered the 'honour' of polite society to be a more durable and reliable motive for heroic action. The net result was a superior form of courage which, though still partly configured in terms of industry, vigour and warriorship, now also required a generosity, eloquence and refinement only attainable by active participation in a modern environment of commercial exchange and polite sociability.[81]

The Chesterfield controversy

From John Locke, to Addison and Steele, to Hume, one of the striking features of late-seventeenth- and eighteenth-century polite theory was the importance attached to the harmony between a gentleman's inner virtue and an external refinement defined more by easiness and accommodation than by the precise dos and (more commonly) don'ts characteristic of earlier forms of behavioural literature.

This, however, is not an interpretation shared by all historians of eighteenth-century advice literature. From her survey of this material, Fenela Childs proposes an alternative trajectory for the development and meaning of politeness during the course of the eighteenth century. Childs suggests a significant shift from a late-seventeenth-century concern to promote 'good breeding' (a combination of 'inner' and 'outer virtues' in the Lockeian sense of the term) to, by the 1730s, a new emphasis on 'politeness' demanding only an external propriety of good manners effectively divorced from their traditional moral foundation. More recently it has been suggested that this shift had significant implications as men seeking a refined reputation gave up a 'high level of inner commitment and character training' for a new 'polite' persona which was now 'a matter of precise and exhaustive calculation'.[82]

The efforts of mid- and late-century behavioural writers to justify the ethical foundation of polite conduct should make us cautious of this argument. As we have seen, many followed Locke's example and continued to advocate 'politeness' as a moral code based on a blend of internal virtues and external refinements. Thus, in 1775 John Harris was still keen to promote a concept of 'politeness' which, originating from 'the sympathetic and generous feeling of the heart', served to 'polish . . . the most virtuous and noble sentiments'.[83]

At the same time, Childs's research reminds us of alternative types of polite advice literature less concerned with the theories of gentlemanliness or conversation than with the minute daily practicalities of refinement. Distinct from the prescriptive fictions of Addison and Steele or the social scientific analyses of Hume and Smith, these guides offered detailed instructions on issues of posture, movement and speech, which many readers clearly considered essential for success in polite society.[84] It was through the acquisition of the 'rules for behaving genteel on all occasions' that, as the Oxford dancing-master Matthew Towle put it, men became 'confined by the laws of Civility'.[85] At the heart of these laws was an essential proficiency in bodily control on which Towle provided instruction in his detailed essay on 'Behaviour at the Dancing School', with particulars on correct posture and the arts of bowing, giving and receiving.[86] Away from the school-room Towle offered advice – much of it by way of negative example – on, among other attributes, the correct way for men to sit (never 'stretch out your Legs and loll in your Chair, yawn, and sit uneasy'); to behave at the dinner table (refrain from eating immoderately or using the same cutlery to serve and eat with); to conduct oneself in the drawing room (do not blow your nose so loudly as to interrupt conversation, or spit anywhere but in your handkerchief); or to walk in the street (avoid walking on the heel or toe of the foot, avoid taking too short or long steps, or swinging the arms).[87] On a subject like walking Towle's advice developed that of earlier writers, among them Adam Petrie, who had similarly encouraged men to practise a style that was neither too fast nor slow, too stiff nor slovenly. Petrie also paid considerable attention to the gentleman's relationship with his fellow pedestrians, advising that male social superiors and women either be allowed to walk on the right, or be given the safety of walking nearest the wall and away from the dirt of the street.[88] If anything, Matthew Towle's instructions were rather more intricate on this aspect of pavement culture. As before, male (and female) superiors were to be given the wall, as were elderly men regardless of social position. Men were also required to walk behind their elders, about two yards from women to avoid treading on their clothing (any more was 'ill Manners'), and in front of one's parents; in open country, superiors were allowed to go first but not if the ground was muddy.[89]

One of the striking features in this and other discussions is the importance of issues of social hierarchy in determining correct forms of polite behaviour. For writers like Petrie and Towle, the supposedly egalitarian sentiments commonly associated with a Spectatorial politeness had to be balanced against the realities of a society just as aware of the intricate practical relationship between superiors, equals and inferiors as those of the sixteenth and early seventeenth century. Towle went so far as to include a chart to instruct readers on the correct form of address for dignitaries ranging from members of the royal family down through the nobility, clergy, officers of the monarch's household, military leaders and judges. As in many similar studies, Towle also commented more generally on the conduct owed to superiors (be deferential, listen carefully) with equals (be respectful but never too familiar) and inferiors (be humane). In placing readers somewhere towards the middle of this social spectrum, Towle clearly aimed his advice towards a restricted social group of what he termed 'genteel and polite Gentlemen', sandwiched between members of a social and professional elite and 'the poor' to whom, he warned, polite readers remained superior by virtue of their posture and dancing skills alone. Part dancing-master's puff, Towle's comment at first appears to draw attention to the relative fineness of the divide between polite and impolite and, in doing so, to reduce the distance between refinement and boorishness to such relatively superficial matters as deportment and gesture. Perhaps aware that the bulk of his advice could be dismissed as instruction merely in the externalities of politeness, Towle, like Locke, also worked hard to demonstrate the symbiosis of what he called the 'moral and social duties', the result being 'Actions, such as walking, standing, sitting, kneeling, speaking' undertaken 'in such a Manner as to Sympathize with thy Soul'.[90]

However, it was clear to many late-eighteenth-century observers that not all writers on politeness were concerned with encouraging this synthesis of manners and morals. For a number of Towle's contemporaries and later conduct writers alike, none proved more reluctant than Philip Dormer Stanhope, fourth earl of Chesterfield (1694-1773) whose 430 letters to his illegitimate son and godson were published by his daughter-in-law a year after the earl's death. Chesterfield's historical reputation has been dominated by his role as a correspondent and, through the nature of his advice, as a cynical exponent of a brand of male refinement characterised by self-advancement disguised under a civil veneer.[91]

In view of this reputation it is worth stating that not all early reviews of the correspondence were critical. The *London Magazine* (1774), for example, thought the letters 'well calculated to form the man', and provided 'many valuable articles . . . for private and public life'.[92] Aspects of Chesterfield's advice also appeared in compilations of conduct literature, such as the 1776 *Polite Preceptor*, alongside selected papers from the *Spectator*.[93] We should also bear in mind those occasions, as in his discussion on dress, when Chesterfield provided instructions almost verbatim to that of, for example, *Spectator* No. 150. As he told his son, a man who dressed above the general standard of his society 'is a fop', though to ignore such standards was also 'unpardonably negligent'. By contrast, the 'man of sense carefully avoids any particular character in his dress', being 'clean for his own sake' but mainly 'for other people's'.[94] Finally, looking back to the comments of earlier polite theorists, we see that Chesterfield was not the first to show how external manners might exist independent of inner virtue. 'Politeness', as Abel Boyer noted, 'does not always inspire a Man with Humanity, Justice, Complaisance and Gratitude' despite providing 'him in appearance what he should be in reality'. David Hume's suggestion that polite men gave 'the appearance of sentiments different from those to which they naturally incline' likewise left open the possibility for duplicity, while Samuel Johnson acknowledged that politeness required one to be 'pleased with a man's work' though only 'when he is present'.[95]

That politeness was open to abuse and would-be polite males prone to cynical affectation – both central issues to the Chesterfield controversy – were thus anxieties with which commentators had lived throughout the century. This said, Boyer, Hume and Johnson were distinguished by their concern either to steer gentlemen away from these dangers or, through a moderate level of false manners, to promote the wider benefits of well-intentioned and pleasing, if not always truthful, conversation. Crucially, what set Chesterfield apart, and what prompted much of the criticism of his advice, was his apparently unrepentant exploitation of the potential gap between external polish and morals. To his detractors, Chesterfieldian manners were motivated not by a sensitivity for others but by a duplicitous bid for personal advancement: 'be upon your own guard', the earl told his readers, 'and yet by a seeming natural openness . . . put people off theirs'.[96]

Critics of such comments drew attention to Chesterfield's wilful misinterpretation of refinement as a gloss of manners, not only stripped of moral integrity but actively employed in exploiting that of others. The schoolmaster

Vicesimus Knox labelled Chesterfield's an 'ornamental education' that led men to adopt 'varnished qualities' and the 'mean motives of self-interest'.[97] Parents wishing to raise a 'wise, considerable, accomplished Man' were likewise warned by the *Westminster Magazine* to avoid the work of a 'late celebrated Nobleman' who had 'combined politeness and insincerity together'.[98] James Fordyce (1720–96), the popular preacher and sermon writer, expressed a similar view, rejecting 'a wretched system of education' intended to make young men 'vain . . . and smooth rather than polite'.[99]

It is highly likely that Chesterfield's advice would have provoked strong reactions among earlier conduct writers. Yet to understand fully the vitality of the controversy we also need to appreciate the specific cultural context in which the correspondence appeared: in part, an era of anti-elite criticism which identified Chesterfield's recommendations as symptomatic of wider aristocratic corruption, but also, and more significantly, a mid- to late-century culture of sensibility, in which polite discourse was reworked in favour of a modified concept of refinement prioritising instinctive sensitivity and greater emotional expression.

We began this chapter by charting the early-eighteenth-century rise of the 'polite gentleman' as a popular exemplar of a new culture of politeness. Easy, accommodating and sociable, the polite gentleman was viewed as a definite improvement on existing figures of refinement, the country gentleman and the courtier. Free to roam beyond the confines of the court, the polite gentleman had communication skills that equipped him for professional and leisure pursuits in the male, and now female, society of the town. To his proponents, the polite gentleman's superiority was guaranteed by his claim to manhood based on the rejection of traditional attributes such as violence, and the appropriation of qualities like self-control and sense for sociable purposes. The effect for conduct writers and academic analysts alike was a new form of manhood that was both more refined and more courageous, industrious and honourable.

Yet, as responses to Chesterfield's letters suggest, there was growing concern that the polite gentleman might also be an agent of duplicity. The Chesterfield controversy was heightened by the then well-established interest in sensibility. Publication of the correspondence was certainly not the 'cause' of sensibility; nevertheless, the tone of its advice provided a rallying point for a number of prominent sentimental writers, among them Vicesimus Knox and James Fordyce, then developing their own ideals of male conduct. As Paul Langford suggests, Chesterfield's advice proved 'peculiarly offensive to an age which had learned to cherish innocence and spontaneity . . . [and] confronted with the man of honour in this shape, the man of feeling could not but revolt'.[100] It is to the characteristics and the context of this latter figure that we turn in Chapter Three.

Notes and references

1. Locke, *Some Thoughts Concerning Education*, pp. 160, 164.

2. *Ibid.*, pp. 246–7.

3. Bryson, *From Courtesy to Civility*, p. 37.

4. Certain English translations, such as Nathaniel Walker's 1663 *The Refined Courtier*, highlight the duration of this association; for the *Galateo*'s title as an index to changing standards of refinement see also p. 50 fn 64.

5. This emphasis on regulation is central to Norbert Elias's concept of increasingly comprehensive 'thresholds of embarrassment' by which successive generations of early modern readers came to view formerly acceptable social practices as incivil, *Civilizing Process*, pp. 56, 492–8. While acknowledging the importance of restraint in early modern notions of civility, Anna Bryson also questions Elias's incremental model, *From Courtesy to Civility*, pp. 96–106.

6. William Fiston, *The Schoole of Good Manners; or a New Schoole of Vertue* (1629), no pagination.

7. James Raven, *Judging New Wealth: Popular Publishing and Responses to Commerce in England, 1750–1800* (Oxford, 1992), ch. 5. Also Felicity Heal and Clive Holmes, *The Gentry in England and Wales, 1500–1700* (Basingstoke, 1994), ch. 8.

8. Raven, *Judging New Wealth*, p. 98.

9. Francis Osborne, *Advice to a Son; or, Directions for Your Better Conduct* (Oxford, 1656), pp. 15, 17–18, 103, 106–7. 'Next to cloaths', wrote Osborne, 'a good *Horse* becomes a Gentleman' (18).

10. 19 Oct 1660, *The Diary of Samuel Pepys*, eds. R.C. Latham and W. Matthews, 10 vols. (1971–83, rpt 1995), I, p. 23. Pepys's companion Sir William Petty likewise thought Osborne's guide one of those 'most esteemed and generally cried up for wit in the world', 27 Jan 1664, *Diary*, IV, p. 27.

11. *Spectator*, No. 150 (22 Aug 1711), II, p. 91.

12. No. 230 (28 Sept 1710), in *The Tatler*, ed. Donald F. Bond, 3 vols. (Oxford, 1987), III, p. 195. Later eighteenth-century opinion tended to accept these earlier verdicts: Samuel Johnson, for example, thought Osborne a 'conceited fellow', Boswell, *Life of Johnson*, pp. 493–4.

13. *Tatler*, No. 30 (18 June 1709), I, p. 226; Boswell, *Journal of a Tour to the Hebrides*, p. 327.

14. Boyer, *English Theophrastus*, pp. 114–19.

15. Spectator, No. 193 (11 Oct 1711), II, p. 257; No. 394 (2 June 1712), III, p. 478.

16. *Scots Magazine*, 55 (1793), p. 500.

17. *Spectator*, No. 240 (5 Dec 1711), II, pp. 433–4. It was no coincidence that the courtier's presence brought confusion to country gentlemen whom the *Spectator* thought wedded to the formalities of previous generations by virtue of their unfamiliarity with modern town manners. Elsewhere, Addison employed the character of the country gentleman rather than the courtier as the outmoded alternative to the polite town-dweller. See below, p. 62.

18. *Tatler*, No. 207 (5 Aug 1710), III, p. 99. Steele's faith in the compatibility of the merchant's self-interest and his broader aptitude for true politeness is distinct from later characterisations of traders, somewhat in the model of the courtier, as duplicitous and uncompromising. For elements of this later image see Michael Roper, *Masculinity and the British Organization Man since 1945* (Oxford, 1994). The impact of a wider city culture on the court's declining intellectual and artistic importance is considered in R.O. Bucholz, *The Augustan Court: Queen Anne and the Decline of Court Culture* (Stanford CA, 1993). Bucholz also discusses contemporaries' complaints against the formulaic and dull forms of sociability then practised at court (246).

19. *Guardian* No. 21 (4 Apr 1713), p. 103.

20. *Spectator* No. 150, II, pp. 91–2.

21. *Ibid.*, No. 631 (10 Dec 1714), V, pp. 157–8.

22. No. 119 (17 July 1711), I, p. 487.

23. No. 49 (26 Apr 1711), I, p. 210.

24. Klein, *Shaftesbury and Culture of Politeness*, p. 4. Peter Burke, *The Art of Conversation* (Oxford, 1993), ch. 3. See also Cohen, *Fashioning Masculinity*, ch. 1; Goodman, *Republic of Letters*, ch. 3, and Gordon, *Citizens Without Sovereignty*.

25. Henry Peacham, *The Compleat Gentleman* (1622), p. 196.

26. Fiston, *Schoole of Good Manners*, ch. 2 'Of gesture and behaviour' (np).

27. Locke, *Thoughts Concerning Education*, p. 252. On seventeenth-century modes of conversation see Bryson, *From Courtesy to Civility*, esp. ch. 5.

28. *Tatler*, No. 45 (23 July 1710), I, pp. 325–6; *Spectator*, No. 169 (13 Sept 1711), II, pp. 165–6.

29. J.R. Woodhouse, *From Castiglione to Chesterfield: The Decline in the Courtier's Manual* (Oxford, 1991), esp. pp. 9–11.

30. *Spectator*, No. 49 (26 Apr 1711), I, p. 208.

31. Trusler, *Principles of Politeness*, pp. 13–14.

32. Joseph Highmore, 'Of politeness and complaisance, as contradistinguish'd', in his *Essays Moral, Religious and Miscellaneous*, 2 vols. (1766), II, pp. 46–9.

33. *The Art of Complaisance* (1673), p. 53.

34. James Forrester, *The Polite Philosopher* (1738), p. 29.

35. Boyer, *English Theophrastus*, p. 104.

36. *Tatler*, No. 21 (28 May 1709), I, p. 165; No. 176 (25 May 1710), II, p. 459.

37. John Constable, *The Conversation of Gentlemen Considered* (1738), pp. 264–5.

38. *The Polite Companion; or, Wit à la Mode* (1760), p. 76.

39. Richard Peers, for example, chastised the drunkard for 'unmanning' himself, and for then repeating an action by which, over time, one 'renounces Manhood', *A Companion for Youth* (1738), p. 84. On the unmanliness of heavy drinking see Foyster, *Manhood*, pp. 40–4.

40. Boswell, *Life of Johnson*, p. 746.

41. *Spectator*, No. 49 (26 Apr 1711), I, p. 210.

42. *Ibid.*, No. 45, I, p. 210.

43. Brian Cowan, 'Reasonable ecstacies: Shaftesbury and the languages of libertinism', *Journal of British Studies*, 37 (1998), pp. 111–38, esp. 118–19.

44. Ellis, *Gentile Sinner*, p. 122.

45. Women's role in cultivating the seventeenth-century French concept of *honnêteté* is discussed by Cohen, *Fashioning Masculinity*, ch. 1. For salons and *salonnières* see Goodman, *Republic of Letters*.

46. William Ramesey, *The Gentleman's Companion* (1672), p. 10. Many reasons were proposed for women's superior refinement: in addition to Ramesey's evolutionary physiological model, women were variously more observant, less bookish, more socially active or possessed a wider vocabulary. Later writers on sensibility also attributed women's refinement to a more delicate and responsive nervous system, Barker-Benfield, *Culture of Sensibility*, ch. 1; Rousseau, 'Towards a semiotics of the nerve'.

47. *Spectator*, No. 57 (5 May 1711), I, p. 242; No. 433 (17 July 1712), IV, p. 21. The implication that men should only mix with virtuous women was common to the majority of guides; the message reminds us that a fear of corruption by members of the opposite sex was not just the preoccupation of women in the period. Hume, for example, spoke only of 'Women of Sense and Education', 'Of essay-writing', in *Essays*, p. 536; Bellegarde likewise advised men to socialise with 'women of virtue . . . respectable for their rank or merit', *Models of Conversation for Persons of Polite Education* (trans. 1765), pp. 296–7.

48. Forrester, *Polite Philosopher*, p. 49.

49. Simon Wagstaff [Jonathan Swift], *A Collection of Genteel and Ingenious Conversation*, (1738, 1755 edn), p. 116; Bellegarde, *Models of Conversation*, p. 302.

50. Hume, 'Rise and progress of the arts and sciences' (1742), in *Essays*, p. 134.

51. Millar, 'Of the rank and condition of women in different ages', in *Observations Concerning the Distinction of Ranks*, p. 71.

52. Swift, 'Hints towards an essay on conversation', in *Works*, IV, p. 95.

53. Hume, 'Rise and progress', in *Essays*, p. 134, Bellegarde, *Models of Conversation*, p. 297.

54. Forrester, *Polite Philosopher*, p. 49.

55. Bellegarde, *Models of Conversation*, pp. 307, 302.

56. Millar, *Observations*, p. 86.

57. *Ibid.*, pp. 89–90. On men's new-found respect for women, and the implications for standards of male conduct as discussed by Millar, see Moran, ' "The commerce of the sexes" '; Christopher Berry, *Social Theory of the Scottish Enlightenment* (Edinburgh, 1997), pp. 109–13; Jane Rendall, *The Origins of Modern Feminism. Women in Britain, France and the United States, 1780–1860* (1985), pp. 25–8.

58. Hume, 'Rise and progress', in *Essays*, p. 134; Smith, *Theory of Moral Sentiments*, p. 205.

59. Discussions of male attributes in conduct literature and personal diaries include Robert B. Shoemaker, *Gender in English Society, 1650–1850: The Emergence of Separate Spheres?* (1998), ch. 2; Alan Bray, 'To be a man in early modern society. The curious case of Michael Wrigglesworth', *History Workshop Journal*, 41 (1996), pp. 155–65; Katharine Hodgkin, 'Thomas Whythorne and the problems of mastery', *History Workshop*, 29 (1990), pp. 20–41.

60. In addition to Bray and Hodgkin see Fletcher, *Gender, Sex and Subordination*; Alexandra Shepard shows how reason was often employed to contain what early modern advice writers regarded as men's naturally passionate and disruptive disposition, 'Meanings of manhood in early modern England, with special reference to Cambridge, *c.* 1560–1640' (Ph.D thesis, Cambridge University, 1997), esp. ch. 1.

61. Amussen is concerned with the problem of civility as it affected the early modern clergy, though she also suggests its relevance to men from other walks of life. ' "The part of a Christian man": the cultural politics of manhood in early modern England', in Amussen and Mark Kishlansky eds., *Political Culture and Cultural Politics in Early Modern England* (Manchester, 1995), p. 223. Refinement was also at odds with Epictetus's brand of stoical teaching which viewed sociability as a challenge to self-identity.

62. Stephen Philpot, *An Essay on the Advantages of a Polite Education over a Learned One* (1747), p. 37.

63. *The Polite Companion* (Birmingham, 1749), pp. 73–4.

64. Oliver Goldsmith, *An Enquiry into the Present State of Polite Learning* (1759), in Arthur Friedman ed., *Collected Works of Oliver Goldsmith*, 5 vols. (Oxford, 1965), I, p. 306. On the compatibility of 'enlightened' academic study with notions of polite gentlemanliness in Scottish universities, see Paul B. Wood, *The Aberdeen Enlightenment: The Arts Curriculum in the Eighteenth Century* (Aberdeen, 1993), esp. pp. 160–3. For James Boswell's praise of Adam Smith as a polite gentleman, see below, p. 188.

65. Bernard Mandeville, *An Enquiry into the Origins of Honour* (1732), ed. M.M. Goldsmith (1973), p. 83.

66. John Cockburn, *The History and Examination of Duels* (1720), p. 229. For Cockburn's contribution to the early-eighteenth-century anti-duelling movement see Donna T. Andrew, 'The code of honour and its critics: the opposition to duelling in England, 1700–1815', *Social History*, 5 (1980), pp. 503–29.

67. *Gentleman's Magazine*, 31 (1761), pp. 58–9. There were of course dissenting voices: Samuel Johnson believed duelling more common among men 'in high degree refined' for 'in a highly polished society, an affront is held to be a serious injury', Boswell, *Life of Johnson*, p. 484.

68. Oliver Goldsmith, *Life of Richard Nash* (1762), in *Works*, III, p. 305.

69. Locke, *Some Thoughts Concerning Education*, p. 310.

70. Philpot, *Essay on Polite Education*, p. 55; James Nelson, *An Essay on the Government of Children* (Dublin, 1763), p. 101.

71. Lewis Lockee, *An Essay on Military Education* (2nd edn, 1776), pp. 29–30.

72. Constable, *Conversation of Gentlemen*, pp. 264–5.

73. Hume, 'Rise and progress', in *Essays*, pp. 131–3.

74. Hume's 1742 paper 'On essay writing', for example, gendered the 'learned' and the 'conversable' worlds as male and female respectively. While aiming to narrow this distinction, Hume still placed more emphasis on socialising the learned than on educating the socially polished. See *Essays*, p. 534.

75. Hume, 'Rise and progress', in *Essays*, pp. 131–3.

76. Richard Campbell, *The London Tradesman* (1749), p. 197.

77. Ellis, *Gentile Sinner*, p. 114.

78. *Art of Complaisance*, p. 118.

79. Bellegarde, *Models of Conversation*, pp. 309–10.

80. *Ibid.*, pp. 309–10.

81. Hume, 'Of refinement in the arts and sciences' (1752) in *Essays*, pp. 274–5.

82. Fenela Childs, 'Prescriptions for manners in English courtesy literature, 1690–1760, and their social implications' (D.Phil thesis, Oxford University, 1984), esp. pp. 102–28; Fletcher, *Gender, Sex and Subordination*, p. 336.

83. Harris, *Essay on Politeness*, p. 24.

84. As we have seen, discussions of conversation typically focused on generalities such as the need to entertain, the unattractiveness of pedantry or delivery and tone of voice. Guides occasionally provided more detailed lists of subjects suitable for polite company, a strategy which ran counter to the theory of spontaneous discourse, but which suggests the practical difficulties of easy, erudite speech and the efforts taken to achieve the desired effect. One such primer, the *Dictionary of Conversation* (1800), offered information on a medley of topics including America, balloons, Descartes, guillotines, 'ladies, *British*', popes, and summer-houses.

85. Matthew Towle, *The Young Gentleman and Lady's Private Tutor* (Oxford, 1771), p. 79.

86. References to the posture of bodies at rest and in motion proved an integral feature of dancing manuals throughout the period. Pierre Rameau, for example, devoted 110 pages and 60 illustrations to men's leg movements and a further 46 pages to use of the arms, *Dancing-Master*. The social as well as the physical benefits of dancing were also highlighted in more general guides for gentlemanly education: James Nelson, for example, encouraged parents to allow their sons to learn an art that 'gives a pleasing Distinction of the bred from the unbred', *Essay on . . . Children*, p. 102.

87. Towle, *Private Tutor*, pp. 130–7, 148–9, 168–9.

88. Petrie, *Rules of Good Deportment*, pp. 6–7.

89. Towle, p. 149. Towle thought 'this kind of Behaviour makes every one take Notice of you for your Politeness' (169). Commenting slightly later, Samuel Johnson believed the rising incidence of men 'giving the wall' an indication of improved standards of manners between his own and his parents' generation. Boswell, *Journal of a Tour to the Hebrides*, p. 297.

90. Towle, *Private Tutor*, pp. 116–27, 86. Towle's spiritual justification for a knowledge of dancing, for instance, drew on Psalm 150: 'Praise Him in the Cymbals and Dances' (181).

91. See Roger Coxon, *Chesterfield and his Critics* (1925). The impact of the correspondence as a juncture in eighteenth-century concepts of good social conduct is analysed by Michael Curtin, 'A question of manners: status and gender in etiquette and courtesy', *Journal of Modern History*, 57 (1985), pp. 395–423.

92. *London Magazine*, 43 (1774), p. 193.

93. For extracts of Chesterfield's advice on men's choice of company, how to please, dress and dance see *The Polite Preceptor*, pp. 209–12, 242–3, 247–9.

94. Chesterfield to Philip Stanhope, 30 Dec 1748, in *Lord Chesterfield's Letters*, ed. David Roberts (Oxford, 1992), p. 128.

95. Boyer, *English Theophrastus*, p. 108; Hume 'Rise and progress', in *Essays*, p. 132; Boswell, *Life of Johnson*, p. 844.

96. Chesterfield, *Letters*, p. xii.

97. Knox, 'On the superior value of solid accomplishment' (1782), in *Works*, II, p. 202.

98. *Westminster Magazine*, III (Jan 1775), pp. 30–1.

99. James Fordyce, *Addresses to Young Men*, 2 vols. (1777), II, p. 175.

100. Paul Langford, *Public Life and the Propertied Englishman, 1689–1798* (Oxford, 1991), p. 542.

CHAPTER THREE

The manliness of feeling

As we saw in the last chapter, the publication of Lord Chesterfield's *Letters to His Son* (1774) prompted considerable interest and strong reactions. The diarist Horace Walpole 'devoured' the correspondence late on the evening of 8 April (the day after publication) and was initially surprised to find that Chesterfield had 'really written from the heart, not for the honour of his head', though Walpole soon modified this view: the letters 'do no great honour to the last, nor show much feeling in the first' he concluded.[1] Several months later, the novelist Fanny Burney commented on her household's preoccupation with the relative merits of Chesterfield's late son, Philip Stanhope (1732–68), and the Tahitian Prince Omai, then visiting London. Opinion clearly favoured the latter. Burney explained how, 'with no Tutor but Nature', Omai had captivated fashionable society with his 'appearance and behaviour *politely easy*, and thoroughly well-bred', while the privileges afforded to Stanhope had produced a 'mere *pedantic* booby'. 'I think,' she concluded, 'this shews how much more Nature can do without *art*, than *art* with all her refinement unassisted by nature'.[2]

Comparisons between an unnatural and unyielding Chesterfieldian and a man of apparently natural refinement were again made several years later. On this occasion the hard-hearted malefactor was the fifth earl, the late earl's godson and the chief recipient of Chesterfield's advice after Philip Stanhope's death. Early in 1777 the fifth earl came to public attention for his determination to prosecute William Dodd, his former tutor and erstwhile chaplain at London's Magdalen Hospital. Dodd, a popular preacher who made his name in the 1760s through his exhortations to philanthropy, now stood accused of forging Chesterfield's signature to acquire funds to repay personal debts. His plight, imprisoned in Newgate, found guilty and hanged, led many to criticise what the *Morning Post* saw as Chesterfield's compassionless refusal 'to sacrifice rigid justice to an impulse of humanity'. The auction of Dodd's possessions was described in the same newspaper as an act of 'men equally devoid of delicacy and feeling'.[3] Dodd, by contrast, was represented as a man of sensitivity and intense emotion who during visits from his wife was 'so much affected as to stop short and burst into a flood of tears'.[4] He was also the subject of widespread public sympathy. Horace Walpole, for one, 'felt exceedingly' for 'poor Dr Dodd', and believed that his trial, 'a scene of protracted horrors', could not 'but excite commiseration in every feeling breast'.[5]

Events like Dodd's case ensured that the fourth earl's correspondence was as enduring as it was disquieting. In the year of the minister's execution, the popular sermon writer James Fordyce felt it necessary to warn young male readers away from a 'wretched system of education' that produced 'pleasing triflers and plausible insignificants'.[6] It is highly likely that Chesterfield's advice would have prompted criticism at other points in the century. The letters provided evidence of the ways in which politeness could be distorted for deception as the relationship between inner and external refinement, central to late-seventeenth-century conduct guides from John Locke onwards, was exploited for self-interest. Yet at the same time, the scale and tone of the criticism points to the existence of new thinking on social refinement encapsulated in a mid- to late-eighteenth-century 'culture of sensibility'.[7]

Horace Walpole's appreciation of heartfelt messages and feeling, or Fanny Burney's elevation of a natural over a formal education, offer examples of some of the key themes of this culture. Burney's praise of Omai as 'politely easy' reminds us that the emergence of sensibility never completely replaced the well-established interest in, and vocabulary of, 'politeness' and 'polite' living. But a distinct concept and language of sensibility was also well established by the 1770s to describe styles of refinement distinguishable from and superior to those of the polite male. Principal among these was the increasing attachment to gentlemen's displays of emotional sensitivity, free from what were now seen as the controls and corruptions of an earlier polite discourse.

It was through such displays that the weeping William Dodd and the palpitating on-lookers at his trial earned their reputation for 'delicacy' and 'feeling' in the newspapers and magazines covering the event. The first part of this chapter looks in more detail at some of the actions expected of the sentimental gentleman. Unlike the polite man of conversation, the man of sensibility was distinguished more by his display of bodily delicacy conveyed, on one level, through sighs, trembles and above all tears. Likewise, whereas the polite gentleman had been a habitué of the town and its public venues, the sentimental man was more frequently depicted as a family man who expressed his true refinement not with strangers but with intimate and trusted loved ones.

These distinctions have led a number of historians to treat the sentimental male, epitomised by the figure of the 'man of feeling', as a markedly feminised individual. A second section on 'Manly ideals' shows how, as with polite manhood, reformers sought to demonstrate the compatibility of sensibility and manliness. Like the debate over politeness, this discussion engaged both academic social theorists and a host of sermon writers, essayists, magazine contributors and novelists, through whom scholarly models of sympathetic exchange and medical theories of the nervous system were conveyed to a wide audience. Both academic and popular studies presented their case with reference to the durability of traditional values now reworked and displayed through a series of idealised personality types – the sensitive genius, the benevolent philanthropist, the tender husband and the caring father – whose qualities were shown to greatest effect in descriptions of real-life heroes.

The corruption of men like Chesterfield confirmed the need for new signs of refinement that could not be faked as easily as polite styles. To its proponents, sensibility restored the link between moral and physical refinement. Yet even now it was not always clear when declarations of refined feeling were genuine. One such celebrated case concerned the emotional tone of the political writer, Edmund Burke, in his criticism of the French Revolution, published in 1790. The debate over Burke's genuine or affected response is often seen by historians as marking the end of the culture of sensibility in ways reminiscent of the Chesterfield controversy and politeness during the mid-1770s. However, as the final section suggests, sentimental writers had been troubled by the abuse of sensibility well before Burke's outburst. Most alarming was the realisation that the culprits of duplicity were not overtly contemptuous figures like Lord Chesterfield but the very men of feeling, including James Fordyce and William Dodd, at the heart of sentimental culture.

Sentimental actions

Many condemned the perceived duplicity of Lord Chesterfield and his acolytes, but few rejected superficial and cynical forms of male refinement with quite the precision of the poet William Cowper in 1785:

> *I would not enter on my list of friends*
> *(Though graced with polish'd manners and fine sense,*
> *Yet wanting sensibility) the man*
> *Who needlessly sets foot upon a worm.*[8]

Here the man of sensibility was distinguished by a sensitivity to his environment which created sufficient 'humanity', as Cowper went on, to 'tread aside and let the reptile live'.[9] How did such sensitivity come about? Several years later Cowper offered one explanation in a letter to Margaret King, the wife of a schoolfriend. More concerned on this occasion to highlight the bonds than the differences between men, Cowper explained sensibility in terms of a common male physiology. Two developments were at work in modern society: first, the physical refinement of men's bodies and, second, the rise of men's capacity for sensitivity or sensibility. For Cowper the latter shift was clearly determined by the former, an argument he illustrated with reference to an unspecified past. Men in an earlier age had been known for the 'sturdiness of their frame' but 'had little feeling' since 'a very robust athletic habit seems inconsistent with much sensibility'; in their descendants, by contrast, 'our feelings have been render'd more exquisite as our habit of body has become more delicate'.[10]

Cowper's observations raise several points pertinent to the practices of sentimental manhood. Most obvious is the attention paid to men's physiology as a basis for sensibility. What Cowper regarded as modern men's unprecedented capacity for sensitivity was directly determined by changes to what he termed the 'human constitution', with the refined physique being, by implication, a principal means for the continued expression of sensibility through a new range of gestures and actions. The themes considered in Cowper's letter conform closely with the views of a number of contemporary conduct writers. If the image of the polite man was predominantly of a responsible and regulated conversationist, that of the sentimental man, if never eschewing the merits of speech, gave greater attention to the watched physical body as a means of indicating refinement. Moreover, whereas polite writers emphasised the body through often detailed instruction on deportment, advocates of sensibility encouraged less regulated and more expressive, if still prescribed, actions as indicative of male feeling.

As with discussions of politeness, complexity and ambiguity are evident within a diverse set of texts of which William Cowper's remains one interpretation. As we saw in Chapter One, Cowper considered men's heightened capacity for feeling as the result of a gradual, centuries-long refinement of the male body caused by life in an increasingly comfortable and materially prosperous society. For others, however, sensibility's appearance was an altogether more recent phenomenon. In these interpretations the shift from hardier but more boorish males to a newly refined ideal was understood to have occurred over a matter of decades or between a single generation. Elsewhere, Cowper himself offered two potentially divergent pictures of the origins and scope of sentimental manhood. In his letter to Margaret King, sensibility emerges as a universal feature in men sharing a common history and social environment. However, in the verse with which we began this section, sensibility exists as a rarer quality characteristic of a limited number of men (Cowper's potential friends) who are contrasted with those 'wanting sensibility' – whether from a deficiency of constitution or, as is implied from the poet's juxtaposition of feeling and social polish, from a conscious rejection of the trappings of sentimental manhood.

To appreciate the subject's complexity is not to deny the existence of a broad range of common sentimental actions by which mid- to late-century men were regularly encouraged to demonstrate new forms of social refinement. Writing to Margaret King, Cowper characterised his own condition in terms of physiology and ill-health, making regular comments on a recurrent eye inflammation, here complemented by rheumatism brought on by temperature changes to which his sensitive 'bodily feelings' were closely attuned. Cowper's ailments, and his understanding of their origin, were typical of those experienced by many eighteenth-century men whom medical and later non-medical literature regularly identified as 'hypochondriacs'. Then a non-pejorative label to describe a defined illness, 'hypochondria, and, more ambivalently, melancholy' were, according to John Mullan, characterised 'as types of susceptibility which tend to be evidence of refinement and "sensibility"'.[11] Traceable to Aristotle, there was little particularly novel in an equation between a purportedly intellectual or civilised lifestyle and physical health. However, added momentum and topicality were now provided by this gradual acculturation of late-seventeenth-century theories of a nervous physiology – the cause of Cowper's 'bodily feelings' – whereby the circulation of sensations along nerves offered an original means of explaining the impact of external stimuli on personal emotions and behaviour. In acute states, the benefits of a delicate nervous system were registered as profound intellect, moral standing and/or creative genius. David Hume, a self-declared hypochondriac, believed that 'a gloomy and melancholy disposition' was often found in 'very worthy persons' possessed of a 'great sense of honour and great integrity', while the Edinburgh novelist Henry Mackenzie, writing after Cowper's suicide in 1800, attributed the poet's 'great genius' to his being 'nervous in constitution'.[12]

That only a limited number of men scaled these creative and intellectual heights was frequently explained with reference to what physicians identified as natural gradations within men's innate nervous condition. It was an idea readily adopted by non-medical authors who, like the Church of Scotland theologian and sermon writer Hugh Blair, spoke of the 'different degrees of constitutional warmth in men's affections . . . For all derive not from nature the same happy delicacy, and tenderness of feeling.'[13] Faced with variations in the quality of male sensibility, sentimental conduct writers concentrated on two particular issues: first, on the means to educate readers – the majority of whom lacked the advanced natural sensitivity of a Hume or a Cowper – in how to recognise expressions of sensibility; and, second, on the ways by which individuals might develop and exercise their limited sensitivity to their own and others' advantage.

As several commentators pointed out, it was not always possible to detect the presence of sensibility simply by reference to the gentility of an individual's social performance. Indeed, on certain occasions and among certain personality types, sensibility could exist in tandem with behaviour far removed from accepted notions of refined conduct. 'Softness of manners', warned Hugh Blair, 'must not be mistaken for true sensibility . . . [since] under a negligent and seemingly rough manner, there lies a tender and feeling heart.'[14] Having himself commented on Samuel Johnson's 'very slovenly' dress, 'uncouth voice' and dogmatic conduct, James Boswell defended his companion with a similar observation taken from Oliver Goldsmith: 'Johnson, to be sure, has a roughness in his manner; but no man alive has a more tender heart.'[15]

Yet, at least among sentimental conduct writers, such boorish sensibility remained an interesting exception, rather than the rule. In most cases a capacity for feeling was believed to produce more pleasing and demonstrably refined modes of social conduct. 'Sensibility', continued Hugh Blair, 'indeed tends to produce gentleness in behaviour', a view shared by John Logan, a fellow Church of Scotland minister, for whom sensibility was the 'refinement which polishes the mind' and produced 'that gentleness of manners which sweetens the intercourse of human society'.[16]

Men in tears

How were refined men of sensibility expected to behave? In answering this question we should again be careful not to create an overly false distinction between notions of polite and sentimental manliness. The language of 'softness' and 'gentleness' so often employed in depictions of sentimental men was, as we saw in Chapter Two, also applied to discussions of polite manhood. Similarly, late-eighteenth-century descriptions of the gentlemanly ideal commonly characterised their subjects as men both of elegant manners and copious feeling. It was said that 'Mr Lorpois', the creation of the dancing-master and author, Matthew Towle, for example, 'distinguisheth himself by his Politeness' while also 'admire him for his Sensibility'.[17] Sentimental styles are therefore best viewed less as a complete replacement for than as a significant reworking of existing definitions of male refinement, whereby the potential for polite artifice was reduced through an accentuated attachment to the value of genuine emotion. The result produced a shift in notions of admirable social behaviour which now saw sentimental styles contrasted favourably with the anachronistic 'polish'd manners' of Cowper's Chesterfieldian-style corrupter.

In place of these formalities, sentimental commentators set out important body-centred additions to the repertoire of mid- to late-century refinement. Sentimental men, like their female counterparts, were encouraged to employ a range of physical gestures – sighing, trembling and facial expressions – to convey and to receive the sympathies on which sentimental sociability depended. Observation, as much as speaking or listening, served as the means to understand the extent of another person's feeling. Advice on such behaviour featured prominently in discussions of good male conduct. In 1777 James Fordyce advised young men to include the 'tender look of fellow-feeling' as an important device for securing and maintaining friend-ships.[18] Later he returned to the subject, developing the various elements of this wordless exchange, and encouraging male readers to seek independ-ence through their adoption:

> And yet this path to joy still open lies,
> Though wealth be absent: sympathetic sighs,
> And tender tears, and pray'rs, and looks of love,
> And friendly smiles, the feeling heart that prove,
> With nameless gentle offices beside,
> Above the richest boons bestow'd by Pride,
> Import a sov'reign balsam to the breast,
> That may be felt, but cannot be expressed.[19]

The idea that sensibility moved individuals to convey emotion through a range of physical, and especially facial, gestures goes some way to explain a late-century revival in the science of physiognomy. The ability to read faces served both as a useful means to evaluate others' sensitivity while indicating the extent of one's own perceptiveness as a sentimental observer. 'Harley', the hero of Henry Mackenzie's hugely popular sentimental novel, *The Man of Feeling* (1771), was described as being especially proud of his physiognom-ical skills – his 'foible' – in which there was said to be 'a very considerable degree of general attention' following the 1789 English translation of Johann Lavater's influential study, *Physiognomische Fragmente* (1775).[20]

Of the gestures listed in Fordyce's poem, it was perhaps weeping and tears – what one mid-eighteenth-century novelist called the 'tokens of sens-ibility' – that received most discussion among rival behavioural writers.[21] This image of the tearful man of feeling remains, moreover, a popular and enduring perception of late-eighteenth-century masculinity derived largely from the enduring tone of sentimental novels, like Mackenzie's, in which 'sensitive men . . . shed tears (gushes, wellings, droplets) over "interesting objects", ranging from blasted trees to crippled dogs'.[22]

It would be wrong to suggest that positive statements on men's weeping were unknown prior to the vogue for sensibility; the mid- to late eighteenth century did not see the first deployment of men's tears in conduct literature. Yet until this point it was still common for weeping to be identified as a distinctly female practice. Writing towards the end of the seventeenth century, Lord Halifax, for example, had considered it an act by which deceitful women influenced their husbands.[23] Thirty years later, Richard Steele also identified weeping as a female activity, though one which he thought motivated by a genuine sympathy for others. The clear implication of both accounts was the unsuitability of men's engagement in similar actions. As Steele claimed in *Tatler* No. 68, while a woman's response to suffering 'inclines her to Tears . . . in a Man, it makes him think how such a one ought to act on that Occasion'.[24] The prohibition on male tears also appears to have extended to boys who, although as yet unfamiliar with the discipline of adult life, were still expected to control their tendency to weep. John Locke set the tone with his denunciation of boys' tears as a 'fault' to be ignored in the inculcation of a 'Brawniness and Insensibility of Mind' necessary for adult life.[25]

Not all commentators were consistent in this hard line. For Richard Steele, for example, the gendering of tears did not rule out all opportunities for adult male weeping. What was required was that men appreciate the inappropriateness of tears in certain circumstances. In view of his comments in *Tatler* No. 68, Steele evidently thought that men's tears should not come before practical assistance at moments of crisis. Male readers were also advised to avoid intemperate behaviour when going about their daily business. An excess of emotion, even in front of close friends, was thought embarrassing and antisocial; 'laughter in one condition', warned Steele, 'is as unmanly as Weeping in the other'.[26] Distressed men who sought the assistance of male peers were also dissuaded from public grief: whereas a female observer was said to respond instinctively to tears, her male equivalent valued 'those whom he observes to suffer in Silence'.[27] Male tears in either the *Tatler* or *Spectator* were usually shed in private and then typically only as a consequence of acute personal experiences. The grieving widower in *Spectator* No. 520, for example, was shown to 'retire and give way to a few Sighs and Tears' before rejoining his companions; more intense outbursts meanwhile, when his 'Eyes gush with grief', took place 'in a serious and lonely Hour'.[28] By the time he wrote his final play, *The Conscious Lovers* (1722), Steele had apparently shifted his attitude to crying in public, if not his emphasis on the need to subordinate emotion to self-control. In the preface he complimented male members of the audience for crying during a touching scene between a father and his daughter. Men whose tears 'flow'd from Reason and Good Sense', he wrote, 'ought not to be laugh'd at for weeping, till we are come to a more clear Notion of what is to be imputed to the Hardness of Head, and the Softness of the Heart'.[29]

In fact, it would seem that for many later writers men's tears were less an indication of mental weakness than of a superior and commendable sensibility. A passage from Peter Shaw's periodical *Man* (1755) provides a good example of this emerging appreciation both of the merits of men's 'softness of heart' and the value of male weeping as a now public expression of this quality. For Shaw, tears served in men and women alike as 'witnesses of the noble disposition of a heart participating in the most amiable manner'.[30] Rather than cause embarrassment or scorn, as Steele had suggested, tears indicated an individual's readiness to offer sympathy to those in distress and for whom sensitive men now wept in demonstrations of sociable exchange. 'Tender tears', as James Fordyce pointed out in 1786, were sure signs of a 'feeling heart'. Of course, in Fordyce's poem weeping took its place alongside a range of physical techniques seemingly equally valued in the development of a sentimental persona. Yet it was a commonly held view that tears best indicated the peak of refinement. The 'degree of sensibility which prompts us to *weep with them that weep*', believed Hugh Blair, was stronger 'than that which prompts us to *rejoice with them that rejoice*'.[31] The schoolmaster and essayist Vicesimus Knox was similarly keen to equate tears with enhanced moral virtue. In place of the 'hardness of heart' displayed by early eighteenth-century men, Knox advocated unapologetically emotional behaviour and asked that modern gentlemen offer no 'blush at being seen to give vent to grief by the floodgates of the eyes'.[32] Formerly an image associated with shame and social exclusion, men in tears had now become one of the foundations on which advocates of sensibility, like Knox, sought to establish superior forms of male sociability.

Men at home

The emergence of a mid- to late-eighteenth-century culture of sensibility clearly brought with it a new appreciation of the value and appropriateness of male weeping. This said, the suitability and extent of men's tears remained, as we shall see later, a subject of some discussion among sentimental commentators. Though Vicesimus Knox judged copious weeping acceptable and indeed desirable, more cautious writers on male sensibility, among them the Glasgow professor of moral philosophy Adam Smith, stressed the need for displays of feeling commensurate with an overt show of forbearance and dignity.

A similar debate surrounded the mid-century gentleman's conduct with his family. Adam Smith, ever guarded in his attitude to sentimental styles of manhood, began his discussion of men's relationship with their children with a customary word of warning. An excess of what Smith called 'paternal tenderness' produced an unacceptable ostentatiousness requiring constant regulation to ensure propriety. Though critical of immoderate conduct, Smith was ultimately reluctant to censure a form of excessive feeling which 'though it may appear blameable, never appears odious'.[33] Elsewhere, he included the 'too indulgent father' as one of several characters who may 'on account of the softness of their natures, be looked upon with a species of pity . . . but can never be regarded with hatred and aversion'. Far less deserving of sympathy was the man:

> who appears to feel nothing for his own children. . . . The stoical apathy is, in such cases, never agreeable, and all the metaphysical sophisms by which it is supported can seldom serve any other purpose than to blow up the hard insensibility of a coxcomb to ten times its native impertinence.[34]

Smith's account of the incompatibility between domesticity and apathetic stoicism followed a more generous recommendation of the relationship between the heart and hearth in David Hume's essay 'Of moral prejudices' (1752). Hume contrasted the lifestyle of the austere ancient stoic with the modern figure of Eugenius, a man whose displays of tearfulness and tenderness he – Eugenius – refused 'to call . . . by the Name of *Weakness*', even in front of his male friends. Central to Hume's approbation of these actions was their origin in the family, for him a key location for male sensibility. Eugenius is described as having enjoyed an intimate relationship with his now deceased wife and their children, with subsequent displays of emotion prompted by his 'fond and tender Recollection of past Pleasures' and by contact with a daughter bearing close resemblance to her mother.[35]

The importance of men's place in family life has not gone unnoticed by historians of sensibility. According to Shawn Lisa Maurer, the period witnessed the development of a model of 'noncompetitive and familial masculinity' epitomised either by the 'exemplary sentimental father . . . who protects, supports, advises, and understands his son', or by an idealised husband in whom, to quote Kathryn Shevelow, 'compassion, concern, and responsibility become the male virtues matching those of prudence and chastity in the woman'.[36] These particular accounts trace such developments to an early eighteenth-century periodical literature dedicated to showing the compatibility of men's displays of familial affection with what the *Spectator* described as 'the most masculine Disposition'.[37] Historians' attempts to date the emergence of such an ideal remain fraught with difficulty, however.

Stimulated by Lawrence Stone's work on nuclear family formation in the 1970s, early modern historians have since found evidence for the emergence of the domesticated male at various points between the sixteenth and the early nineteenth centuries.[38] Alongside the problem of tracing the origin of more affectionate parenting, we also need to be cautious about attributing the eighteenth century's interest in men's domestic conduct simply to a vogue for sensibility. Guides to politeness did occasionally consider the behaviour of husbands who were warned against criticising or flattering their wives in public (deemed irritating for the spouse, embarrassing for onlookers), while both husbands and wives were encouraged as members of 'the really well-bred part of the world' to adopt 'a genteel, and easy carriage to one another'.[39]

Even so, it is still possible to appreciate the particular importance of the domesticated ideal in mid- and late-eighteenth-century discussions of male conduct. Two themes distinguish these accounts from many earlier conduct studies of the polite gentlemen. First, for the majority of its theorists, politeness had been a public phenomenon primarily concerned with men's behaviour in places of work and leisure populated by strangers, clients and patrons, as well as intimate friends and selected relations. Discussions of this public world focused much attention on conduct at newly emerging sites of polite sociability. Consideration of behaviour within the home, if not excluded from this literature, dwelt simply on the transferability of social skills between the public and domestic spheres. Consequently, there was rather less focus on men's intimate conduct within the nuclear family. Men who refused to take their refinement home did indeed come in for criticism, but this chastisement focused specifically on their failure to socialise with invited guests rather than family members. As one guide from the early 1730s had claimed, many tradesmen while 'very considerable Figures in their Coffee-Houses' turned out to be incivil in their homes, unable to sit correctly at the table or to enter a room 'with decency'.[40]

A second distinction was also evident in mid-eighteenth-century efforts to redefine the meaning of the home and the style of good conduct required therein. Previously a relatively unimportant extension of a public world of politeness, from mid-century the home became more closely identified as a key venue for truly refined behaviour, domestic conduct becoming what Samuel Johnson described in the *Rambler* (1750) as 'the most authentic witness of any man's character'. Within a community now defined as immediate family members rather than invited guests, Johnson identified refined manliness as one's ability to control the power which the majority of adult men held over their wives and children: only as a loving rather than a disciplinarian husband or father was a man able to show that his 'heart is pure'.[41]

The decades following Johnson's statement saw the development of the considerate husband and the sensitive father as influential images in contemporary thinking on idealised manliness. As the range of venues for the would-be man of refinement shifted to include these more intimate spaces, so discussions paid closer attention to the merits of women's company as wives rather than as platonic social acquaintances. Time and again, sentimental commentators proposed the benefits of a loving marriage, in which male and female qualities were blended to produce a superior composite form. Like their predecessors, male readers of behavioural literature in the 1760s and 1770s were advised of the benefits of refining their conduct, though now it was intimacy and affection, rather than public discourse, by which this transformation was expected to occur. Through what James Fordyce called 'honourable love' there came a 'powerful softness of the fiercest spirit . . . which converts the savage into a man'.[42] In the same year (1765), readers of the *Scots Magazine*'s 'Picture of true CONJUGAL FELICITY' were able to see this process in action in the marriage of Amanda and the aptly named Manley who, as a result of his love for a 'mild and endearing' wife, learned to 'soften to become happy' and gained 'the character of a good man'.[43]

Second only to the intimacy of husband and wife was that expected between what Fordyce labelled those 'Bosom Friends', a father and his son. In its idealised form, paternal, like conjugal, affection benefited both adults – Fordyce spoke of men being 'softened into the love . . . of superior graciousness' – and their children, producing 'mildest and noblest feelings' across the age gap.[44] To encourage common emotions was not to downplay the importance of domestic hierarchies between the sexes or the generations within what proved to be an often distinctly conservative sentimental conduct tradition: Amanda remained dependent on a kind but ever resourceful Manley, while filial feeling manifested itself through unswerving obedience.

Patriarchal authority was further buttressed by the precise roles that fathers were expected to fulfil, specifically in relations with their male children. Adult men were encouraged to play to their innate strengths as wise counsellors able to guide their offspring through the difficult transition from adolescence to manhood: instructions on beginning an apprenticeship or on starting at university were two of the tasks highlighted in Thomas Gisborne's 1795 guide for middle-class fathers.[45] In doing so, conduct authors like Gisborne made clear their belief that domestic practices need not impede men's proficiency in more 'society-based' roles centred around work, citizenship, public duty, intellectual activity and religious worship with which adult manliness had long been associated. This said, reformers remained alert to the potential threat posed to manliness by focusing on domestic actions, from which, without careful regulation, the chances of producing men like Adam Smith's pitiful and 'too indulgent father' remained acute. More generally, the popularity of a sentimental refinement encouraging supposedly feminine attributes, such as physical delicacy and weeping, demanded a similar awareness of the need to convince sceptics of the compatability of sensibility and manliness.

Manly ideals

For some early exponents of sensibility this connection seemed elusive. After the success of *Pamela* (1740–1) and *Clarissa* (1747–8), tracing the fortunes of two sentimental heroines, the novelist Samuel Richardson turned to an equivalent study of the 'good man'. The task, however, caused Richardson considerable difficulty. 'Can you help me to such a one as is required of me?', he wrote to a female correspondent in 1750: 'how can we hope that ladies will not think a good man a tame man?' The result of Richardson's deliberation, *The History of Sir Charles Grandison* (1753–4), is now regarded as a less successful novel, in which the eponymous hero exists as 'more than anything else, an effect of feminine awe' in a 'text now scarcely readable . . . for which *aficionados* of Richardson often tend to apologize'.[46] Interestingly, for the novelist and later literary critics alike, the weakness of the novel's sentimental protagonist rests principally with Sir Charles's gender. Richardson clearly remained conscious of the limitations of men acting as exemplars of sensibility. 'A good woman is my favourite character', he explained to Lady Bradshaigh, with whom 'I can do twenty agreeable things . . . none of which could appear in a striking light in a man. Softness of heart, gentleness of manners, tears, beauty, will allow pathetic scenes in the story of one, which cannot have place in that of the other.'[47] Richardson's belief in the difficulties of representating male sensibility fits broadly with the chronology of changing attitudes to, for example, male weeping as outlined above. His correspondence with Lady Bradshaigh took place at a time when, as we have seen, ideals of manliness were still largely determined with reference to earlier eighteenth-century discourses of refinement: thus in other correspondence Richardson outlined the need for his idealised 'good man' to be less sentimental than, above all, 'wonderfully polite'.[48]

A later generation of novelists, reflecting opinions then current in much conduct literature, were clearly less reticent about depicting their male heroes as, quite literally, embodiments of sensibility. Yet it is striking how recent accounts of these novels identify and criticise their sentimental male characters as feminised or imperfect forms of manhood. For Janet Todd the archetypal 'man of feeling' of the 1770s and 1780s possessed a 'weakened and ageing' body, 'avoided manly power and assumed the womanly qualities of tenderness and susceptibility', substituting the 'masculine sign of honour' for 'the more feminine posture of grief'. G.A. Starr suggests that late-eighteenth-century readers passed the same verdict on a character type whose conduct was associated 'with infancy or femininity, but not with masculine adulthood'. A similar attitude can be discerned in historians' treatment of the broader culture of male feeling. Kevin Sharpe and Steven Zwicker consider the 'sentimental hero, that composite of masculine form and feminine sensibility' as 'almost hermaphrodite', while Dror Wahrman includes the 'lachrymose, tender "man of feeling"' in a trio – completed by male transvestites and fops – of late-eighteenth-century 'gender transgressive figures . . . traversing or bending gender boundaries'.[49]

On the basis of such statements we might be tempted to draw one of two conclusions about late-eighteenth-century representations of the man of feeling and, by implication, the wider concept of sentimental manhood. First, that the presence of enervated men of feeling indicated a historical moment at which social commentators actively encouraged the adoption of styles understood as feminine within distinct models of male social behaviour. Alternatively, we might infer that eighteenth-century writers intended the man of feeling to serve not as a depiction of ideal conduct but as a representation of failed manhood, pushed by his overt sentimentalism into a world populated by fops and cross-dressers. It is my aim in this section to show that neither interpretation accurately reflects a late-eighteenth-century debate over the relationship between manliness and sensibility.

The problems of assessing this debate owe much to historians' readiness to identify late-eighteenth-century fictional men of feeling, notably Henry Mackenzie's Harley, as synonymous with expressions of idealised male conduct as depicted within a wide-ranging academic and conduct literature. However, as several recent studies point out, ambiguity exists over the novelist's own opinion of a character whose sensibility resulted in admirable levels of sympathy but also in levels of social marginalisation, weakness and ineffectiveness criticised elsewhere in Mackenzie's journalism.[50]

While many eighteenth-century commentators indeed identified sensibility as a particularly female quality, an active promotion of new styles of sentimental manliness was seldom expected to blur gender identities. In his discussion of the virtue of weeping, for example, the periodical essayist Peter Shaw made little distinction between male and female tears. In other papers, however, Shaw provided evidence of a clear gender demarcation based on what he regarded as modern men's enduring physical superiority and the accompanying male virtues of fortitude and courage. Men who failed to display these attributes were guilty of timorousness, a female quality, and were judged too 'despicable . . . to become the male character'.[51]

James Fordyce later informed young female readers that 'modesty, sympathy, generosity, the desire of pleasing . . . the promptness to cherish tender sentiments' were 'all so natural to the worthiest part of your sex.' What was 'beauty' among virtuous women proved 'in the male composition . . . certainly a blemish'. Nevertheless, as a vigorous proponent of the softening of male manners, Fordyce was also convinced of sensibility's contribution to definitions of idealised manhood. It was his and others' intention to promote specifically masculine forms of sensibility in which similar values of compassion, humility, sympathy and tenderness were combined with – and, in Fordyce's opinion, enhanced – more established masculine qualities.[52]

In considering eighteenth-century discussions of the manliness of feeling we would do well to remember John Dwyer's comment on the 'complex nature of the relationship between emotion and self-control within the sentimental genre', and the error of 'positing a gulf between the language of reason and the language of sentiment'.[53] In arguing this, Dwyer is particularly mindful of Adam Smith's understanding of the dynamics of the sympathetic community, as detailed in his *Theory of Moral Sentiments* (1759). Smith claimed that all worthwhile exchanges depended on a capacity for reasonable sympathy both on the part of the sufferer and the potential alleviator of his or her sorrows. In each case, reason served to control the natural proclivity of self-interest and to produce a mutually beneficial outcome. Whereas earlier essayists like Addison and Steele stressed the need for self-command to avoid offence in conversation, Smith emphasised its place in facilitating comprehension in a social bond of expressions and gestures. Central to his theory was a belief in the impossibility for spectators, however well meaning, to appreciate fully the experiences of another person, and to enter into a sympathetic relationship with that person unless the observed individual moderated his or her feelings, reducing them, as Smith put it, to a 'certain mediocrity' that 'the spectator can go along with'. Smith had little time for distressed individuals who displayed their emotions in an intemperate and, for him, incomprehensible manner. Such figures lacked 'the virtues of self-denial, of self-government, of the command of the passions' which brought 'the dignity of every passion . . . down to what others can enter into!' Failure to control one's passions resulted not just in incomprehensibility but in social rejection – a disgusting sight of 'clamorous grief, which . . . calls upon our compassion with sighs and tears and importunate lamentations', far removed from the widely praised virtue of a 'reserved . . . silent and majestic sorrow'.[54] As Dwyer shows, Smith's emphasis on self-command within a sympathetic community drew heavily on a socially responsible form of Epictetan stoic philosophy, the 'spirit and manhood' of which, in Smith's opinion, 'make a wonderful contrast with the desponding, plaintive, and whining tone of some modern systems'. Yet Smith's project always involved more than just the insertion of classical republican values into modern community relations, entailing in addition an emphasis on stoicism's role in stimulating the mechanisms of sympathetic exchange on which such communities were based. Thus, at a fairly trivial level, men who remained cheerful during 'frivolous disasters' were deemed 'genteel and agreeable'; meanwhile, greater acts of resolve – possibly in the face of death – produced greater compassion among spectators 'more apt to weep . . . for such . . . as seem to feel nothing for themselves'.[55]

Self-command was also required when reacting to the sight of others' distress. Smith considered practical assistance the best response to well-regulated displays of passion. As he noted, this outcome invariably required a degree of altruism on the part of sympathisers: 'we never are generous except when in some respect we prefer some other person to ourselves, and sacrifice some great and important interest of our own to an equal interest of a friend or of a superior'. So considerable was this sacrifice that Smith made no attempt to explain generosity in terms of an ability directly to imagine or seek to alleviate the hardship of others. Rather, generosity remained a consequence of the capacity to comprehend a situation not from the perspective of the afflicted but from that of a third, independent on-looker or 'impartial spectator'. Seen through the eyes of this spectator, all possible sacrifices appeared less significant than they did to the individual who stood to lose out in any subsequent altruistic act. It was this alternative perspective that prompted men to undertake even life-threatening actions. Thus, in Smith's opinion, the soldier risked death not because he thought a cause worth dying for, but because he was, through sympathy with an impartial spectator (here manifest as the patriotic nation at large), prompted to sacrifice time, material wealth and ultimately his life for what he was able to understand, if not feel, to be a greater good.

Significantly, Smith identified these intellectually motivated acts of 'generosity' as male, which he defined in opposition to an equivalent female quality, 'humanity'. What might appear initially as associated virtues were distinguished, at least for Smith, by a clear gender polarisation. 'Humanity', a quality consisting 'merely in the exquisite fellow-feeling which the spectator entertains with the sentiments of the persons principally concerned', demanded 'no self-denial, no self-command, no great exertion of the sense of propriety' and was hence 'the virtue of a woman'. By default, certain qualities stand out in Smith's understanding of 'generous' male manifestations of sympathy. First, the subordination of personal emotions to the arbitration of an impartial spectator demanded powers of 'reflection', 'speculation' and 'self-command' which he believed more common among men. Second, distinctly 'generous' acts served as the well-spring for traditionally manly actions: hence the soldier behaved heroically on account of his ability to sympathise with the national interest. In a separate example, Smith revealed how Brutus, founder of the Roman republic, had been able to quell his paternal affections to sanction the execution of his traitorous sons in a similar act of 'exalted propriety'.[56]

Smith's method for illustrating the manly elements of sympathetic exchange presents a model of virtuous male behaviour far removed from many of the images of sentimental manliness discussed elsewhere in this chapter. Brutus's extreme actions were not widely condoned by popular sentimental writers, many of whom favoured a more benign image of father-hood. This said, Smith's emphasis on the proximity of male sensibility and stoicism proved more popular and certainly locates him as one in a series of intellectual and popular commentators eager to demonstrate the symbiosis of 'modern' feeling with 'classical' self-discipline.[57]

Among other sentimental writers, the merits of self-command were likewise acknowledged as the means to moderate potentially excessive displays of natural feeling. Vicesimus Knox's identification of true sensibility as 'reserved' rather than 'forward, noisy and ostentatious', or David Hume's promotion of 'strong sense' and 'soundest judgement' in men possessed of 'delicacy of passion', provide instances of the value of such regulation. Indeed, Hume believed that judgement not only limited excessive passions but also 'improves our sensibility', replacing 'rougher and more boisterous emotions' with 'tender and agreeable passions'.[58] Elsewhere, Hume prefigured Smith's call for men's displays of refined feelings to be evaluated in terms of their provision of practical assistance. As a result, Hume's 'man of virtue' combined the 'softest benevolence' with 'most undaunted resolution' to produce a man of action who, even when 'bathed in tears', possessed sufficient 'sentiments of humanity' to 'brighten up the very face of sorrow'.[59] Later papers from Henry Mackenzie's *Lounger* periodical (1785–7) likewise praised men who combined the 'habits of action' with those 'of contemplation', identifying the embodiment of this ideal in 'one of the most illustrious men that ever lived' (and also the subject of Adam Smith's praise), the Roman stoic Marcus Aurelius Antonius. In the same issue, Mackenzie contrasted the manly Marcus Aurelius with a critical picture of a modern would-be sentimental male whose failure to translate his declarations of feeling into constructive acts revealed a personality remarkable less for manhood than 'indolence, languor, and feebleness'.[60]

If the connections between these various statements are clear, then so too are variations in tone and definition. In contrast to Adam Smith's association of 'humanity' with uncontrolled emotion, passivity and femininity, other writers apparently had little hesitation in recommending that male readers behave in a humane manner. David Hume's stoic was compelled to act precisely because of his 'sentiments of humanity', while for Vicesimus Knox 'the noblest distinction of human nature, is emphatically styled HUMAN-ITY'.[61] To an extent, these variations in meaning might be ascribed to inconsistencies of application between different writers over time – thus, aside from the name of their virtue, Smith's 'generous' man bears many similarities to Hume's 'humane' stoic. However, variations in word use do point to more substantive differences in the characteristics of sentimental manliness as defined by these writers. Hume's description, for example, argu-ably proposed a more generous and openly emotional personality compared to the Smithean ideal. Where Smith saw sympathy as self-interest over-ruled by the impartial spectator, the humane stoic possessed 'softest benevolence' and 'tenderest sentiments'; and whereas Smith called for no more than a mere 'swelling of the eyes', Hume praised the stoic for having sufficient compassion to be 'bathed in tears'.

This appreciation of more demonstrative displays of sensibility is also evident in later conduct guides. Unlike Smith, whose ideal of manly gener-osity drew on reason and sacrifice, Vicesimus Knox downplayed these est-ablished values, encouraging men to indulge more fully in their emotions and, in part, to derive their manly identity directly from this capacity for sympathy and compassion. Knox's description of inadequate men as those who ranked 'sense, courage, fortitude, or philosophy' above sensibility sug-gests a distinction between traditional and newer, sentimental models of manliness. In place of these established qualities Knox praised 'tenderness' and 'susceptibility' as superior values through which the reader was encour-aged 'to feel as a man'.[62] William Cowper's letter to Margaret King charted a similar shift from a hardy and athletic to a more delicate and sensitive manliness. Cowper remained notably sanguine with regard to this change which, like Knox, he interpreted less as a decline in absolute standards than as the development of new qualities unknown to previous generations. Though clearly less vigorous, modern men were able to experience sensibil-ity – 'the sine qua non of real happiness' – for which, in Cowper's opinion, 'we have no course to complain' being 'rather gainers by our degeneracy'.[63]

As we have seen, Cowper's interpretation focused specifically on the changing quality of the male physique: men's feelings became 'more ex-quisite' as their 'habit of body has become more delicate'. This concept of delicacy was an important one to promoters of refined manliness, with implications for definitions of both acceptable social and gender behaviour. The association between delicacy and social refinement occurred regularly in eighteenth-century dictionary definitions: for Nathan Bailey, 'delicate' meant being 'dainty, neat, nice, tender, polite'; while Samuel Johnson (1755) likewise defined 'delicacy' in one instance as 'politeness; gentleness of man-ners'. The latter also provided an additional meaning which came closer to Cowper's particular application in his letter to Margaret King. Thus

Johnson identified two of the more common definitions for delicacy as 'daintiness' and 'anything pleasing to the senses'.[64] Both qualities were clearly significant for those sentimental writers who regarded refinement as feelings communicated via a sensitive and physically slight body. Delicacy necessarily became an important aspect of the sentimental man, and one that commentators were obliged to address in their attempts to establish the manliness of feeling.

Various strategies were followed with regard to this issue. William Cowper, for instance, acknowledged the loss of traditional manly qualities but claimed that, as modern men now enjoyed higher standards of refined sociability, they had no cause for complaint. Others, by contrast, sought to disassociate delicacy from failing standards of manliness. The mid-century essayist Nathaniel Lancaster identified delicacy as synonymous with a sympathy and fellow feeling common in some degree to all men. Productive of a 'warm sensibility' to everything 'pure, regular, and polite', delicacy emerged as a feature of the modern, manly character, with the important consequence of instilling an abhorrence of 'unnatural, effeminate and over-wrought ornaments of every kind'.[65]

A similar debate over the impact of sensibility on manliness can be seen if we return to the ways by which mid- to late-century advice literature dealt with the place and propriety of men's weeping. Despite the popular image of Georgian men freely and confidently indulging in tears, it would be wrong to suggest that the eighteenth-century association between femininity and tears was broken, even at the height of the vogue for sensibility. The frequency with which readers of sentimental fiction and advice literature were informed that tears were *not* unmanly reminds us that this shift in attitudes is better understood as a struggle in which successive generations sought to overcome a traditional and much reiterated equation of emotion expression with (feminine) weakness.

It was as part of just such a debate that Vicesimus Knox offered his 1788 investigation 'On the unmanliness of shedding tears'. Knox's statement provides a particularly good example of the ways in which sentimental writers stressed the compatibility of manliness with broader patterns of advanced social behaviour. At first sight, the essay appears to reassert well-established civic concerns that modern lifestyles threatened men's readiness to act with hardiness, public spiritedness and honour. However, Knox went on to dispute this interpretation in his understanding of the qualities of desirable manliness. Modern living did indeed contribute to corruption but in the reverse direction, leading not to weakness and effeminacy but to a hard-heartedness among men contemptuous of those who displayed their feelings. This contempt, argued Knox, was not true manhood but shameful insensitivity masquerading under 'the appellation of manly fortitude'. Real manliness, by contrast, while maintaining a commitment to public duty, did so not through stoical resolution but sympathetic exchange, of which weeping was an essential component. Tears, far from being a sign of 'weak understanding', were evidence of the 'tenderness and susceptibility' by which truly noble manhood was defined.[66] By implication, their absence put manliness in doubt: 'it may be questioned', claimed the periodical essayist Peter Shaw, 'whether those are properly men, who never weep upon any occasion'.[67]

Those needing further confirmation were reminded of the power and significance of tears when shed by other men. Knox was one of a number of sentimental writers who referred to Christ's weeping at the death of Lazarus as evidence of the acceptability of similar actions by modern men. As Jeremy Gregory shows, this depiction of Christ *on earth* as a tangible and imitable ideal became increasingly popular with the rise of an early seventeenth-century Arminian theology. From this date, representations of Christ provide an insight into both conceptions of Christianity and also some of the suitable male behavioural traits by which these ideals were to be expressed. In view of the differences between these depictions, we should be cautious of extrapolating too much about attitudes to manliness from isolated early modern representations ranging from Christ as warrior – 'fenced with the breast-plate of righteousnesse, and shield of Faith, as well as his body with armour and weapons of steele' – to philanthropist whose life was 'one continued illustrious expression of kindness and charity'.[68] This said, it is noteworthy how far mid- to late-eighteenth-century authors developed this latter, benevolent image in their presentation of Christ as man of feeling to be imitated for the 'tenderness', 'gentility' and 'sensitivity' of that charity.

Hugh Blair's sermon 'On the compassion of Christ' offers a striking example of this image. Rejecting the 'hard indifference' of classical thought, Christ here proposed a 'tender and exquisite' sensibility through which, crucially, he confirmed his masculine status by having 'felt as a man'. Much was made of Christ's propensity to weep, the commendable act of one who, for Blair, 'indulged all the amiable feelings of our nature' and which, in James Fordyce's opinion, showed modern readers that 'nothing [is] more becoming than the tear of generous sorrow'.[69] It should be remembered that the popularity of religious weeping in the 1770s and 1780s, especially among Moderate Church of Scotland ministers, followed the overt emotionalism common to Methodist meetings, and in particular those of Whitefield's Calvinist Methodists, during the late 1730s and 1740s. To their attendants, the propriety of men's participation in such displays was guaranteed by the concomitant communion with God, though critics of Methodism regularly judged these performances immoderate and unrefined. By contrast, John Wesley's sermons often provided a less visceral account of the benefits of feeling. Quoting his brother Charles, Wesley called on male and female listeners to 'excite your softest sympathy' and 'weep with them that weep', while, elsewhere, readers were encouraged to follow the sentimental Christ's example of 'kind, soft, benign' love 'inspiring thee with the most amiable sweetness . . . and tender affection'.[70]

Heroes and villains

Benevolent, compassionate and gentle, the popular late-eighteenth-century image of Christ offered one means by which conduct writers sought to construct and validate a manly sentimental ideal. But more surprising role models were also held up for emulation. Vicesimus Knox's essay on men's weeping, for example, also noted the tears of such familiarly hardy and vigorous warriors as the Greeks Ulysses and Achilles, and the Trojan hero Hector. In doing so, Knox argued not only for the compatibility of sentimental display with courage, but also for a redefinition of military heroism as characterised, in part, by the capacity for feeling itself. This idea owed much to earlier studies, notably Richard Steele's *The Christian Hero* (1701), which had underlined the importance of forgiveness and fellow feeling in definitions of courage within civilised society. That true and manly courage was determined by self-control, consideration and ultimately compassion became a common eighteenth-century theme that played readily into the more pronounced equation of sensibility and militarism evident from the late 1750s.[71] Despite this emphasis, reformers were again keen to show how, in encouraging new forms of sentimental soldierhood, they were simply reinterpreting practices long recognised, to quote one mid-century author, as 'among the most conspicuous Virtues, with which the greatest heroes among the Ancients were said to be embued'. From definitions of courage as feeling developed the idea that heroic actions were attributable to an individual's sensitivity to others, 'men of sensibility being generally Persons of the strictest Honour and most exalted Courage'.[72] Hugh Blair set out a similar relationship when he equated the desire to behave benevolently with the motivation required to act courageously. 'Manliness and sensibility', Blair argued, 'are so far from being incompatible, that the truly brave are, for the most part, generous and humane; while the soft and effeminate are hardly capable of any vigorous exertion of affection.'[73]

There was a range of opinions as to how, and to what degree, soldiers' sensitivities were best expressed. Adam Smith, as we have seen, while clearly appreciating the value of sympathy, remained uneasy about the levels of sensibility that military men should be permitted to develop and display.

Male readers of 'too exquisite sensibility' were warned to 'not wantonly embrace the profession of a soldier'.[74] Just what form this excessive sensibility might take was not made clear by Smith. However, in the context of his comments on the unseemly nature of open grief or his admiration of Brutus's sacrifice of his sons, Smith's ideal would evidently have shied away from some of the more overtly sentimental acts deemed appropriate by later writers.

In marked contrast to Smith's depiction of Brutus, Knox's discussion of Hector occurred not in an account of war or civic responsibility, but in an essay, 'On the happiness of domestic life' (1782), which depicted the Trojan hero at home playing with his son. Knox clearly found this a beguiling scene; modern readers would, he assumed, be 'pleased to see the arm, which is shortly to deal death and destruction among a host of foes, employed in caressing an infant son with the embraces of paternal love', safe in the knowledge that these domestic affections would not compromise his warriorship. That affectionate fatherhood was compatible with the fulfilment of public responsibilities, whether these be work or warfare, was a popular theme for authors conscious that many men still identified parenting, like tears, as a feminine activity. Knox explained that his essay had been prompted by a desire to confound those men who looked on parental duties as 'satisfying none but the weak . . . and the effeminate', and how he intended the multi-faceted Hector to show that enjoyment of an intimate family life was 'by no means unmanly'. Indeed, if anything, Knox expected readers to be most appreciative of Hector as the caring father: when 'he is taking off his helmet, that he may not frighten his little boy with its nodding plumes'.[75]

Suggestions that classical authors had always appreciated the valour of sensibility, or depictions of figures like Hector as a complex weave of bravery and compassion, were clear attempts to identify and validate the manliness of feeling as a historical commonplace exemplified by legendary male heroes. However, this interest in established figures did not preclude discussions of more recent role models for commentators who were equally keen to depict sensibility as the particular manifestation of an advanced, refined society.

Although cautious in his appraisal of the merits of social 'progress', Adam Ferguson, Edinburgh professor of moral philosophy, provided a scholarly assessment to this effect, comparing representations of the military hero in classical and modern literature. The result was a somewhat less sympathetic interpretation of the classical characters than that offered by many of Ferguson's contemporaries. In Greek poetry military heroes had, in Ferguson's opinion, been wrongly praised for their 'maxims of animosity and hostile passion', which he likened to theories of idealised combat in a less advanced, non-European environment (the 'woods of America' being his example). Ferguson thought it symptomatic of the classical ideal that Homer had refused to evoke sympathy for the beaten Hector who 'falls unpitied' by Greek soldiers and poets alike. Such callousness was noticeably absent in what Ferguson described as 'modern romance literature' in which heroes emerged as more rounded personalities, combining 'ferocity' and 'love of blood' with 'gentleness' and 'sentiments of tenderness and pity'.[76] Vicesimus Knox's 1778 essay 'On sentiment' provided a similar statement on the superiority of contemporary military ideals. This did not mean that Knox abandoned the idea of ancients and moderns being jointly 'furnished by nature with every feeling in great perfection'. Rather, what distinguished the latter was not their capacity but their greater opportunity to express feeling in a modern, sophisticated society in which, away from the battle-field, soldiers now enjoyed a diverse range of civilising recreations compared to the stark choice between war and politics available to many of their classical forebears.[77]

One of these civil recreations, as it had been for the admirable Hector, was the home. Indeed, for Knox and for many other sentimental commentators, domestic engagements provided a suitable, indeed necessary, aspect to the modern image of heroism. This ideal was certainly prominent in many eighteenth-century accounts of real-life soldiers in the 1750s, 1760s and 1770s – in good supply at a time of frequent warfare – who appeared either in sentimentalised military biographies or as role models in general guides to manly sensibility. Readers of the *London Magazine* (1759), for example, were informed of the admirable character of General William Blakeney (1672–1761). Blakeney, whose defence of Minorca from the French proved one of the few British successes during the early encounters of the Seven Years' War (1756–63), was a 'great and good officer . . . not more remarkable for his publick than for his private conduct'.[78] Similar qualities were displayed by the naval officer John Bentinck (1737–75), whom James Fordyce praised in 1777 for his 'masculine character in an uncommon degree'. In addition Fordyce thought Bentinck 'peculiarly interesting' for his combining military service with 'many liberal acquirements . . . illuminated by a large share of sentiment, as well as vivacity, and tempered by the happiest domestic affections'.[79]

For many mid- to late-century writers, including Fordyce, the desired blend of courage and sentimental refinement was at its apogee in the figure of General James Wolfe (1727–59). As the commander-in-chief of the British army in Canada, Wolfe mounted a successful attack on Quebec which resulted in the defeat of the French forces in September 1759 and led to Wolfe's death from wounds sustained during the battle. It would be wrong to suggest that subsequent references to Wolfe's personality consistently played up his reputation for feeling. As Kathleen Wilson shows, many discussions depicted the general as the saviour of 'patriotism and manliness through the imperial cause' whereby manliness was understood in terms of 'courage, aggression, martial vigour [and] strength'.[80] Descriptions of Wolfe's hardiness, sobriety, honesty and sense of public duty certainly did much to cast him in a traditional model of civic heroism. Much, however, was also made of Wolfe's sensitive and refined character. To one early biographer, Wolfe was 'polite, affable, gentle, free, and unreserved in Conversation', combining 'the Sweets of particular Attachments' with 'a more extensive Spirit of Benevolence' to become 'truly brave, truly noble, friendly and candid, gentle and beneficent, great and glorious!'[81] His death also provided excellent opportunities for others to display their own sensitivity through grief. Soldiers in Quebec had, according to the *Annual Register*, shared 'a glorious grief/And while they gather'd laurels wept their chief'. Sir John Pringle, Wolfe's biographer, similarly described how each soldier 'mourns his loss in him', and on news of the death: 'the Eye is seen to mourn' and the 'whole Body' clothes 'itself with a Garb expressive of Sorrow', recalling the wordless physicality proposed in accounts of idealised sentimental males.[82]

Villains

The attractions of a mid- to late-century fashion for sensibility validated displays of male grief or intimacy, and permitted conduct writers to style these as indicative of new brands of manliness. Sensibility's appeal owed much to its being a statement of genuine sociability moderated by established ideals of male behaviour: the possible femininity of feeling nullified, as we have seen, by a peculiarly male synthesis of moderation, self-discipline, benevolence and sincere sympathy. In the aftermath of episodes such as General Wolfe's death, few questioned the integrity or the manliness of those whose mourning was described in the pages of an overtly patriotic periodical literature.

However, at times of greater political debate such unanimity was far from guaranteed. One good example is the response to Edmund Burke's survey of the early stages of the French Revolution, and the ensuing discussions over the nature of British political opinion during the late 1780s and 1790s. In contrast to his previous defence of the American rebels, Burke's *Reflections on the Revolution in France* (1790) launched a bitter attack on the European revolutionaries and their British supporters. Central to his criticism was a belief that, even in its early stages, the revolution threatened the dominance of the nobility and the church – for Burke the twin pillars of order, prosperity and civilisation or chivalry, which he believed generic to all refined states. Such views, as J.G.A. Pocock argues, resembled those of an earlier generation of Scottish academic theorists for whom high standards of modern inter-personal relations also owed much to the rise of chivalry in medieval society.[83] In a passage with clear similarities to John Millar's 1771 *Observations Concerning the Distinction of Ranks*, Burke spoke of the superiority of a 'system of opinion and sentiment . . . [with] its origin in the antient chivalry' which had endured 'even to the time we live' in a '[French] nation of gallant men . . . [and] men of honour'.[84] Yet, for Burke, the centuries-long benefit of chivalry was now being challenged and contorted by agents opposed to the *ancien régime*. Recent events, he argued, had seen 'a consider-able revolution in . . . politeness' among political radicals who thought it 'the most refined strain of delicate compliment' to abuse and humiliate the French monarchy by forcibly removing the royal couple, Louis XVI and Marie Antoinette, from Versailles to Paris in October 1789. Burke's ima-gined account of this event, the most provocative passage of his study, dwelt particularly on the suffering of the French queen – that 'delightful vision, glittering like the morning star' – who had been forced to flee 'almost naked' from an act of barbarity that struck simultaneously at the notion of chivalry as the key to both refined gender and social relations.[85]

To his defenders, Burke's emotional description of Marie Antoinette's plight was symptomatic of a man who followed chivalry's course to its logical and sentimental conclusion. Horace Walpole, who thought 'every page' of the *Reflections* 'shows how sincerely he is in earnest', declared him-self 'charmed' with Burke's 'enthusiasm' which he compared favourably with those political writers whose declarations 'never seem to flow from the heart'.[86] 'Burke, thy heart, by juster feelings led/Mourns for the Spirit of proud Honour fled' was how another summed up his contribution to an age where now 'the graceful sympathies depart/That wak'd with gentlest touch th'according heart.'[87]

But many who praised the revolution, at least in its early stages, were less impressed by Burke's character or by the tone of his defence of *ancien régime* France. From these commentaries there emerged an alternative image of Burke the sentimentalist as someone who, if experiencing genuine distress, contorted and corrupted his true feelings for the benefit of political argument. In 1791, in what was then, and remains, the best known of these attacks, the radical politician Thomas Paine criticised Burke's faulty interpretation of events, and the emotive style in which this 'fawning character' and 'friend to none, a COURTIER' had couched his argument. Like many others, Paine paid particularly close attention to Burke's eulogy for Marie Antoinette, dismissing the tribute's energy and emotion as mere 'theatrical exaggeration'. This, coupled with Burke's failure to appreciate the suffering of ordinary French people before the revolution, further indicated someone motivated not by 'the reality of distress touching his heart' but by its 'showy resemblance' – by the 'plumage' not the 'dying bird'.[88]

This idea of Burke as a manipulator was also central to an equally important attack on the *Reflections* by the writer on women's rights, Mary Wollstonecraft. Rejecting Burke's self-promotion as a man of feeling with a 'heart of flesh', Wollstonecraft viewed Burke's defence of the French monarchy as an example of the ease with which 'sympathy . . . was made to give way to party spirit and the feelings of a man . . . to the views of a statesman'. For Wollstonecraft, Burke's readiness to manipulate his emotions for political ends was also evident in the light of earlier responses to domestic events, notably George III's personal suffering induced by 'madness' during the Regency crisis (1788–9). In order 'to promote ambitious or interested views', Burke had then shown little sympathy for a monarch whom Wollstonecraft herself described in markedly sentimental terms as a 'father torn from his children, – a husband from an affectionate wife, – a man from himself'. 'Where', she concluded, 'was your sensibility? . . . Go hence, thou slave of impulse [and] look into the private recesses of thy heart.'[89]

Wollstonecraft's comparison of Burke in 1788 and 1790 is interesting for two further reasons. First, as John Barrell argues, it reveals the incorporation of sentimental imagery into late-eighteenth-century representations of monarchy, and offers a further instance of modern sentimental heroism in the form of an ailing or imprisoned king as caring family man.[90] Second, Wollstonecraft's identification of Burke as a 'slave of impulse' extended the range of abuses committed by a self-styled man of feeling who was now accused not only of manipulating sentiment for effect but also of indulging in excessive feeling. Burke had, she believed, 'an antipathy to reason', his principal argument in defence of the *ancien régime* being that 'our *feelings* should lead us to excuse . . . the venerable vestiges of ancient days'.[91] In response, Wollstonecraft emphasised the value of behaviour which combined the merits both of reason and of a genuine, educated and active sensibility. The result was a 'truly sublime' man far superior to his two antitheses, whom she identified as the excessively emotional 'dupe of his feelings' or the ultra-rational man of 'clearer head and colder heart'. Over-reliant on emotion at the expense of rationality, and simultaneously calculating in his expression of these sentiments for effect, Burke here embodied both inferior male personalities. In many of these points Wollstonecraft's criticism bore clear similarities to that proposed by Thomas Paine. Where Wollstonecraft differed from Paine, however, was in her readiness to identify Burke's faults as a sign of his effeminacy. Thus Wollstonecraft belittled Burke's self-image not just as the promoter of feeling and propriety but also as a self-styled guardian of 'manly sentiment'. In her depiction, the now 'feminine' Burke existed as a 'vain man' penning 'unmanly sarcasms and puerile conceits' both swept up by and pandering to the current trend for sensibility – Wollstonecraft's *'manie of the day'* – with what for a man she identified as an unbecoming attachment to triviality and current fashions.[92]

Vicesimus Knox and the pretty preacher

Edmund Burke was not the only supposed sentimentalist to draw Mary Wollstonecraft's scorn. In her account of 'writers who have rendered women objects of pity', from *A Vindication of the Rights of Woman* (1792), she discussed the deleterious effects of several leading mid- to late-century male conduct writers, among them the popular sermon writer James Fordyce. Like Burke, Fordyce was at fault both for his interpretation and the tone of his sensibility. His was a language of extremes, a 'sentimental rant' of 'pumped-up passions', designed to identify the virtuous female reader (Wollstonecraft limits her discussion to Fordyce's 1765 *Sermons to Young Women*) as the epitome of sensibility characterised as beauty, innocence and sensitivity. Similarly, just as Burke was guilty of duplicity, so Fordyce's declarations were to be seen less as the product of genuine feeling than as a topical artifice aimed at subordinating women to their expected domestic roles, condemned by Wollstonecraft as 'a display of cold artificial feelings', a mere 'parade of sensibility' that would never reach the heart 'though the ear may be tickled'.[93]

In view of her distinctive sexual politics it is not difficult to understand Wollstonecraft's antipathy to Fordyce's delivery of a message which she identified as central to the construction of a restrictive and demeaning image of virtuous femininity. More striking is the mixed reception Fordyce received from other, male sentimental conduct writers from whom we might have expected agreement rather than criticism. Of course, to some Fordyce remained a forceful preacher and a paragon of modern sensitivity and refinement: a man who combined 'powers of eloquence and the fervour of piety' in the pulpit with a 'heart of sensibility . . . peculiarly tender and affectionate' in his domestic relations, according to two later biographical sketches.[94] Others, however, remained sceptical of the sincerity of these undoubtedly popular presentations at London's Monkwell Street Chapel, where Fordyce ministered between 1760 and 1772. Through the eyes of one anonymous satirist, Fordyce's sermons appeared more the stuff of an amateur dramatist than a sober moralist. Sighing, groaning, hand-wringing and sobbing were all employed to 'express aright the passion of his heart' and to ignite similar emotions among his congregation. However extreme these manners might have seemed to earlier eighteenth- or indeed late-twentieth-century observers, there appears to have been nothing intrinsically out of place in such actions in a culture in which, as we have seen, physical displays of sensitivity as social refinement were actively encouraged in advice literature and fiction. Fordyce's error was again identified as the motive behind his actions; namely the bid by this 'hero of affectation' to ingratiate himself with, and sexually arouse, his predominantly female audience. In the light of the on-going debate concerning the possible reconciliation of sensibility with manliness, it is interesting to note how, for this unknown satirist at least, histrionic duplicity earned Fordyce – or 'Miss James' as he was dubbed – an effeminate persona, regardless of his own protestations of 'manly eloquence'.[95]

It was attributes such as these that led the Tonbridge School master, Vicesimus Knox to identify Fordyce as an example of the modern phenomenon of the 'pretty preacher'. In several essays, Knox set out Fordyce's shortcomings, criticising – in a tone prefiguring Wollstonecraft's – a preaching and writing style characterised by its florid tones and meaningless sentiments.[96] The ambivalence shown towards Fordyce closely parallels the mixed review of the conduct of William Dodd, the popular preacher hanged for forgery in 1777. As we saw at the start of this chapter, Dodd's supporters made much of his capacity for feeling, of which many found evidence in his powerful Magdalen Hospital sermons during the 1760s and early 1770s. At the time, for example, Horace Walpole had commented on Dodd's 'haranguing . . . very eloquently and touchingly' with the effect that his congregations 'sobbed and cried from their souls'.[97] Later tributes spoke of the benevolence of his preaching through which 'he shone conspicuously'.[98] Yet even in the aftermath of Dodd's execution, authors did not shy away from criticising the very style that Walpole had previously seen employed to such good effect. In addition to his shining philanthropy, Dodd was also 'by many charged with Affectation, and possessing too much of the Stage Eloquence and Action for the Pulpit'.[99] Though such characteristics did not earn him, like Fordyce, a reputation for femininity, they did contribute in 1773 to his being dubbed the 'macaroni parson' – macaronis being then popular Italianate men of fashion – who was best equipped to minister to 'the present polite world [that] must have sermons suited to their polished ideas and enforced with dramatic energy'.[100]

What should we make of these contests? In the case of Thomas Paine's attack on Edmund Burke, or Mary Wollstonecraft's criticism of Burke and Fordyce, much of the antagonism clearly rests with their sharp difference of opinion over issues of sexual and radical politics. Such confrontations are often interpreted by historians as beginning the decline of a culture of sensibility now found wanting both by radicals and conservatives at a time of international political crisis. Likewise, the rather more surprising contest between Knox and Fordyce may partly be attributed to a personality clash between rival popular moralists, one of whom sought to tarnish the other's reputation with accusations of corrupting the ideals demanded of congregants. At the same time, however, we might also detect a more deep-seated ambivalence towards the value of sensibility in these confrontations. That it was manifestly possible for sentimental (like polite) commentators to manipulate and mislead realised the tensions and inherent dangers within the discourse at large: namely, the potential for an excessive indulgence in feeling devoid of moderating sense, or the exploitation of a reading or listening audience through the manipulation of emotion for personal gain.

Accusations of this kind recall those levelled at the Chesterfieldian code of duplicitous politeness with which we began this chapter. For Chesterfield, of course, such advice had been justified in terms of its realistic and practical assistance in fashioning his son in the model of a refined gentleman. Fordyce, we might presume, also saw his work as a genuine attempt to produce a virtuous manliness characterised by sensitivity, compassion and friendship. In challenging the credibility of these authors, critics regularly undermined these claims of a new manliness. Fordyce as 'Miss James' or the 'unmanly' Burke, author of 'pure foppery', were clearly ill-placed to offer constructive advice, as was that 'Frenchified fop', Chesterfield.[101] In seeking to promote refined manliness, polite and sentimental commentators were continually faced with an unpalatable alternative, the underside of the male civilising process creating not manly role models but effeminate fools. To identify the source of this corruption in the shape of a single writer was a convenient way both of encapsulating the problem and, as in the case of Wollstonecraft's attack on Burke, castigating a political adversary. Ultimately, however, individual critics knew the debate over the dangers of male refinement to be more complex and far reaching than a few errant authors. It is to some of the contexts, meanings and cultural images of this crucial debate that we now turn.

Notes and references

1. Horace Walpole to William Mason, 9 Apr 1774, in *The Yale Edition of Horace Walpole's Correspondence*, ed. W.S. Lewis, 48 vols. (New Haven CT, 1937–83), XXVIII, p. 146.

2. Fanny Burney, *The Early Journals and Letters of Fanny Burney*, ed. Lars E. Troide, 3 vols. (Oxford, 1988–94), II, pp. 62–3. Omai (*c.* 1753–*c.* 1780), the first Tahitian to visit England, proved a source of endless fascination to members of fashionable society versed in then topical debates on the merits of the 'noble savage'.

3. *Morning Post* (11 Feb 1777), quoted in Gerald Howson, *The Macaroni Parson. A Life of the Unfortunate Dr Dodd* (1973), pp. 134, 166.

4. *Morning Chronicle* (15 Mar 1777), quoted in *ibid.*, p. 168.

5. Horace Walpole to Lady Ossory, 29 June 1777, in *Correspondence*, XXXII, p. 360. The anonymous pamphlet *A Tear of Gratitude* (1777) captures the mood of many of the publications marking Dodd's death.

6. Fordyce, *Addresses to Young Men*, II, p. 175.

7. G.J. Barker-Benfield, *Culture of Sensibility*.

8. William Cowper, 'The Task' (1785), in *The Poems of William Cowper*, eds. John D. Baird and Charles Ryskamp, 3 vols. (Oxford, 1980–95), II, p. 251. Earlier, Cowper had addressed Chesterfield directly as 'Thou polish'd and highfinish'd Foe to Truth,/Graybeard Corrupter of our list'ning youth', Cowper to John Newton, 21 Jan 1781, in *Letters and Prose*, I, p. 435.

9. 'Task', in *Poems*, II, p. 251. The novelist and follower of Rousseau, Thomas Day (1748–89), was famously said to have refused to stand on a spider, claiming 'not to know that I have a right to kill it', quoted in George W. Giguilliat, *The Author of* Sandford and Merton. *A Life of Thomas Day* (New York, 1932), p. 123. On the sentimental mania for the welfare of anything from worms to foxes to lobsters see Langford, *Polite and Commercial People*, pp. 503–5.

10. Cowper, *Letters*, III, p. 180.

11. Mullan, *Sentiment and Sociability*, p. 207.

12. Quoted in *ibid.*, p. 210.

13. Hugh Blair, 'On sensibility' (1790), in *Sermons*, III, p. 26.

14. *Ibid.*, III, p. 36.

15. *Boswell's London Journal*, p. 260; Boswell, *Life of Johnson*, p. 400.

16. Blair, 'On sensibility', *Sermons*, III, p. 36; Logan's sermons delivered during the 1770s were published posthumously in 1826, quoted in Dwyer, 'Clio and ethics', p. 49.

17. Towle, *Private Tutor*, pp. 144–5.

18. Fordyce, *Addresses to Young Men*, II, p. 92.

19. Fordyce, 'Epistle on various subjects', in *Poems* (1786), p. 259.

20. Henry Mackenzie, *The Man of Feeling* (1771), ed. Brian Vickers (Oxford, 1967), p. 44; 'Physiognomy' in *Dictionary of Conversation*, p. 79. The 1789 translation of Lavater appeared as *Essays on Physiognomy*.

21. The comment by Sarah Scott appears in Ellis, *Politics of Sensibility*, p. 96. Sir George Ellison, the eponymous hero of Scott's 1766 novel, is a man given to tears over the treatment of West Indian slaves.

22. Claudia L. Johnson, *Equivocal Beings. Politics, Gender and Sentimentality in the 1790s* (Chicago IL and London, 1995), p. 5; Henry Morley's 'Index to tears' in his 1886 edition of *The Man of Feeling* records Harley weeping on 47 occasions in just 135 pages.

23. On Halifax's comments, offered as part of *The Lady's New Year's Gift* (1688) to his daughter, see Shoemaker, *Gender in English Society*, p. 103.

24. *Tatler*, No. 68 (15 Sept 1709), I, p. 472.

25. Locke, *Some Thoughts Concerning Education*, p. 217. Steele warned of a similar effect in reverse, whereby a mother's copious weeping induced an 'unmanly Gentleness of Mind' in her son, *Tatler*, No. 181 (6 June 1710), II, p. 484.

26. *Spectator*, No. 143 (14 Aug 1711), II, p. 67.

27. *Tatler*, No. 68, I, p. 472.

28. No. 520 (27 Oct 1712), IV, pp. 350–1.

29. *The Plays of Richard Steele*, ed. S.H. Kenny (Oxford, 1971), pp. 299–300.

30. *Man, a paper for ennobling the species*, No. 43 (22 Oct 1755), p. 5.

31. Blair, 'Of sensibility', in *Sermons*, III, pp. 24–5.

32. Knox, 'On the unmanliness of shedding tears' (1788), in *Winter Evenings; or Lucubrations on Life and Letters*, 2 vols. (1788, 2nd edn, 1790), II, pp. 182–3.

33. Smith, *Theory of Moral Sentiments*, pp. 142–3.

34. *Ibid.*, p. 40.

35. Hume, 'Of moral prejudices', in *Essays*, p. 541.

36. Shawn Lisa Maurer, '"As sacred as friendship, as pleasurable as love": father–son relations in *The Tatler* and *The Spectator*', in Beth Fowkes Tobin ed., *History, Gender and Eighteenth-Century Literature* (Athens GA, 1994), pp. 15, 25; Kathryn Shevelow, *Women and Print Culture: The Construction of Femininity in the Early Periodical* (1989), p. 143.

37. No. 236 (30 Nov 1711), II, p. 418.

38. Lawrence Stone, *The Family, Sex and Marriage in England, 1500–1800* (1977); commentaries on styles of early modern and modern fatherhood include – in addition to Fletcher, *Gender, Sex and Subordination* and Davidoff and Hall, *Family Fortunes* – John Tosh, *A Man's Place. Masculinity and the Middle-Class Home in Victorian England* (New Haven CT and London, 1999).

39. *The Polite Miscellany*, p. 75. Good domestic manners often differed little from those of male strangers at the coffee-house. 'The conversation of a married Couple cannot be agreeable for Years', warned the mid-century conduct author Wetenhall Wilkes, 'without an earnest endeavour to please on both Sides.' Quoted in Vickery, *Gentleman's Daughter*, p. 72.

40. *The Man of Manners*, p. 7.

41. 'Every man chiefly happy or miserable at home', *Rambler*, No. 68 (10 Nov 1750), in Johnson, *Works*, III, p. 361. On the late-eighteenth- and early-nineteenth-century relocation of courtship from public assembly to private dining-room see Stana Nenadic, 'Middle-rank consumers and domestic culture in Edinburgh and Glasgow, 1720–1840', *Past and Present*, No. 145 (1994), pp. 122–54, esp. pp. 150–4.

42. Fordyce, *Sermons to Young Women*, I, p. 24.

43. *Scots Magazine*, 27 (1765), pp. 393–4.

44. Fordyce, *Addresses to Young Men*, I, p. 329; II, pp. 19–20.

45. Thomas Gisborne, *An Enquiry into the Duties of Men*, 2 vols. (1795), II, pp. 444–6. Additional examples of fatherly roles are provided in Shoemaker, *Gender in English Society*, pp. 123–5.

46. Mullan, *Sentiment and Sociability*, pp. 81, 83, 86.

47. Quoted in *ibid.*, pp. 61–2.

48. *Ibid.*, p. 81.

49. Janet Todd, *Sensibility. An Introduction* (1986), pp. 89, 99; G.A. Starr, 'Sentimental de-education', in Douglas Lane Patey and Timothy Keegan eds., *Augustan Studies* (1985), p. 253; Kevin Sharpe and Steven N. Zwicker, 'Introduction', to *idem* eds., *Refiguring Revolutions. Aesthetics and Politics from the English Revolution to the Romantic Revolution* (Berkeley CA, 1998), p. 13; Dror Wahrman, '*Percy*'s prologue: from gender play to gender panic in eighteenth-century England', *Past and Present*, No. 159 (1998), p. 123.

50. For this discussion see Sheriff, *Good-Natured Man*, ch. 6; Barker-Benfield, *Culture of Sensibility*, pp. 137–48.

51. *Man*, No. 14 (2 Apr 1755), pp. 2–5.

52. Fordyce, *Sermons to Young Women*, II, pp. 233, 226.

53. John Dwyer, 'Enlightened spectators and classical moralists: sympathetic relations in eighteenth-century Scotland', in Dwyer and Richard B. Sher eds., *Sociability and Society in Eighteenth-Century Scotland* (Edinburgh, 1993), p. 103.

54. Smith, *Theory of Moral Sentiments*, pp. 23–4, 27. See also John Dwyer, *Virtuous Discourse: Sensibility and Community in Late Eighteenth-Century Scotland* (Edinburgh, 1987), ch. 6.

55. Smith, *Theory of Moral Sentiments*, pp. 283, 48. On the interaction of stoicism and sensibility in Smith see Julie Ellison, 'Cato's tears', *English Literary History*, 63 (1996), esp. pp. 594–5.

56. Smith, *Theory of Moral Sentiments*, pp. 190–2.

57. Brutus's example gained more praise within British and French neo-classical schools of history painting: Angelica Kauffmann's *Brutus condemning his sons to death for treason* (1788) and Jacques-Louis David's *The lictors returning to Brutus the bodies of his sons* (1789) contrast a father's 'manly' stoicism with the grief of his sons in the former and with their nurse in the latter. See Gill Perry and Michael Rossington eds., *Femininity and Masculinity in Eighteenth-Century Art and Culture* (Manchester, 1994).

58. Knox, 'On the inconsistency of affected sensibility' (1788), in *Winter Evenings*, II, p. 161; Hume, 'Of the delicacy of taste and passion', in *Essays*, p. 6.

59. 'The stoic', in *ibid.*, p. 151.

60. No. 77, *The Lounger* (1785–7), 3 vols. (2nd edn, 1787), III, pp. 85, 87.

61. Knox, 'Unmanliness of tears', in *Winter Evenings*, II, p. 182.

62. 'On the inconsistency of affected sensibility', in *ibid.*, II, p. 158.

63. Cowper, *Letters*, III, p. 180. Earlier comments suggest that Cowper's equation between refined conduct and a fragile physique was not intended as blanket praise for all manifestations of male physical refinement. Unlike the sensitive but sympathetic man of sensibility, the foppish 'delicate BILLY SUCKLING' described in his 1756 periodical essay was representative of what Cowper considered a breed of trivial, selfish and 'lady-like gentlemen', *ibid.*, V, pp. 3–6.

64. *OED* traces this association of delicacy with 'exquisite fineness of feeling' and 'a refined sense of what is becoming' to the early eighteenth century. These definitions developed from an existing connection between delicacy and luxuriousness.

65. Nathaniel Lancaster, *The Plan of an Essay Upon Delicacy* (1748), p. 55. Lancaster's interpretation seems particularly useful, given his 1747 satire of the enervating effects of false refinement on manhood, *The Pretty Gentleman; or the Softness of Manners Vindicated*.

66. Knox, 'Unmanliness of tears', *Winter Evenings*, II, p. 179.

67. *Man*, No. 43, p. 4. Literary disavowals of tears as a sign of male weakness include Laurence Sterne's novel, *Tristram Shandy* (1759–67): 'Tears are no proof of cowardice, Trim. – I drop them oft-times myself, cried my uncle Toby' (IV:4), quoted in John Mullan, 'Sentimental novels' in John Richetti ed., *The Eighteenth-Century Novel* (Cambridge, 1996), pp. 242, 247.

68. William Gouge, *The Dignitie of Chivalrie* (1626), quoted in Shepard, 'Meanings of manhood', p. 51; John Sharp, archbishop of York (1694), quoted in

Jeremy Gregory, 'Homo-religiosus', in Hitchcock and Cohen eds., *English Masculinities*, p. 100.

69. Blair, 'On the compassion of Christ' and 'On the moral character of Christ', in *Sermons*, II (1780), p. 122; V (1801), p. 68; Fordyce, *Sermons to Young Women*, II, p. 232. John Dwyer also notes the appreciation of another Old Testament figure, Joseph, whose tears Blair described as the 'effusions of a heart overflowing with all the tender sensibilities of nature', *Virtuous Discourse*, pp. 59–60.

70. Wesley, 'On pleasing all men' and 'Sermon on the Mount XIII', in *Sermons*, III, p. 424; I, p. 697.

71. The alternative to true courage was 'physical' bravery, an inferior quality characterised as reckless and self-serving aggression. It was for such 'criminal' conduct that Johnson wished to consign, among others, Julius Caesar and Peter the Great to 'obscurity and detestation', *Adventurer*, No. 99 (16 Oct 1753), in W.J. Bate, J.M. Bullit and L.F. Powell eds., *The Idler and the Adventurer* (1753–60) in Johnson, *Works*, II (1963), p. 433. For sentimental soldierhood in transatlantic context see Sarah Knott, 'A cultural history of sensibility in the era of the American revolution' (D.Phil thesis, Oxford University, 1999), esp. ch. 5.

72. Stephen Fovargue, *A New Catalogue of Vulgar Errors* (Cambridge, 1767), pp. 127–8.

73. Blair, 'On sensibility', *Sermons*, III, p. 37.

74. Smith, *Theory of Moral Sentiments*, p. 245.

75. Knox, 'On the happiness of domestic life' (1782), in *Works*, I, p. 214.

76. Adam Ferguson, *An Essay on the History of Civil Society* (1767), ed. Fania Oz-Salzberger (Cambridge, 1995), p. 190.

77. Knox, 'On sentiment', *Essays Moral and Literary* (1778), p. 4.

78. *London Magazine*, 28 (1759), p. 579.

79. Fordyce, *Addresses to Young Men*, II, p. 226.

80. Kathleen Wilson, 'Empire of virtue. The imperial project and Hanoverian culture, *c.* 1720–1785', in Lawrence Stone ed., *An Imperial State at War. Britain from 1689–1815* (1994), pp. 146, 150. For an excellent discussion of literary and pictorial representations of Wolfe's death see David H. Solkin, *Painting for Money. The Visual Arts and the Public Sphere in Eighteenth-Century England* (New Haven CT and London, 1992), pp. 206–13.

81. John Pringle, *The Life of General James Wolfe* (1760), pp. 3, 5, 17.

82. *Annual Register*, 2 (1759), pp. 452, 283. To see this promotion of soldiers' tears as part of an on-going debate over the appropriateness of men's weeping we must also acknowledge the persistence of more traditional opinions:

The Tears of the Foot Guards, upon Departure for America, 2nd edn (1776), wherein a cowardly, 'effeminate' soldier protests against the boorishness of war, offers one example.

83. Pocock, *Virtue*, pp. 196–9.

84. Edmund Burke, *Reflections on the Revolution in France* (1790), in L.G. Mitchell ed., *The French Revolution, 1790–1794*, in *The Writings and Speeches of Edmund Burke*, 9 vols. (Oxford, 1981–97), VIII (1989), pp. 126–7. Pocock also notes the differences between Millar's and Burke's historical interpretation: whereas Millar saw chivalry as a crucial but undeveloped stimulus to later, more advanced refinement, Burke regarded it as the enduring feature of a more circumscribed noble elite, *Virtue*, p. 199.

85. Burke, *Reflections*, pp. 120, 126.

86. Walpole to Lady Ossory, 1 Dec 1790, in *Correspondence*, XXXIV, p. 98.

87. W.L. Bowles, *A Poetical Address to the Right Honourable Edmund Burke* (1791), pp. 2–3.

88. Thomas Paine, *Rights of Man* (1791), ed. Mark Philp (Oxford, 1995), pp. 189, 110, 102.

89. Mary Wollstonecraft, *A Vindication of the Rights of Men* (1790), in *Political Writings*, ed. Janet Todd (Oxford, 1994), p. 25.

90. John Barrell, 'Sad stories: Louis XVI, George III, and the language of sentiment', in Sharpe and Zwicker eds., *Refiguring Revolutions*. Barrell's principal focus is on popular presentations of Louis XVI as a man of feeling in reports of his final meeting with his family before execution in January 1793. On George III see also Linda Colley, *Britons: Forging the Nation, 1707–1837* (New Haven CT and London, 1992), esp. pp. 232–3.

91. Wollstonecraft, *Vindication*, pp. 25, 8.

92. *Ibid.*, pp. 6–7, 17. This contest is further discussed by Virginia Sapiro, *A Vindication of Political Virtue. The Political Theory of Mary Wollstonecraft* (1992), pp. 188–207; Susan Khin Zaw, ' "Appealing to the head *and* heart": Wollstonecraft and Burke on taste, morals and human nature', in Perry and Rossington eds., *Femininity and Masculinity*.

93. Wollstonecraft, *A Vindication of the Rights of Woman* (1792), in *Political Writings*, pp. 167–8.

94. *Memoirs of the Late Mrs Henrietta Fordyce* (1823), p. 14; James Lindsay, *A Sermon on the Occasion of the Death of James Fordyce* (1797), pp. 38, 48, 54.

95. *Fordyce Delineated: A Satire in Verse* (1767), pp. 10–11, 16.

96. Knox, 'Cursory remarks on the eloquence of the pulpit' and 'On preaching, and sermon-writers' (both 1782), in *Works*, II, pp. 196, 215–16.

97. Horace Walpole to George Montagu (28 Jan 1760), in *Correspondence*, IX, p. 274.

98. *The Life and Writings of the Rev. William Dodd* (1777), p. 3.

99. *Ibid.*

100. *Town and Country Magazine*, V (1773), p. 681. In this, probably the original application of what became an enduring label, Dodd was also accused of fine dressing and, like Fordyce, womanising. For more details of the macaronis and their place in the debate over acceptable and unacceptable styles of manhood, see Chapter Four.

101. The accusation of 'pure foppery' came from Burke's political ally, Sir Philip Francis, who commented on drafts of the passage on Marie Antoinette. Francis did not question the validity of feeling *per se*, rather the sincerity of this specific declaration. Burke subsequently restated his credentials as a genuinely sentimental male: 'the abominable Scene of 1789 ... did draw Tears from me and wetted my Paper', a response that would occur 'as long as Men – with their Natural feelings exist'. Quoted in Johnson, *Equivocal Beings*, p. 4. The association of Chesterfield with foppery occurred in William Hayley, *Two Dialogues: Containing a Comparative View ... of Philip, the late Earl of Chesterfield and Dr Samuel Johnson* (1787), p. 216. Other satires, among them *The Fine Gentleman's Etiquette* (1776), depicted the earl as a vain man in 'macaroni' dress.

CHAPTER FOUR

Effeminacy, foppery and the boundaries of polite society

The previous two chapters have shown how proponents of polite conduct distinguished modern manners from pre-existing forms of civility associated with a social elite located either at the court or in the country. In contrast to the selfish, deferential courtier or the formal rural gentlemen, the early-eighteenth-century polite male was expected to be more relaxed or 'easy' in company, to move more freely across social divisions (while not ignoring the need to respect social superiors), and to seek to please his audience through displays of self-control and genuine fellow feeling. The rise of a culture of sensibility prompted mid-century writers to rework the respective merits of these two qualities in a complementary discourse of male refinement defined in large part by displays of sympathy and constructive benevolence.

Central to both discourses, whatever their specific strategies of communication, was a confidence in the harmony between inner virtue and social expression. Without this correlation the essential complaisance of politeness or the benevolence of sensibility could be reduced to a series of gestures designed to ingratiate and deceive. We have seen how, as in the case of Vicesimus Knox on Lord Chesterfield and James Fordyce, for example, these dangers posed a very real problem for writers on polite society. As the nature of Knox's criticism indicates, these accusations operated simultaneously at several levels: thus Chesterfield and Fordyce's errors were, in part, the personal failings of corrupt individuals; in addition, the earl's advice was deemed representative of an elite social group seemingly detached from the values of a respectable majority fortified by sensibility. However, Chesterfield's vilification during the 1770s and 1780s also needs to be seen in the context of a longer-running eighteenth-century debate over concepts of refinement, and the implications of these for standards of gentlemanly conduct and broader discourses of manliness.

This chapter focuses on several aspects of this debate. Proponents of politeness worked hard to equate new standards of refined living with a manliness based on a synthesis of traditional and modern values. However, many also remained sceptical as to the wisdom of this redefinition: as David Hume reported, it was common for 'the more zealous partisans of the ancients' to decry 'modern politeness', and especially men's engagement in female society, as 'foppish and ridiculous . . . a reproach, rather than a credit, to the present age'. This was not a view Hume shared, though he too remained alert to the deleterious effects of excess refinement. Though critical of ancient manners as liable to collapse 'into rusticity and abuse', Hume also acknowledged the instability of a modern form of polite sociability which 'naturally so ornamental, runs often into affectation and foppery, disguise and insincerity', so reducing the benevolent acts by which 'the male sex, among a polite people, discover their authority' to the product of a 'foppish and affected' individual.[1] Polite and sentimental discourses were evidently not unproblematic, and in their various responses to the dangers, both critics and defenders drew frequently on Hume's contrast between genuine politeness and insincerity or unbecoming triviality, vividly brought to life in the contrast between the 'manly' gentleman and the 'effeminate' fop.

Ceremony and affectation

For its late-seventeenth- and eighteenth-century advocates, the equation of politeness with relaxed and genuine sociability proved an essential means of establishing the originality and merits of new modes of social refinement. Topical, enjoyable and virtuous, politeness was a substantive improvement on existing forms of gentlemanly behaviour criticised for over-regulation and stiff formality encapsulated in the idea of ceremony and ceremoniousness. By the time that Samuel Johnson defined 'ceremonious' conduct as 'formal to a fault' in 1755, generations of gentlemen had learned to regard it as one of the qualities against which desirable behaviour was now defined. This did not mean that eighteenth-century instructors failed to appreciate the value of formalities, especially for those setting out to acquire the ways of refined social interaction. Young men in particular were encouraged to show others what John Locke described in the 1690s as 'that common ceremony and Regard which is in civility due to them'. It was through the 'ceremonious parts of Breeding' that young men came to understand 'what is most becoming' in the adult world.[2] Furthermore, the importance attached in later guides to the rules of refined conduct, often imparted by dancing-masters turned author, suggests to some extent the enduring value of respectful and deferential ceremony in eighteenth-century definitions of polite manhood.

At the same time, ceremony required careful regulation and manage-ment, without which it became, as Locke put it, 'a fault in good Manners'.[3] Over the next half-century it is possible to detect a shift in meaning as a result of which the social errors attributed by Locke to an '*excess of Ceremony*' became, with the emergence and consolidation of polite discourse, a char-acteristic of 'ceremonious' *per se*. Among eighteenth-century polite theorists, 'ceremony' came to be associated typically with imperfect or underdeveloped forms of gentlemanly conduct. Writing in 1711, Joseph Addison, for example, attributed the unattractive manners of past societies to their being 'entirely lost under Form and Ceremony'.[4] In the early 1760s Oliver Goldsmith provided a more detailed, pseudo-conjectural history in which 'ceremony' featured as an intermediary stage in the evolution of modern refined soci-ety, being the necessarily meticulous response to earlier boorishness and the prelude to contemporary ideals as 'the trouble of being ceremonious at length produces politeness, elegance and ease'.[5] Those who persisted with ceremony were, like the *Spectator*'s Restoration-style country gentleman, now thought anachronistic. Others considered ceremony the mark of upstart pretenders to true refinement. The young Edmund Burke, for example, had deemed it the tendency of the 'Vulgar . . . to judge of politeness as a number of ceremonious observances' – an idea 'exploded amongst people of good sense and breeding'.[6] However identified, the ceremonious man's predomin-ant characteristic remained his capacity to irritate and weary companions of a more polite disposition. Mr Spectator's dinner engagement with formal country gentlemen proved 'very troublesome to a Man of my Temper'.[7] An essay from the *The World* periodical (1753–6) likewise described the incon-veniences experienced by club members in the company of 'a man of CEREMONY' or 'person of very FINE BREEDING' who used meetings not as a means to socialise but to demonstrate his civility. The result was a protracted series of greetings followed by elaborately formal conversation which, if well mannered, was, as one member described, 'certainly the dullest I ever heard in my life'. A better man, it was added, would have acknow-ledged his limitations and left the club.[8]

Such obvious social faults rendered men of ceremony more ridiculous than harmful. However, as many behavioural writers were aware, ceremo-niousness could also be employed more deviously, and dangerously, to dis-guise personal self-interest behind a veneer of seemingly refined and sincere sociability. The result was a second, and more serious, social misdemeanour: affectation. As a show of external refinements devoid of accompanying inner civility, affectation directly challenged polite theorists' claims to morality. In a bid to dissuade young men from this course, writers pointed out the obviousness of such behaviour to experienced men of society. John Locke, for example, defined affectation as manners 'plaister'd on' that 'at best sit but untowardly'.[9] Nearly a century later, Hester Chapone claimed that 'affected gestures [and] manners ... [were] obvious to every understanding', and hence commonly ridiculed. At the same time, Chapone admitted the damage caused when duplicitous conduct went undetected, especially by the young: thus by concealing 'every passion of his own heart', the affected corrupter 'takes advantage of others'.[10] Fears of social treachery led the sentimental sermon writer James Fordyce to propose that genuine male friendships were only truly possible between a father and son, secure from the 'smoothest talkers' and 'specious haranguers' who populated the social spaces of traditional polite society.[11]

Both Chapone and Fordyce had Lord Chesterfield firmly in mind when they commented upon an apparent late-century increase in false refinement. However, the fear of affectation had a much longer history. In terms of substance, if not perhaps intensity, such concerns had been expressed since Baldassare Castiglione defined the Renaissance courtier's gracefulness as much on the grounds of political expediency as genuine fellow feeling. Over time the tone and content of this debate had undergone changes. As Anna Bryson shows, during the seventeenth century claims of affectation were regularly directed against Puritan gentlemen whose pretensions to a Godly synthesis of manners and morality were deemed hypocritical by their Cavalier critics. Bryson goes on to suggest that the decline of this tension after the Restoration saw concern over the compatibility of 'moral integrity and the social imperatives' decrease 'markedly in later seventeenth-century texts'.[12] This argument would appear to substantiate that of Fenela Childs and Anthony Fletcher who, as we saw in Chapter Two, suggest a conscious shift in early-eighteenth-century notions of 'politeness' away from a moral code to a series of external civilities designed to ingratiate the recipient, regardless of true feelings. However, as we also saw in Chapter Two, polite theorists, along with writers on deportment like the dancing-master Matthew Towle, continued to stress external manners as a product of inner virtue. In view of this, it is perhaps more useful to see eighteenth-century concerns over affectation as not in decline but rather as undergoing redefinition, from an earlier equation with religious hypocrisy to new preoccupations such as with the effects of men's foreign travel to French and Italian centres of ostentatious, and hence false, refinement. In a century of near-continuous warfare, the image of the affected Frenchman peddling false compliments, or the Frenchified British gentleman who appropriated these manners to become modish, proved a stock-in-trade both of confident Francophobic satires and more alarmist commentaries on the national condition.[13] Eighteenth-century interest in affectation also paralleled flashpoints in the debate surrounding the subsequent condition of British refinement: for example, during the mid-1770s, when sentimental writers revealed the duplicity of the (conveniently) 'Frenchified fop', Lord Chesterfield; or when, in the 1790s, critics exposed Edmund Burke's sympathy for the French monarchy as 'ornamental feelings'.[14]

The debate over Burke's comments is often seen as shattering the faith in sensibility as a corrective to the duplicity that many believed a feature of earlier forms of polite society. In fact, anxiety over the affectation of sensibility again pre-dated the 1790s. As early as 1755, the essayist Peter Shaw had informed readers of the distinction between men's 'moral weeping', when tears flowed from genuine social affection, and 'physical crying' – a mechanical act calculated to impress, but devoid of corresponding mental or emotional sentiments. Vicesimus Knox, an ardent defender of men's tears, wrote in 1788 of his concern that once seemingly clear statements of sensitivity were being 'brought into disrepute [by] very artful people . . . who weep from habit or affectation'; the one means to detect the devious being their 'usual error . . . to weep to excess'.[15] As we saw in Chapter Three, such concerns were integral to the culture of sensibility and testimony to its popularity, especially in the 1770s and 1780s, as a marker of social refinement. It was this popularity which prompted late-century images of the affected gentleman not just as Frenchified but now also as a man of false feeling.

Effeminacy and excess

Commentaries on ceremonious or affected refinement variously depicted practitioners as anachronistic, pedantic or corrupt. But for writers like Vicesimus Knox it was also of great importance to characterise the man of false refinement as failing in his gender identity; not only ridiculous but also unmanly – a 'lady-like gentleman', as he described one such exponent in his 1788 essay 'On the inconsistency of affected sensibility'. On this occasion, Knox offered scant explanation for his equation of artifice with loss of manliness, failure being implicit in the affected individual's corruption of an admirable moral and behavioural code required to 'feel as a man'.[16] Elsewhere, this relationship between affectation and effeminacy was set out more clearly. Many, for example, saw affectation less in terms of corruption than as an unregulated attempt to cultivate a reputation for refined feeling. In such cases, the fashion for refinement pushed men towards ever more elaborate displays of delicate, polished or sensitive behaviour. On certain occasions, notably misguided individuals such as Lord Chesterfield were accused of encouraging both trickery and excessive delicacy among their readers. In his essay on the 'Superior value of solid accomplishment' (1782), for example, Knox presented a fictional dialogue between the earl and the Roman philosopher Cicero – the embodiment of classical sociability – who was depicted criticising the *Letters* for promoting deception and a state of hyper-refinement that 'has a connection with effeminacy'.[17] Contemporary critics saw a similar link between Chesterfield's preoccupation with the externalities of refinement and young men's excessive interest in their appearance and deportment. The correspondence, claimed the *Westminster Magazine*, reduced politeness to 'the outside recommendations of the glittering suit of cloaths', and diminished the once admirably refined gentleman to a mere 'pretty, painted, lacified popinjay'.[18]

Such performances remained, for some, the conscious posturing of a wayward individual or members of an exclusive social elite. However, many believed excessive refinement as a more integral feature of modern, sociable living. This was a potentially more disturbing interpretation in that it increased the numbers at risk from rising levels of material temptation and the concomitant pressure for greater behavioural sophistication within a polite society, broadly defined. Fear of actual or imminent social ruin proved a popular and enduring theme in eighteenth-century social commentaries, which sought to explain a series of British domestic and international set-backs then being experienced by a once vigorous nation. Books, periodical essays, magazine articles, songs and verse were devoted to charting the loss of traditional male virtues such as moderation, sense, public duty, integrity and independence for which, in this often unashamedly nostalgic literature, British manhood had once been famed and feared. In its place had come the tyranny of self-interest from which sprang the social evils – luxurious consumption, social competition and preoccupation with fashionable trivia – bemoaned by pessimistic observers throughout the period.

In making these claims commentators revived an early modern civic humanist concept of social evolution, itself drawn from classical models, in which states developed from a primitive to an advanced condition before degenerating into tyranny and a return to barbarity. In contrast to medieval models, which interpreted decline as a combination of cosmic and natural factors, Renaissance theories had given more attention to man-made influences – notably the unregulated rise of commerce – as the principal dynamic in rotating the historical cycle. Thus, social change required careful regulation if currently virtuous societies were to avoid degeneration, in terms of the loss of political liberties, the erosion of national health and vigour, and falling cultural and moral standards.

In an early manifestation during the 1670s, civic discourse served to unify 'Country' politicians against the ruling 'Court' group whose hold on power was seen as a serious threat to political liberty. Modifications of the Country stance in the face of later episodes of ministerial corruption – including opposition to Robert Walpole's 'Robinocracy' during the 1730s, the duke of Newcastle's incompetence in foreign affairs during the mid- to late 1750s, or the earl of Bute's alleged tampering with the constitution in the early 1760s – ensured political events remained a key feature of eighteenth-century civic assessment. The perceived extent of political corruption was such that otherwise progressive commentators also drew attention to the damage caused, notably by Walpole's oligarchical administration. Writing in the 1750s, Oliver Goldsmith claimed that rising levels of political patronage and manipulation were now sufficiently widespread to be discerned in changing social customs which saw the 'laced player' favoured over the 'man of virtue', and 'wisdom, wit and innocence' replaced by 'a laced coat, a pliant bow, and an immoderate friendship'.[19]

Goldsmith's complaint also suggests a significant development in eighteenth-century civic analysis. A first generation of Country critics had advocated a strictly political ideology in an attempt to preserve liberty through the actions of a landowning, and therefore independent, male citizenry. They were now followed by commentators for whom the social implications of change – primarily the accelerated development of a post-1688 consumer economy – proved of equal importance. Considerable attention was paid in these discussions to the impact of changing social conditions on standards of manliness. In line with a shifting focus from political to social corruption, eighteenth-century civic commentators revealed how the temptations and comforts of consumerism were weakening men's mental and physical resolve, reducing not just politicians, but military leaders and their subordinates, churchmen, traders and other professionals, to a state encapsulated in the much evoked notion of 'effeminacy'.

It was a common argument in civic assessments that the refinements required for inclusion in modern polite society were incompatible with, and indeed destructive of, established male values. Many believed this an insoluble conundrum, the effects of which were thought to increase from decade to decade, giving renewed energy and relevance to an otherwise repetitive discourse. It was this fear that allowed successive generations to berate their contemporaries for sinking to new levels of enervation as fresh political or military crises demonstrated the spread of polite socialisation to (supposedly) untouched spheres.

During the 1740s and 1750s, a period of particular alarm over rising levels of effeminacy, civic commentators paid especial attention to the impact of polite society on the armed forces. The image of the enfeebled soldier who preferred the comforts of civilian life to the rigours of war was a commonplace in both mid-century satires and sober social documentaries.

In the aftermath of the 1745 Jacobite rising, and the initial disorganisation of the British army's response, the novelist and editor Eliza Haywood offered a timely essay on 'Effeminacy in the army censured'. Haywood's concern at the 'over-delicacy . . . among the military Gentlemen' set out the popular equation between rising material consumption and falling standards of manliness among those who 'find it an insuperable Difficulty to bring themselves to that Hardiness and Neglect of personal Ornaments, which suits the Life of a Soldier'.[20] Discussions over the condition of the armed forces, intertwined with the scale, duration and course of actual military engagements, reached their height a decade later after severe set-backs during the early stages of the Seven Years' War (1756–63). For John Brown, author of an *Estimate of the Manners and Principles of the Times* (1757–8) – then and now the best known of these jeremiads – military losses were the consequence of a navy reduced to 'the School of *Avarice*, to the *Ends of Effeminacy*', and to an army, now the '*School*, not of Honour, but of *Effeminacy*', governed by officers preoccupied with 'Dress, Cards and Tea'.[21] Brown explained declining standards in terms of the military's over-exposure to the *Estimate*'s principal theme: an already (and increasingly) 'effeminate' civilian population.

In keeping with civic discourse, Brown treated effeminacy as a broad and multi-faceted state arising from the loss of traditional male qualities: physical health, hardiness, courage, rational thought, sense, public duty, and political and financial independence. Brown attributed declining standards of manliness to Britain's having reached the 'third and highest stage' of commercial activity, naturally begetting 'gross Luxury, or effeminate Refinement'.[22] Social refinement was believed to stimulate effeminacy through various channels, each of which revealed the destructive effects of an advanced commercial economy. The subsequent distortion of politeness led to a preoccupation with delicacy, and to the production of previously unknown states of mental and physical weakness. Thus, devotion to new polite fashions resulted in a loss of personal independence. At the same time, the promotion of mixed company forced men to adopt the habits and interests of female companions – clothes shopping, tea-drinking and so on – while innovations such as the Italian opera exposed audiences to what one earlier critic had described as 'soft and effeminate Musick' harmful to 'the Minds and Manners of Men'.[23] Those who failed to be genuinely enervated through refinement were said to affect a reputation for what Brown called 'false Delicacy', itself productive of 'effeminate Manners' (in a relationship later revisited by Vicesimus Knox in his essay on Chesterfield) through a loss of manly independence and sense.[24]

Over time, developments in the discourse of refinement also led to modifications in the image of the excessive and exquisite gentleman. By the third quarter of the century many commentators, including sentimental writers, defined effeminacy in terms of an excess of feeling. In certain cases, this excess derived from attempts to gain a reputation for social refinement. The man of 'too great sensibility' described in a mid-1770s reworking of Giovanni della Casa's *Il Galateo* had become a figure of such 'excessive delicacy' that he was now capable only of an 'effeminacy of manners . . . very unbecoming, especially in men' and suitable only to the 'sillier part of the female sex'.[25] In other instances, it was commonly suggested that, among certain men, excessive feeling was the result of an innate physiological state. Fineness of nerves, while accounting for intellectual ability and sensitivity, contributed in extreme conditions both to physical ill-health – hypochondria, vapours, spleen – and to psychological disorders in men, described by Hume as 'subject to a certain delicacy of passion, which makes them extremely sensible to all the accidents of life'.[26] At worst, the effects of this sensitivity led to uncontrollable melancholy and even suicide. At best, afflicted men were driven not towards but away from polite society, repelled by what they saw as the minute horrors of daily life. The result was a similar loss of manly reason and responsibility. As Vicesimus Knox argued, men of excessive sensibility were afflicted by an 'effeminacy of mind' manifest in their flight from 'vigorous pursuits and manly exertions'. Hence 'disgusted with men and manners', such an individual 'either seeks retirement . . . or weakened . . . conducts himself with folly and imprudence'.[27]

Debating effeminacy

Mid-eighteenth-century readers of texts like John Brown's *Estimate* may justifiably have thought theirs a society abandoned to enervating luxury, trivial fashions and unprecedented levels of individual and collective effeminacy. Such views did not, however, go unchallenged. Chapter Two showed how academic theorists like David Hume argued for the compatibility of manliness with modern commercial activity and polite conduct. Indeed, Hume thought it likely that modern manners would lead to new forms of manliness, combining traditional virtues such as moderation, industry and courage (themselves improved by refinement) with more innovative qualities, notably a consideration for and intimacy with female society. Redefinition necessarily had implications for debates concerning the relationship of effeminacy to polite society. In reinterpreting formerly corrupt personality traits as manly, progressive authors reappraised the meaning of effeminacy and the range of activities that threatened manly identity and, as a result, re-estimated national health in the context of an emerging polite society.

This appraisal took several forms. For some, reassessment prompted not a critique of an established civic paradigm but a fresh look at current statements on the national condition. Written at the height of the military crisis during the Seven Years' War, Charles Hanbury Williams's *Real Character of the Age* (1759) praised the motive behind recent alarmist studies, like John Brown's, while questioning their accuracy: 'effeminacy' was indeed 'a great Foible' of the population, but had not yet become a 'Characteristick of the *English* Nation'. Modern living, argued a sympathetic contemporary, 'only threatens us with effeminacy of manners: we are not yet sunk into it'.[28]

Other more intellectually ambitious studies proposed a radical break from the civic association of effeminacy with commercial 'progress'. One theorist to have already taken a considerable step in this direction was Bernard Mandeville. In his provocative treatise, *The Fable of the Bees* (1714), Mandeville challenged the civic humanist equation between personal vice and communal decline. While accepting a traditional association of luxury, refinement and effeminacy for individuals, he simultaneously denied any connection between the enervated man and declining national standards of manhood.

Mandeville based his explanation on the division of labour. Personal utility was dependent on one's occupation, as he made clear in his own rather more optimistic discussion of the British military. Thus a strong army required that the majority of common soldiers be isolated from the corrosive effects of social change, something Mandeville thought inevitable given that most members of the rank and file were drawn from 'the working slaving People' employed in peacetime to produce luxury goods for the wealthy. It was, he argued, of no consequence if elite men were now less adept at traditionally manly acts, since as officers they were merely required to give orders and were able to 'destroy Cities a-bed, and ruin whole Countries while they are at Dinner'.

At this level, Mandeville's thesis of private interests and public benefits was shocking and profound. But his argument went further, to suggest that male refinement within the army, rather than simply failing to undermine courage, positively enhanced national fortitude. Unlike many civic commentators who saw the military as the last bastion of manliness in a degenerate society, Mandeville considered the army one of the 'greatest Schools of Breeding and good Manners . . . to polish the Men'. He based his contention on the claim that the quest for honour proved the surest route to male refinement. In their pursuit of and desire to retain the respect of their colleagues, soldiers became both more refined – they 'excel each other in Finery of Equipage . . . [and] Politeness of Entertainments' – and more courageous. The result was the bizarre spectacle (according to Mandeville, recently borne out during the War of the Spanish Succession [1701–13]) of 'puny young Striplings . . . tenderly Educated' acquitting themselves in battle with a bravery becoming 'the most stinking Slovens'.[29]

The influence of Mandeville's equation between politeness and courage, and his identification of effeminacy as a subjective category conditioned by personal context, is clearly evident in later (albeit critical) Scottish enlightenment studies in which his thesis was subjected to social-scientific analysis. As Adam Smith demonstrated, seemingly absolute standards of manhood were in fact conditioned by a particular society's position in the stadial sequence of social evolution. Thus, acts which modern, enlightened writers regarded as desirable signs of social affection continued to be seen as the 'most unpardonable effeminacy' to the 'Spartan' natives of North America.[30]

To reconceptualise the characteristics, origins and scope of effeminacy was not of course to deny its existence. In his 1752 essay 'Of refinement in the arts and sciences', David Hume described modern-day Italians as a 'civilised people' distinguished by their lack of 'courage and a martial spirit'. The 'effeminacy of the ITALIANS' was not attributable to their civilised state, however. As Hume explained, Britain and France were equally known for 'their luxury, or politeness, or application to the arts' but here, in his opinion, courage and refinement coexisted. Hume accounted for the Italians' peculiar situation with reference not to universal models of cyclical social development, but to specific historical events that had resulted in government by a factious aristocracy, priests, women and mercenaries. In historicising the Italian condition, Hume effectively disassociated political corruption from socio-economic improvement and hence negated the threat of these dangers in a British context.[31] In this and in his earlier essay, 'Of the rise and progress of the arts and sciences' (1742), Hume achieved something of a high watermark in the enlightenment's attempt to redefine the relationship between politeness and effeminacy. His breaking of the link between refinement and male degeneration was here coupled not only with the assertion (like Mandeville's) that modern manners improved standards of courage, but also with a critique of Mandeville's unpalatable equation of honour with self-interest, and of polite society with a circumscribed social elite.

Over the next two decades, however, there were clear signs that this confident separation of refinement and male degeneration was coming in for renewed scrutiny within the Scottish moral philosophical and conjectural historical tradition. Subsequent studies provided grounds for fresh concern over modern manners by reasserting the destructive effects of misjudged refinement on both male social and political life. The Edinburgh moral philosopher Adam Ferguson was a leading exponent of this newly cautious attitude in the late 1760s. Ferguson claimed that many contemporary conduct writers had lost sight of the true meaning of 'politeness' – from the Greek *polis*, defined by Ferguson as 'the state of nations in respect to their laws and government' – and had replaced it with a social attachment defined as 'proficiency in the liberal and mechanical arts, in literature, and commerce'.

Such developments were not in themselves a threat to the individual and national condition. However, Ferguson feared that former associations with public service and political freedom were once again vulnerable to current notions of politeness which promoted the values of personal over public interest. Freed from patriotic duty and encouraged to 'pursue . . . private advantage', the modern man became more 'effeminate, mercenary, and sensual' as classical standards of egalitarian citizenship were replaced by artificial social skills 'infecting all orders of men, with equal venality, servility, and cowardice'.[32]

What certain civic-minded analysts regarded as the inevitable outcome of cyclical social development, others saw more straightforwardly as the effects of an irresponsible younger generation. Thus, the 1760s, a decade which Ferguson identified with falling standards of true politeness and rising levels of effeminacy, later seemed relatively healthy to a fellow Edinburgh resident and Mirror Club member, the publisher William Creech. Along with many of his club associates, Creech claimed that he lived at a time when once simple manners were deteriorating under the weight of 'indolence, sensuality, vice and corruption' and currently (1783) 'hasten to decay'. Specifically, Creech's understanding of falling standards focused less on effeminacy than on other flawed forms of fashionable manliness. It was a shift he neatly illustrated with reference to changing patterns of Edinburgh street language whereby the 'fine fellow' of 1763 – a man of 'an accomplished mind, added elegance of manners, and a conduct guided by principle' – had become, twenty years on, 'one who could drink three bottles . . . who swore immoderately and before ladies . . . [and] disregards the interests of society'.[33]

Blackguards and bad behaviour

William Creech thought the conduct of oafish youths reprehensible and not to be encouraged. Yet other critics of modern manners were prepared to countenance the advantages of a little less social polish. As a typical civic tract from the late 1750s put it, the 'bravest' and 'honestest' men were inevitably the 'roughest'.[34] A later guide to male sensibility likewise called for overly sensitive recluses to be pushed into the 'roughness' of daily business.[35] Even early reformers like John Locke had admitted that 'Plain and rough Nature left to itself, is much better than an Artificial Ungracefulness, and such studied Ways of being ill fashion'd.'[36]

Given the apparent tide of refined effeminacy, it is worth noting the existence of a counter-culture of anti-civility propagated by, in the seventeenth century, male groups such as the 'hectors' and 'blades' and, in the eighteenth century, by fraternities including the 'bloods' and 'greenhorns' – unschooled in the details of polite society – or like the early-eighteenth-century 'mohocks', who rejected their civilised upbringing for a life of insult and violence.[37] To this catalogue of anti-social personalities we might also add the 'blackguard', a character who to some extent encapsulated both behavioural styles.

Dating from the mid-sixteenth century, the term 'blackguard' had been variously used to denote a menial servant or an attendant to a group of thieves. The characters encountered by the early-eighteenth-century satirist Ned Ward, for example, combined slovenly and criminal conduct, being 'poor wretches . . . as ragged as old stocking mops [and] hungry as so many catamountains' who took pleasure from their 'villainy, ignorance, laziness, profaneness, and infidelity'.[38] 'Dick Poney', grand-master of the fictional mid-century 'Black-guard Society of Scald-Miserable-Masons', was similarly unashamed to head a fraternity whose members 'stink in the Nostrils of all whom we come within reach of', and 'carry Links of a Night, which we thrust in Peoples Faces under pretence of giving them Light, whilst we pick their Pockets'.[39] To the majority of respectable citizens, 'blackguard' was a term of abuse, denoting low status both in use and implication: as Samuel Johnson put it in 1755, 'a cant term amongst the vulgar, by which is implied a dirty fellow of the meanest kind'.[40]

In view of the anxiety over excessive refinement it is perhaps not surprising that certain commentators positively appropriated the blackguard character as an alternative to modern, effete forms of manhood. The two decades after Johnson's definition witnessed a high point in the blackguard's fortunes. This was due in large part to the popularity of the radical politician John Wilkes, a prominent critic of the earl of Bute's corrupt ministry (and its legacy) during the 1760s. Wilkes's attack on what he identified as the 'effeminate' manners of a ruling social elite, coupled with his self-presentation as an unaffected manly character espousing patriotic and liberal politics, found favour among advocates of political reform.[41] The merits of plain and vigorous manhood were similarly welcomed by many social observers. Writing in 1775 under the pseudonym 'Blackguard', the dramatist George Colman looked back fifty years to a virtuous and heroic age populated by such 'bold manly wits' as the novelist Jonathan Swift and the dramatist John Gay. Colman contrasted these figures with modern, fashionable gentlemen in this 'frippery age' whom blackguards, and presumably other, equally manly readers, were expected to ridicule. The epitome of delicate gentlemanliness in the 1770s were the flamboyant Italophilic 'macaronis', then much ridiculed in literary and early forms of visual satire. It was, wrote the author of a 1771 magazine essay on 'The profligacy of the times', the responsibility of 'every true English blackguard' to criticise macaroni fashions, and what Colman saw as their 'delicacy of manners that produces effeminacy'.[42]

Though useful to individual commentators during the 1770s, the black-guard character ultimately failed to achieve a redefinition from vulgarian to standard bearer of healthy manliness. As the boorish antithesis to the refined gentleman, the blackguard offered an equally unappealing image of manliness to a middle-class readership wary of the excesses and corruptions, rather than the idea, of social refinement. The place of the Wilkite radical movement is again important for an appreciation of this ambivalence. As recent studies show, the implications of an unprecedentedly populist movement were alarming for moderate political reformers who appropriated the civic identity of virtuous manliness precisely as a means of distancing themselves from what they saw as a feckless and self-seeking multitude. Prominent among these concerns was the emphasis given, especially in Wilkite versions of manly patriotism, to a rapacious male hetero-sexuality which many would-be respectable political reformers saw leading to an uncomfortably potent combination of the libertarian and libertine.[43] Published in the wake of the next significant expression of popular political activity in the mid-1790s, John Caulfield's definition of the blackguard as 'a shabby dirty fellow . . . derived from a number of dirty tattered and roguish boys' certainly suggests a loss of any former positive connotations and a reversion to type.[44]

Nevertheless, Colman's positive application of the blackguard character, though perhaps unusual, does draw attention to the role of literary stereotypes in debates on the effect of polite society on male behaviour. The blackguard, while exposing the excesses of his antithesis, the modern gentleman, did so in ways that were equally alienating to would-be members of polite society. The alternative was to ridicule directly the character of the overly polite and effeminate man, personified by generations of eighteenth-century social observers in the character of the fop. More complex, meaningful and prominent than the blackguard character, the fop type embodied a series of social and gender failings against which men were expected to define themselves when cultivating a successfully polite and manly persona.

The fop

'The years of the Restoration', writes the theatre historian, J.L. Styan, 'scintillate with fops and beaux, coxcombs and gallants'. Indeed, much the same can be said for our period as a whole. Touring England in the early eighteenth century, Henri de Valbourg Misson recalled how 'the playhouses, chocolate-houses, and parks in spring, perfectly swarm with them', while the *Sentimental Magazine* later described how in London the macaronis (foppish men of fashion prominent in the late 1760s and 1770s) 'had generated so much . . . that they form at present no inconsiderable Group in most of the public Circles about Town'.[45] Nor were fops simply a feature of metropolitan society. Fashionable spa towns such as Tunbridge Wells attracted 'a Medley of all sorts', including 'Fops majestick and diminutive'.[46] The polite resort of Bath, claimed Ned Ward, outdid fashionable London for '*Fops* [and] *Beaus* . . . and consists of greater variety of Persons, Remarkable for some Vice or Folly'.[47] According to the *Tatler*, even 'the ancient Simplicity in Dress and Manners' of Scotland was threatened, there being 'in the good Town of *Edinburgh*, Beaus, Fops and Coxcombs'.[48] A popular subject for Restoration playwrights, the fop character, as these examples indicate, also featured prominently in the work of later dramatists and satirical pamphleteers as well as of contributors to new literary genres – the essay periodical, the magazine, the novel – and, from the mid-eighteenth century, new visual media, notably the caricature print.[49]

Foppish historiography

Research on representations of fops has to date produced two lines of argument. Scholars of late-seventeenth-century drama have charted the rise of the type as a staple of comedy theatre in roles such as Sir Fopling Flutter in George Etherege's *The Man of Mode* (1676); the eponymous Sir Courtly Nice of John Crowne's 1685 play; Sir Novelty Fashion in Colley Cibber's *Love's Last Shift* (1696); and, perhaps best known, Lord Foppington, who featured in John Vanbrugh's *The Relapse* (1702) and Cibber's *The Careless Husband* (1704). Between Etherege's Sir Fopling Flutter and Cibber's portrayal of Foppington, the theatre historian Lois Potter identifies a shift in authors' and audience's attitudes to the stage fop, from hostility to gentle sarcasm. Potter explains this development in terms of actor/dramatist Colley Cibber's attempts to popularise his own roles and, more generally, as a consequence of the increasingly benevolent and genteel tone of late-seventeenth- and eighteenth-century comedy theatre. Taking up this second point, Susan Staves suggests that changes in theatrical representations of fops were part of 'deeper shifts in attitudes about what ideal masculine behavior should be' with the result that, by the mid-eighteenth century, fops' refinements were viewed as 'characteristic of new sex-role ideals for men' favoured by sentimental commentators promoting more family-friendly styles of manliness.[50]

The second picture of the fop could not in some ways be more different from that of the benign comic hero or the sensitive man about the house.

For Michael Kimmel, early-eighteenth-century representations of the fop symbolised a 'crisis of masculinity' which many contemporary social observers attributed to an apparent increase in female independence within a pluralistic urban society. Randolph Trumbach also sees the development of London, and changing gender relations there, as a factor in the early-eighteenth-century emergence of a city-based male homosexual subculture, populated by the often transvestite 'molly' type, exclusively interested in sex with other men. Trumbach argues that the concomitant reappraisal of what it meant to be effeminate or manly (here defined in terms of sexual preference and actions) was such that the 'effeminate' Restoration fop was subsumed by this new equation of effeminacy with sodomy. In contrast to the later-seventeenth-century type, deemed unmanly on account of his elaborate clothing and exquisite manners, 'after 1720 the fop's effeminacy . . . came to be identified with the effeminacy of the then emerging . . . exclusive adult sodomite – known in the ordinary language of his day as a *molly*'. For Trumbach, the resulting association demanded that heterosexual men eschew 'elaborate clothes and enthusiastic forms of greeting' which retained the stigma of foppery and effeminacy, but now also left men vulnerable to accusations of being sodomitical mollies.[51]

That modern scholars have located fops within a variety of styles of normative as well as deviant manhood suggests the mutability of a character cited in a range of literary and visual genres for a variety of purposes. However, inconsistencies and variations in definition do not prevent us from sketching some of the essential characteristics, as well as some of the more significant variations, among late-seventeenth- and eighteenth-century representations of the fop; nor from analysing changes in discussions of the type, and suggesting its principal function within debates over the implications of an emerging polite society.

From this examination we can see the need to rethink the image of the fop as presented in recent scholarship. Thus, while it is certainly true that the eighteenth-century fop did feature as the subject of gentle satire, the often bitter attacks on, say, the macaronis during the 1770s suggest that attitudes did not necessarily soften with the rise of a sentimental literary tradition. Likewise, the enduring utility of the fop as a commentary on standards of manhood suggests that the type should not be treated as a response to a specific 'crisis' but to an on-going debate over the fortunes of manliness in polite society. Finally, while certain representations did equate foppery and male homosexuality, it was more common for fops' effeminacy to be explained in terms of social, not sexual, inadequacies and misdemeanours. Foolish, vain and immoderate, the fop like his early modern forerunners provided male readers or theatre-goers with lessons in how to conduct themselves in line with the traditional manly values of sense, self-control and independence. At the same time, by locating the type within the public arenas of eighteenth-century polite society, satirists and conduct writers also deployed the fop as a means to push men towards more manly forms of refinement.

From fools to men of fashion

Derived from the Latin *fatuus*, the term 'fop' – traced in *OED* to the mid-fifteenth century – was used then and during the next two centuries as an alternative, critical label for a fool. In this 'old broad sense', as Robert Heilman shows, 'fop' was commonly applied to rough country gentlemen who were critical of the more refined manners of the courtier.[52] By the third quarter of the seventeenth century this well-established association was giving way, largely through the efforts of Restoration dramatists, to a more precise type of foolishness specifically characterised by a preoccupation with fashionable dress and conduct.

As a result of this development, late-seventeenth-century descriptions of the type took on some of the personality traits previously associated with Tudor and Jacobean characters, including 'gulls' and 'gallants'. Ostentatious, self-indulgent, exhibitionist, flamboyant, elitist and would-be urbane, the early-seventeenth-century gallant was in many ways the forerunner of the fop. Classic accounts such as Thomas Dekker's spoof conduct guide, *The Guls Horne-book* (1609), depicted gulls or gallants as extravagant men of fashion – sporting silk stockings, broad garters, long hair and feathered hats – and as men of display, promenading slowly and conspicuously in London's fashionable venues, including the playhouse and the aisles of St Paul's Cathedral. Samuel Butler's mid-seventeenth-century 'modish man' or 'orthodox gallant' was likewise keen to see and be seen, 'not varying in the least article of his life, conversation, apparel and address from the doctrine and discipline of the newest and best reformed modes of the time'.[53] Both Dekker's and Butler's depictions also contained a number of similarities to Clement Ellis's 1660 'Silly *Gloworme*' of a gallant 'so tricked up in *Gauderies*' and '*studied* imitation of all the *vanities* Imaginable'.[54]

By the 1670s, references to the gallant were being superseded by discussions of the fop. In rewriting Dekker's guide, Samuel Vincent described his work as a study of the 'behaviour and Character of a Fop'. A rival account, *The Character of the Town Gallant* (1675), likewise defined its subject as an ignorant, vain, proud and debauched man best conceived as 'a silly Huffing thing three parts Fop and the rest Hector'.[55] The following year saw the first public appearance of George Etherege's celebrated stage fop, Sir Fopling Flutter, who appropriated the gallant's mantle of man of fashion. First referred to in a description of his appearance, on stage Sir Fopling is teased for his 'very fine' dress of tasselled pantaloons, tight coat and heavily fringed gloves scented with orange water. The ridicule is completed by his reaction. Misinterpreting these jibes as flattery, Sir Fopling plays down his 'slight suit' while boasting of the modishness of his French fashions.[56] This shift in the fop character from fool to foolish man of fashion is further evident in later dictionary definitions which, throughout the eighteenth century, rooted the fop's idiocy in a preoccupation with the finer points of his own and others' (especially women's) dress. The fop was, as Thomas Dyche put it in 1735, 'a whimsical empty fellow, one whose mind is totally taken up with modes and fashions'.[57] Samuel Johnson later thought the fop 'a man of small understanding and much ostentation', while the *Dictionary of Love* (1795) referred to him as passing 'most of his time in ogling himself in a glass; primming his figure, and caressing his curls and toupee'.[58]

Few eighteenth-century descriptions of the fop type passed up an opportunity to mock and marvel at the results of this preoccupation. In fact, fops' dress typically differed little from the three-piece suit – waistcoat, breeches and frock coat – periwig (or later bag wig) and tricorn hat favoured by gentlemen for at least the first three quarters of the century. Where fops stood out was in the colourfulness, quality and, in some cases, the sheer scale of their clothing. Yellow pantaloons, red silk stockings, coats tied with multi-coloured streamers or, from the 1770s, fastened with large polished metal buttons, and shoes with high yellow or more typically red heels were regular features in representations of the fop type from John Evelyn's 1661 satire on modern fashion, *Tyrannus,* to the macaronis' excess over a century later.[59] Not only lurid, fops' dress was also noteworthy for its combination of delicate fabrics. Rejecting the domestic woollens and linens deemed both materially and metaphorically coarse, fops chose a costume of imported Belgian lace or French embroidery and velvet, typically finished off with a pair of soft chicken or dog-skin gloves.

Finally, while regularly depicted in slim, flattering clothes, when it came to wigs the fop favoured a voluminous, even monumental style. A required element of middling- and upper-class male dress at least until the final quarter of the eighteenth century, wig-wearing – while viewed, as Marcia Pointon suggests, as 'vanity or fashionable aspiration for a woman' – remained for men a symbol of 'masculine authority', connoting formality, prosperity, professional standing and social status.[60] However, through what was deemed an excessive interest in the spectacle of their hair-piece, fops undermined the wig's symbolic effect, reducing it to a marker of vanity, irresponsibility and indolence. Indeed, as understood by Vanbrugh's Lord Foppington, the wig tended more to obscure than confirm male identity. Foppington's new wig, 'so long and so full of hair, it will serve for hat and cloak in all

Figure 4.1   J. Bretherton after Henry Bunbury: The St James's Macaroni (1772). © Copyright the British Museum.

weathers', was initially rejected as too small: a 'full periwig' must, he declared, 'be like a mask to a woman, nothing should be seen but [the] eyes'.[61] From the 1720s, the periwig's replacement by the smaller, cap-like 'bag wig' with side curls and short tail brought a decline in images of fops hidden from view by masses of false hair. Rather, in later depictions, notably of the 1770s macaroni type, fops' flamboyance was shown by the fashion for extending the wig's foretop to a tower of between two and five pounds of false hair, and elongating a thick 'club' or 'queue' hanging between the shoulders. Such was the wig's weight that George Stevens, satirist of modern coiffure, announced the invention of 'self-moving machines' to carry the bulk and 'lighten the heads of our modern fine gentlemen'.[62]

Whatever the wearer's claims to novelty, it is clear that many of the new fashions were in fact developments of those favoured in earlier representations of deviant manhood. The macaronis' taste for impractically high wigs, for example, might be seen as a throwback to the mid-seventeenth-century gallant fashion for tall, conical 'sugar-loafe-like Hats'. Similarly, gallants' habit of wearing brightly coloured 'ribband bushes' from their cod-pieces suggests parallels with Evelyn's slightly later Westminster fop and his descendants.[63] However, as this last example indicates, there remained one significant characteristic differentiating representations of modish fops from those of the fashionable gallant. In discussions of the gallant, an interest in appearance might be ridiculed as a sign of pride, selfishness or foolish naivety, but it was seldom thought to undermine the wearer's claim to manliness in the way that it did for the fop. Indeed, calls by Thomas Dekker for gentlemen to affect a slovenly garb, or to wear fashions that drew attention to the cod-piece and the genitals, were clear attempts to inflate the gallant's reputation as an (albeit ridiculous) swaggering, emancipated and sexually rapacious male. Clement Ellis's account was typical in attributing gallants' irresponsibility and profanity directly to their desire for an overtly manly persona: 'Divinity and morality are supposed [too] much to *mollifie* and *emasculate* the brave soule of a *Young Gentleman* . . . To instruct him how *hereafter* he should manfully resist his Enemies, he shall first be taught to fight against *God* and *Goodnesse*.'[64]

The predominant image of late-seventeenth- and eighteenth-century fops, by contrast, was of figures whose fascination in dress undermined manliness, resulting in the very effeminacy gallants dressed up (or down) to avoid. George Etherege's *Man of Mode* provides us with an instance of this divergence between the gallant and fop type in its comparison of the characters of the libertine Dorimant and the supine Sir Fopling Flutter. At first sight, both characters appear to share important traits. Like Flutter, Dorimant is concerned about his appearance (as he tells his valet, 'I love to be well dressed sir, and think it no scandal to my understanding'). Like

Dorimant, Sir Fopling expects his modish taste to impress the opposite sex, and vows 'to have a gallantry with some of our English ladies'. However, Dorimant and his rakish colleagues remain unconvinced by what they regarded as hollow claims and desires, ridiculing Sir Fopling for thinking himself 'the pattern of gallantry' when simply 'the pattern of modern foppery'.[65] What divided the traditional gallant from the new-style fop was less dress *per se* than issues of style and the consequences of this preoccupation. Thus, the gallant was prepared to be seen in states of undress, used clothing to impress and seduce women, and, despite being eager to look modish, rarely entered into detailed discussions about the quality of particular fabrics. Fops, on the other hand, seldom appeared except in full dress, and, while occasionally boasting of their sexual attraction to women, were typically less interested in courtship than gossip. Moreover, fops were especially eloquent when discussing the minutiae of male and female fashions, and actively engaged in the 'feminine' accessories of dress: tellingly, while Sir Fopling bases his chances of gallantry on his wearing orange-scented gloves, Dorimant rejects the offer of perfume from his valet in order to 'smell as I do today', it being 'no offence to the ladies' noses'.[66]

Sexuality and gender identity

Representations of fops had clear implications for discussions of gender identity. Due to their interest in dress, fops were frequently depicted as having adopted a distinctly feminine persona. What was commonly regarded as women's natural predilection for vanity was deemed unacceptable among men. What 'makes a *Woman* elegant', wrote one critic of modern gender relations in the 1730s, 'makes a *Man* deformed; as the dress and ornaments which add grace and dignity to her beauty, but serve to make him a sinical, pragmatic, enervate coxcomb'.[67] Deformed and enervated, fops' participation in female rituals of self-presentation invariably resulted in an identification with effeminacy. It is this association which has led historians like Randolph Trumbach, equating effeminacy with sodomy, to suggest that early-eighteenth-century representations of the type became part of a debate by which normative and deviant standards of manliness were principally determined with reference to male sexual activity. There is something to be said for this thesis. Variations in definitions of terms such as 'fop', 'beau' and 'coxcomb' made for differences in the characteristics and applications of these types as described by individual authors. Thus, accounts did occasionally describe fops participating in sodomitical acts. Mary Evelyn's late-seventeenth-century satire referred to fops' habit of kissing when greeting other men. Her reference to James I and Robert Villiers, first duke of

Buckingham, popularly identified by eighteenth-century commentators as favouring same-sex over 'heterosexual' relationships, suggests Evelyn understood kissing as a prelude to sexual intimacy:

The world is chang'd I know not how,
For Men kiss Men, not Women now.
A most unmanly nasty Trick
One Man to lick the other's Cheek;
And only what renews the shame
Of J. the first, and Buckingham:
For who that loves as Nature teaches,
That had not rather kiss the Breeches
Of Twenty Women, than to lick
The Bristles of one Male dear Dick?[68]

Instances of fops as sodomites crop up in discussions of the type throughout our period. Ned Ward, in his early-eighteenth-century essay on Sir Narcissus Foplin, made a similar point to Evelyn, though his Grub Street style made for a blunter approach. Having 'so cool a Sense of female Favours', Sir Narcissus spurned the 'Charms of a Petticoat . . . for the loathsome Condescensions of a fricatizing *Catamite*, who is beast enough to ease his *Sodomitical Desires*'. Later discussions of the 1770s macaroni type posited a similar connection between their emergence and 'the frequency of a crime which modesty forbids me to name', it being regrettable, claimed the *Public Ledger* newspaper, that the 'vengeance of heaven' could not destroy 'every Macaroni Sodomite's erectness of stature'.[69]

However, that fops were occasionally accused of sodomy does not substantiate the claim that the eighteenth century witnessed the collapse of the character into a sexually defined molly type. The target of Mary Evelyn's scorn was no clandestine transvestite, but a man of fashion dedicated to cultivating a reputation for extravagant dress and refined manners; similarly, Ward's Sir Narcissus was a man who dressed in 'Finery', sporting a wig 'curl'd into the newest fashion'. The popular image of macaronis during the late 1760s and 1770s was likewise not of a secretive, but a conspicuously self-promoting, society of would-be men of fashion. A more prudent approach is to treat these and other cases as indications of a complex picture, where eighteenth-century representations of the sodomite continued to take a variety of forms, one of which was the earlier image of the homosexual male as well-dressed libertine, not transvestite molly.[70]

It was far more common for discussions of fops' sexuality to focus on their relations with female, not male, company. At first it might appear that fops would have made good partners for women. It was common for stage and literary presentations of the type to be forever declaring their love for unfortunate and unresponsive females, showered with a torrent of *billets doux*. Statements of affection may have been wearying but they had much to recommend them when compared with the carnal and deceitful wo-manising of the gallant who, addicted to the 'most delicious Recreation of *Whoring*', played 'with Women as he does Cards'.[71] By contrast fops' affection-ate courtship was, we might assume, both pleasing and reassuring; as one mid-eighteenth-century magazine put it, 'no woman ever owed her ruin to a Macaroni', a virtue expressed, as Susan Staves suggests, in increasingly sympathetic theatrical portrayals of the fop as domestic hero.[72]

Whatever the possible developments on the stage, the predominant image in other forms of literary satire was of fops as ineffectual lovers, with humour or criticism frequently derived from the contrast between elab-orate declarations of affection and their bathetic conclusion. Commentators provided various reasons why fops were reluctant to carry through their promises. Some, while willing, clearly did not have the capacity to pursue a physical relationship; the *Westminster Magazine* believed fops lacked 'the strength of manhood to do those rites which they would wish to be thought pursuers of'; 'smooth-chinned, hair-brain'd Maccaronies' were similarly said to want 'the vigour to experience the joys of womankind'.[73] Foolish women who married such figures soon became frustrated and were forced to cuckold their husband in the search for sexual gratification:

> The wishing Bride, instead of Rapture finds
> Enervate Bodies, unimpassion'd Minds;
> Ye tinsel'd Beaux, who flutter, lie and boast
> As flimsy Silk is known to rustle most.[74]

John Courtenay's identification of fops as men with 'unimpassion'd Minds' provided satirists with a second explanation for their dismal showing. It was a common accusation that fops were not aroused by the opposite sex because of an infatuation with themselves. Women served merely to confirm vain men of fashion in their own high self-regard. Some fops courted women because it was thought modish to have a mistress, while others boasted that women who merely glanced in their direction were instantly captivated by irresistible charms and an elegant appearance.

In these instances, fops presented the semblance of heterosexual desire, albeit for motives other than sexual congress. More typical, however, were those who pursued women's company because of their preference for female recreations. The lure of feminine society began early. Accounts of fops' upbringing typically highlighted the domineering presence of parents, and especially mothers, who either through over-protectiveness or snobbery demanded that their sons be educated at home. Denied the boisterous and intellectual school community necessary to develop a healthy physique and a rational mind, these young men gained only a knowledge of trivial subjects like household management.

Such had been the fate of Florentus, a fictional contributor to Samuel Johnson's mid-century *Rambler* periodical, and the subject of Johnson's essay on 'The education of a fop'. An only son, Florentus had received a cosseted upbringing and was prevented from attending school – an unrefined place where boys could not 'sit at the table without some awkward uneasiness' – in favour of a fawning domestic tutor. Aged twelve, he had learned how to pick up a fan and receive a tea-cup; at fourteen, how to talk knowledgeably about French fashions and, at fifteen, how to perform at the assembly room. The result had left Florentus suited only to female society and his days had been spent dressing for, talking with and visiting women eager to be associated with such an ostensibly refined individual. Plans to break into male society had ended in failure and he now found himself the butt of coffee-house humour, 'hunted from all masculine conversation' with only a few 'grave ladies' for company.[75]

In many ways the epitome of the type, Florentus proved something of an exception in his bid to break free of female society. Other foppish characters made no such attempt; Maiden in Thomas Baker's play *Tunbridge-Walks* (1703) declared that he 'cou'd never abide the Boys' at school and had as an adult no time for 'lewd Rakes' at the tavern. For him, as for others, female society proved far superior: 'I lov'd mightily to play with the Girls, and dress Babies', and sought only to 'Rattle with the Ladies, Dance with them, and Walk with 'em in publick'. Far from being embarrassed by their interests, fops boasted of their skills in perukery, wax-works or tea-table chat, even like Maiden 'vying with them [women] in their Accomplishments'.[76] Through such depictions sober male readers were presented with both the unseemliness of unregulated integration into female society – 'the Dregs of our Sex' was how one mid-century critic described those who preferred female to male company – and its challenge to men's gender identity, reducing them to 'lap-dogs', 'danglers', 'pet monkeys' and 'pretty dolls'.[77] The popular image of fops mixing with female company serves to further distance the type from the effeminate, often misogynistic molly defined by an active same-sex sexuality. This is not to suggest that fops' effeminate status bore no relation to their sexual orientation, rather that as sexual non-performers theirs was a loss of manhood more often attributed to asexuality than 'homosexual' activity.

It is important to note that commentators categorised fops' deficiencies in ways other than sexual behaviour. In the majority of what we might term 'respectable' eighteenth-century conduct books, periodicals and magazines, the prevailing image was of fops as social deviants ridiculed for unbecoming conduct in an emerging network of polite public spaces. A number of social faults – foolishness, vanity, immoderate self-indulgence and exhibitionism – were, as we have seen, traits common to the earlier gallant type. Continuing denunciations of these characteristics within depictions of the new fop type suggest the durability of more desirable qualities, such as self-regulation and intelligence, to ideals of manhood throughout the early modern period and beyond.

Men of fashion to men of excess refinement

The success of the fop character also owed much to its flexibility and adaptability as a social type. Late-seventeenth- and eighteenth-century representations combined a discussion of traditional features of failed manhood with an exposition of new social habits pertinent to a theatre-going or reading public for whom the type served as a specific commentary on aspects of men's conduct in a modern, predominantly city-based, polite society. Up to a point, these shifts were less reflections of new notions of social error than of changes in a built environment undergoing significant development during a 'renaissance' of metropolitan and provincial urban culture. Thus, foppish vanity and exhibitionism were now located at, in addition to the traditional sites of cathedral aisle or playhouse, the coffee-house, park, promenade, assembly room and, from the 1730s, the pleasure garden. Parallels existed between the censure of conduct in old and new locations. Thomas Dekker's deliberate and showy St Paul's gallant anticipated those in a 1770s spoof guide in which macaronis were encouraged, when in the pleasure garden, to walk 'stately and slow . . . turning your face to your company with a smile [and] all the time . . . twisting your cane'.[78] The theatre-going gallants' habit of parading on stage was likewise imitated by fops aware that this provided 'the best place to shew a handsome person in an elegant suit of clothes'.[79] Such displays, made easier by the provision of stage seating in early-eighteenth-century theatres, allowed characters like the *Spectator*'s 'sort of beau' both to flaunt himself before a performance of Beaumont and Fletcher's play *Philaster* and then to appear on set 'frequently in the Prince's Apartment . . . and the Hunting Match' in Act 4, and 'very Forward at the Rebellion' in Act 5.[80]

As we saw in Chapter One, promoters identified polite venues as arenas in which male and female visitors were expected to behave with a heightened sense of refinement unknown to their forebears or less civilised peers. Yet involvement in these arenas – often a new experience indicative of improved social standing – was also potentially treacherous: the importance attached to men's good dress, to self-display, to seeing and being seen were the stigmatised preoccupations both of gallants and fops. It had been a function of the vain, boisterous, and sexually predatory gallant to demonstrate some of the undesirable characteristics of public behaviour to an early-seventeenth-century readership. By the century's close, a preoccupation with politeness required that the fop type also offer a more eloquent commentary on issues of refinement. In addition to demonstrating traditional challenges to manhood, such as vanity and immodesty, depictions of fops, provided information on the distinction between men of admirable refinement and those guilty of ceremony, affectation and excessive social polish.

Fops' failures were in precisely those areas elsewhere deemed essential for the polite gentleman. In conversation – for many the keystone of polite sociability – fops were found wanting in terms of both subject matter and vocabulary. In part harking back to traditional associations of foppery and foolishness, eighteenth-century satirists made much of fops' misdirected education in fashionable arts or domestic economy. Various depictions characterised the type as interested in creating only an impression of learning. Vanbrugh's Lord Foppington, for example, boasted a large collection of books and considered it 'the most entertaining thing in the world to walk and look upon 'em', though he confessed they remained unread.[81] This did not prevent Foppington and others from holding forth on a variety of subjects. Opinionated and self-absorbed, the archetypal fop was often ridiculed for pedantry, a cardinal error in new models of easy and polite sociability, and one also associated, as we saw in Chapter Two, with the anti-social scholar. Other literary representations saw fops using venues like the coffee-house for self-display, not learned and reciprocal debate. An early-eighteenth-century 'gaudy crowd of fellows' who made up the 'fluttering assembly of snuffing peripatetics' at Man's coffee-house in London anticipated later figures like Frank Fopling who, at a similar venue in St James's, 'flutters up and down . . . and while he is adjusting his hair, takes occasion to contemplate his legs, and the symmetry of his breeches'.[82] Worse still was fops' habit of interrupting serious exchanges to express their own thoughts on trivial or offensive subjects such as fashion or society intrigue. These interjections, delivered in characteristically affected speech patterns – Foppington's 'bax' for 'box', for example, or the clipping of words to monosyllables – reduced fops' conversation from the centre-piece of polite manliness to the 'chattering', 'gossiping' and 'prattling' typically expected of intemperate female company.[83] The daintiness which characterised much foppish speech was also evident in descriptions of their public perambulations. In contrast to the swaggering gallant, fops were identifiable by what the *Tatler* described as a 'Trip in their Gate' or the dramatist John Gay as their 'nicest Tread'. Gay's fop received further censure, for in avoiding the

Figure 4.2   A fop with the 'nicest tread': detail from Plate II (Noon) of William Hogarth, *The Four Times of the Day* (1738). © Copyright the British Museum.

curb and the street (in order to protect his clothes from dirt), he contravened the polite practice of 'giving the wall' to women and male superiors.[84]

Fops were also self-deluded in seeing themselves as the arbiters, not the destroyers, of politeness: the 'refined Youths of this *cultivated Age*' at the fore-front of attempts to 'polish the *British* Manners', as the satirist Nathaniel

Lancaster mocked the 'pretty gentlemen' of 1749.[85] Lancaster's ironic tone would have been evident to readers aware of the strong connection between continental, and especially French, culture and foppish misconceptions of the polite male. This association, which emerged forcefully in depictions of the Restoration type, became a key feature in the development of a specifically new social fop, distinct from the gallant in terms of his continentalism and, significantly, the further reputation for effeminacy that such interests brought. Lancaster's claim that fops were little more than 'Sons of Delicacy' was readily substantiated by critics who repeatedly equated the fashionable, invariably imported, modes of refinement with physical and mental enervation.

Such connections are seen particularly clearly in discussions of foppish diet and lifestyle. As was typical of many satirists, Lancaster offered a variation on 'you are what you eat' to explain fops' preference for dainty, exotic foods and the subsequent deleterious effects of diet on physiology and personality. As 'Old *English* Roast-Beef is indeed properly adapted to *English* Manners' so 'at the Table of a *Pretty Gentleman*, you never see the Flesh of a full-blown Animal. Chickens of a Week old, Veal Sweet-breads, or a leg of Lamb . . . are highest Indulgence'.[86] When it came to drink, fops invariably substituted the tavern, one of gallants' favourite haunts, for the tea-table (visits to the coffee-house being usually for display, not consumption). Alcohol was rejected as damaging to the complexion and was often replaced with green tea or, in the case of macaronis, with milk, 'the finest thing for the constitution' of these self-professed 'delicate beings'.[87] Taverns were also avoided on account of their clientele, being popularly identified as locations of potential boorishness. Such venues, along with coffee-houses, presented the additional danger of smoking, the fop being 'no great Friend of the Tabacconist, for Fear of his Lungs'.[88] To contemporaries, these sensitivities were suggestive less of a quest for good health than of physical weakness and over-susceptibility to illness. Given the link between ill-health and delicacy, and delicacy and social refinement, fops were also regularly depicted playing up their symptoms: '*Effeminate* Fops . . . drink Milk and Water . . . and in a Counter-tenor Voice, complain of *Vapours* and the *Spleen*' was how *The Female Tatler*'s editor, Mrs Crackenthorpe, put it in 1709. Later representations of men similarly afflicted with nervous illness featured in commentaries on the effects of unregulated sensibility. Thus, when ridiculed for their tastes, the milk-drinking macaronis labelled their critic a 'barbarian' antithetical to 'such delicate beings . . . whose fine feelings are sensible of the slightest pressures'.[89] Not all late-century fops were cast as followers of the new fashion for feeling, however. Illustrating the complex relationship between politeness and sensibility, men of fashion were depicted either, like the milk-drinkers, as slavish followers of the latest sentimental trends, or as critics who dismissed feeling as inferior to the decorous and elegant styles required for polite behaviour. In the opinion of many sentimental conduct writers, fops took on the persona not of immoderate men of feeling but of aloof critics and cool Chesterfieldian corrupters. Young men beware, warned the sermon writer James Fordyce at the tail-end of the macaroni phenomenon, of 'fops of an Italian appellation' with a 'courtly simper' and an 'unfeeling heart'.[90]

The function of foppery

James Fordyce's warning implies two assumptions: namely, that macaronis were a real-life feature of modern urban society whom unsuspecting readers might encounter and, second, that these Italianate fops were recognisable from other men. But what did other correspondents, satirists and conduct writers have in mind when they commented on the macaronis? Writing in 1764, Horace Walpole understood the term to relate to the 'travelled young men who wear long curls and spying glasses' recently returned from the Italian stage of the grand tour. Several years on, they reappeared as the last remaining summer residents in fashionable London: 'there is scarce a soul', he wrote to Viscount Nuneham in 1773, 'but Maccaronies lolling out of windows at Almack's like carpets to be dusted'. James Boswell meanwhile identified one of their number away from its natural city habitat. Fearing that Samuel Johnson was losing his resolve to continue their tour of the Scottish Highlands, Boswell chided his companion: 'I said, "Why, sir, you seemed to me to despond yesterday. You are a delicate Londoner; you are a maccaroni; you cannot ride."'[91]

While employing the same terminology, it is evident that Fordyce, Walpole and Boswell each understood and applied the 'macaroni' label in distinctive ways. Walpole's initial letter to Lord Hertford, for example, described a select body of Italophile gentlemen who made up the members of the self-styled Macaroni Club established off St James's Square in London. In his second description the macaronis appear as a less specific yet still fashionable collection of club-based city dwellers. It is this application that comes close to Boswell's labelling of Johnson. In this instance 'macaroni' serves as a form of gentle satire encapsulating a series of undesirable characteristics – here excess urbanity and effeteness – by which Boswell sought to goad Johnson into action. Fordyce, by contrast, while ridiculing the individual macaroni, applied the term more generally and more seriously as a label for a faceless, but apparently very real, breed of social miscreants.

Across each of these examples it is possible to trace an evolution in the type's definition and application, individual references being consonant with the meaning then most commonly in use. During the course of the late 1760s and 1770s the 'macaroni' label shifted from an association with real-life individuals to a descriptor for a character embodying a range of behaviours – some of which Walpole and Boswell claimed to detect in actual people, and which Fordyce saw as common to a more nebulous though still distinguishable group. The story of this development was also one of redefinition. By the early 1770s, with the macaroni phenomenon at its height, the term signified a social type drawn from diverse social backgrounds, and characterised by vanity, affectation and unregulated refinement. The shift saw the macaroni, a period-specific character, subsumed within the well-established eighteenth-century fop type, albeit as a manifestation of this generic character modelled and labelled in tune with the culture and fashion of the time. Later definitions bear out this shift. According to an edition of Nathan Bailey's dictionary, the macaroni was 'a fop, a fribble, one who dresses fantastically', while Walpole, writing in 1779, thought him 'synonimous to the *Beau, Fop* [and] *Coxcomb*'.[92]

Recent interest in the history of stereotyping has highlighted the place of this mechanism in the formation of social attitudes in early modern society. Studies continue to draw on the American journalist Walter Lippmann's pioneering work. Lippmann defined the stereotype as a constructed, typically deviant, personality whose characteristics reveal much about the prejudices and anxieties of those, however categorised, who develop and disseminate the type. Well-known stereotypes create what Lippmann describes as a 'quasi-environment' requiring observers to judge individuals less according to the reality of their situation than in terms 'which our culture has already defined for us'.[93] In this capacity, categorisations fulfil the function of what Michael Echeruo calls an 'exo-cultural stereotype'; that is, a personality used to represent an alien 'other', usually taking the form of members of a foreign country, with which the labellers claim to experience no shared identity. Echeruo illustrates the function of this particular stereotypical form with reference to the depiction of a theatrical figure whose presence unites an audience for whom 'it is impossible . . . to see the character as other than an example of some other group'. The regularity with which late-seventeenth- and eighteenth-century theatre-goers (as well as readers of satire or scrutinisers of prints) were presented with images of French men as innately foppish, for example, provides an instance of the 'exo-cultural stereotype' in action. But representations of fops involved, as we have seen, something more complex than a simple association with a clearly demarcated 'other'. A recurrent theme in eighteenth-century discussions of the type was a concern that, once an identity reserved for French or elite Francophiles or later Italophiles, fops had become or were becoming native to all ranks of domestic society. Returning to Echeruo's theatrical model, fops now took on the role of a 'cultural stereotype' equally effective for commenting on the behaviour of the audience as on that of those excluded from its number.[94]

In speaking of the use of fops as mechanisms for self and social scrutiny we need to be careful not to suggest an overly deterministic model in which all presentations of the type are seen conforming to a set agenda proposed by a like-minded group of authors or later caricaturists. Yet while being cautious to avoid overly sweeping statements, it appears reasonable to consider the type's effectiveness in terms of its contribution to the on-going debate concerning the consequences and implications for men of the emergence of polite society.

To appreciate this contribution requires us to acknowledge the growing sophistication of an early modern genre of character literature by which fops' traits were made known. Typically taking the form of a free-standing verse or prose essay, the character sketches of mid-seventeenth-century writers like Samuel Butler provided a rounded picture of a discrete personality whose attributes were set out in a list of his or her opinions and behavioural idiosyncrasies.

The continued popularity of the character genre should not obscure important changes, notably prompted by the late-seventeenth-century French author La Bruyère, whose overtly literary style placed each personality within a discursive account of contemporary society. Aspects of both traditions are evident in numerous eighteenth-century character guides. Abel Boyer's 1702 essay on 'A Beau', for example, provided a detailed description of Sir John Foppington's daily routine through which readers learned much about an individual fop's vanity, idleness and love of fashion and gossip. But by locating the fop in society, this new form of sketch provided additional insight into the characteristics of deviant manliness as well as the social pressures – Boyer's 'manners of the age' – that were thought to produce and sustain such a character. Its breadth of attributes made the fop type a useful literary device for general commentaries on a wide range of subjects including dress, fashion, urbanisation, gender relations, sexuality and changing codes of social behaviour. Fops provided social commentators with a type of sufficient sophistication and variety to function as a plausible 'cultural stereotype', whatever the complexity, aim or tone of a particular characterisation. By appreciating fops' ridiculousness, readers could show themselves to be aware of and superior to unacceptable forms of refined conduct which, if eloquently encapsulated by the stereotype, often proved more diffuse, ill-defined and even attractive in their experience of daily life.

To civic critics of modern living, fops provided in microcosm a powerful illustration of the effects of luxurious consumption and superficial socialising which, writ large, threatened the moral and physical integrity of a 'foppish' and effeminate nation. Polite theorists employed the type if not as a critique of socio-economic change *per se* then as an indicator of the perils of unregulated change. Within polite behavioural literature, the type functioned not to prevent but to facilitate the development of new standards of male conduct, by providing images of failed social refinement in reaction to which readers might come to appreciate more acceptable modes of conduct. Of course, not all eighteenth-century advice manuals referred to the fop, just as not all chose to discuss the relationship of refinement to gender identity. When they did, however, it was common for foppish errors to be juxtaposed with instructions on correct behaviour, more often distinguished in terms of intent and degree rather than content. As one conduct writer reminded would-be polite gentlemen, the 'well-bred man lies under the same obligations to cleanliness, Civility &c, that a Fop can well undertake to defend', the difference being 'that a Person of Breeding remits of Forms, when it is proper to be free; whereas a Fop is the same formal stiff Creature wherever he comes'.[95] The *Spectator* likewise considered a polite man as one 'endowed with the natural Bent to do acceptable things', while 'the Affectation of that Character is what constitutes a Fop'.[96] The ideal husband, advised a contemporary conduct book, was a 'Man of Manners . . . tho' by no means foppish'.[97] Later in the century, the dancing-master and author Matthew Towle bolstered his discussion on correct forms of male posture and deportment with a concurrent narrative on the errors of 'that inimitable Fop Mr Gaudy'. In contrast to the understated behaviour of the genuinely polite gentleman, Gaudy drew constant attention to himself by rubbing and admiring his hands, adjusting his shirt, playing with his wig and twirling his cane. That Gaudy's actions were not to be imitated was made clear in Towle's warning that 'even the Ladies are so ungenteel and ungrateful as to join in the laugh'.[98] In this instance the fop's errors were ones of appearance and manner. But, as the *Spectator*'s description suggests, the type also proved antithetical to a more complex concept of refined manliness in which external conduct was the product of an inner moral integrity closely related to a Christian ethic scorned by the spiritually void fop.[99]

This chapter has looked in detail at some of the prominent characteristics of late-seventeenth- and eighteenth-century representations of the fop. A striking feature of the type remains the unchanging nature of its salient personality traits. In his vanity, posturing and pursuit of things fashionable and trivial, the Restoration stage fop differed little from the macaroni a century on. To this list we might also add fops' enduring association with effeminacy, which derived in part from their abandonment of traditional male attributes such as moderation and reason, but also, and more topically, from their irresponsible and inadequate pursuit of refinement. That fops' excesses proved enervating, in a way that those of gallants did not, owed much to the particular requirements of eighteenth-century polite society which they observed to the point of absurdity: abstention from traditionally male recreations and locations; closer platonic integration into female company, and participation in a commercial market-place closely associated with the import of goods and manners from what many regarded as an inherently effeminate French nation.

Civic critics of social change traced fops' loss of manly status to their activities within a modern culture which left them physically and mentally weakened so as to be more like women or children than adult men. Those who challenged such appraisals were equally ready to gender this debate. As we have seen, their approach was not to deny the existence of effeminacy but to seek its redefinition from an absolute category to an extreme consequence of unregulated social change, the characteristics of which, at least in discussions of men's behaviour, were signalled by foppish practices. What unites both uses was the idea that fops' effeminacy resulted not from a conscious abandonment of claims to manly identity, but from the incorrect means by which such characters, in their various guises, sought to achieve manliness within polite society. Thus the comedy provided by eighteenth-century depictions of the type owed much to the juxtaposition between fops' pretensions to an enviable manly refinement and the conduct of ideal gentlemen, however defined. In part, therefore, fops' durability as a social stereotype indicates the enduring popularity of a joke which flattered those men able to solve the conundrum of being both polite *and* manly. Yet durability also suggests the persistence of a puzzle to which successive generations, tormented or stimulated by the vagaries of fashionable, modern living, saw themselves coming afresh. Just how three men handled this challenge is the subject of the next chapter.

Notes and references

1. Hume, 'Rise and progress of the arts and sciences' (1742), in *Essays*, pp. 130–3.

2. Locke, *Some Thoughts Concerning Education*, pp. 249–51.

3. *Ibid.*, p. 249.

4. *Spectator*, No. 209 (30 Oct 1711), II, p. 318.

5. Goldsmith, *Life of Nash*, in *Works*, III, p. 307.

6. Burke, 'The character of the fine gentleman' (nd), in T.O. McLoughlin and James T. Bolton eds., *The Early Writings*, in *Writings and Speeches*, I (1997), p. 63.

7. *Spectator*, No. 119, I, p. 487. See above, p. 62.

8. *World*, No. 42 (18 Oct 1753), I, pp. 255–6.

9. Locke, *Some Thoughts Concerning Education*, p. 160,

10. Chapone, 'On affectation and simplicity', in *Miscellanies*, p. 8.

11. Fordyce, *Addresses to Young Men*, I, pp. 329, 280.

12. Bryson, *From Courtesy to Civility*, pp. 218–21.

13. Cohen, 'Manliness, effeminacy and the French'; Newman, *Rise of English Nationalism*, pp. 68–84, 123–56.

14. Hayley, *Two Dialogues*, p. 172; Wollstonecraft, *Vindication of the Rights of Men*, in *Political Writings*, p. 6.

15. *Man*, No. 43 (22 Oct 1755), p. 2; Knox, 'Unmanliness of tears', in *Winter Evenings*, II, pp. 183–4.

16. Knox, 'On the inconsistency of affected sensibility' in *Winter Evenings*, II, p. 158.

17. 'On the superior value of solid accomplishment', in *Works*, II, pp. 199–202. Knox's dialogue finally sees Chesterfield acknowledge the error of his ways and the 'gracefulness of virtue, and the beauty of an open, sincere and manly character' (202).

18. *Westminster Magazine*, 5 (1777), pp. 22–3, 69.

19. Goldsmith, *An Enquiry into . . . Polite Learning*, in *Works*, I, p. 311.

20. Eliza Haywood, 'Effeminacy in the army censured', in *The Female Spectator*, (1744–6) ed. Gabrielle M. Firmager (1993), p. 30.

21. John Brown, *Estimate of the Manners and Principles of the Times*, 2 vols. (1757–8), II, p. 176, I, p. 101. For Brown see David Spadafora, *The Idea of Progress in Eighteenth-Century Britain* (New Haven CT and London, 1990).

22. *Ibid.*, p. 153.

23. John Dennis, 'An essay on the opera's after the Italian manner' (1706), in E.N. Hooker ed., *The Critical Works of John Dennis*, 2 vols. (Baltimore MD, 1939), I, p. 389.

24. Brown, *Estimate*, I, p. 101.

25. *Galateo: or a Treatise on Politeness*, pp. 45–8.

26. Hume, 'Of the delicacy of taste and passions', in *Essays*, pp. 3–4.

27. Knox, 'On extreme delicacy and sentiment' (1782), in *Works*, II, p. 186.

28. Charles Hanbury Williams, *The Real Character of the Age* (1759), p. 33; *Observations on the Theatre* (1759), p. 15.

29. Mandeville, *Fable of the Bees*, I, pp. 120–2.

30. Smith, *Theory of Moral Sentiments*, p. 205.

31. Hume, 'Of refinement in the arts and sciences' (1752), in *Essays*, p. 275.

32. Ferguson, *Essay on the History of Civil Society*, pp. 195, 237, 241.

33. Creech, *Letters*, p. 39; post-Humean responses to social change in Scotland, including that of Creech, are considered in John Dwyer and Alexander Murdoch, 'Manners, morals and the rise of Henry Dundas, 1774–1784' in Dwyer, Murdoch and Roger Mason eds., *New Perspectives on the Politics and Culture of Early Modern Scotland* (Edinburgh, 1982), esp. pp. 220–30. On the importance attached by the Mirror and Lounger Clubs to stoicism and traditional civic values enshrined in landownership, see Dwyer, *Virtuous Discourse*.

34. *The Tryal of Lady Allurea Luxury* (1757), p. 77.

35. John Aiken, *Letters from a Father to a Son*, 2 vols. (1793), I, p. 13.

36. Locke, *Some Thoughts Concerning Education*, p. 161. Locke listed poorly taught dancing as a principal source of ungraceful conduct, and later made known his preference for natural, if clumsy, manners over the 'apish, affected Postures' of one taught by an 'ill fashion'd Dancing-Master' (310).

37. Daniel Statt, 'The case of the Mohocks: rake violence in Augustan London', *Social History*, 20 (1995), pp. 179–99; on hectors and a late-seventeenth-century 'anti-civility' culture see Bryson, *From Courtesy to Civility*, p. 249.

38. Ned Ward, *The London Spy*, No. 2 (1703), ed. Paul Hyland (East Lansing, 1993), p. 37.

39. *An Epistle from Dick Poney, Esq . . . from his House in Dirty Lane, Westminster* (1742), p. 2.

40. Johnson, *Dictionary*.

41. On the gendering of Wilkes's politics see Kathleen Wilson, *The Sense of the People: Politics, Culture and Imperialism in England, 1715–1785* (Cambridge, 1995), pp. 219–23. The connection between anti-civility and freedom was common to many earlier male types, though employed for different purposes. Whereas Wilkes combined personal with political freedoms, the hectors of the Restoration court had used rule breaking to indicate their superiority over would-be refined city gentlemen. Bryson, *From Courtesy to Civility*, pp. 264–5.

42. *The Gentleman*, No. 2 (July 1775), in George Colman, *Prose on Several Occasions*, 3 vols. (1787), I, p. 172; *London Museum*, 4 (July 1771), p. 23.

43. Wilson, *Sense of the People*, pp. 234–5. Anna Clark also sees criticisms of Wilkes's dissolute and sexually aggressive manliness as a factor in explaining the move of property-owning radicals 'from libertinism toward the domesticity of middle-class patriarchy', *The Struggle for the Breeches. Gender and the Making of the British Working Class* (1995), p. 143.

44. John Caulfield, *Blackguardiana; or Dictionary of Rogues* (1795). For the use of 'black-guard' as a term of abuse within the radical community see Iain McCalman, *Radical Underworld. Prophets, Revolutionaries, and Pornographers in London 1795–1840* (Cambridge, 1988), ch. 2.

45. Henri Misson, *Memoirs in his Travels over England* (1719) quoted in J.L. Styan, *Restoration Comedy in Performance* (Cambridge, 1986), p. 70; *Sentimental Magazine*, 5 (1777), p. 281.

46. Thomas Baker, *Tunbridge-Walks; or, the Yeoman of Kent* (1703), I.i. p. 2.

47. Ned Ward, *A Step to the Bath* (1700), p. 14.

48. *Tatler* No. 144 (11 Mar 1710), II, p. 322.

49. Foppish characters in novels include Beau Didapper in Henry Fielding's *Joseph Andrews* (1742) and Mr Lovel in Fanny Burney's *Evelina* (1778). Macaronis' flamboyant appearance proved popular with many visual satirists whose work was sold individually or in collections such as Mary and Matthew Darly's *Caricatures, Macaronies and Characters* (1771–3).

50. Lois Potter, 'Colley Cibber: the fop as hero', in J.C. Hilton *et al.* eds., *Augustan Worlds* (Leicester, 1978), pp. 153–64; Susan Staves, 'A few kind words for the fop', *Studies in English Literature, 1500–1900*, 22 (1982), p. 428.

51. Michael S. Kimmel, 'From lord and master to cuckold and fop: masculinity in seventeenth-century England', *University of Dayton Review*, 18, 2 (1986/7), pp. 93–109; Trumbach, 'Birth of the queen', p. 134.

52. Robert B. Heilman, 'Some fops and versions of foppery', *English Literary History*, 49 (1982), pp. 363–95. Heilman highlights the diversity of meanings attached to 'fop' and 'foppery' even in the late seventeenth century: lecherous men, failed lovers, idiots, rustics, roués, ceremonious town-dwellers and Whigs (by Tories), to name but a few.

53. Thomas Dekker, *The Guls Horne-book* (1609), ed. R.B. McKerrow (New York, 1971), pp. 27–39, Samuel Butler, *Characters* (nd), ed. A.R. Walker (Cambridge, 1908), p. 240.

54. Ellis, *Gentile Sinner*, pp. 16, 28.

55. Samuel Vincent, *The Young Gallant's Academy* (1674), v; *The Character of a Town-Gallant* (1675), p. 2.

56. George Etherege, *The Man of Mode; or, Sir Fopling Flutter* (1676) ed. Gamini Salgado (1986), I.i. p. 59; III.ii. p. 89.

57. Thomas Dyche, *A New General English Dictionary* (1735).

58. Johnson, *Dictionary*; *The Dictionary of Love* (1795), p. 55.

59. Evelyn's gallant 'dress't like a May-Pole . . . and the Colours were Red, Orange, and Blew [*sic*] of well gum's Sattin', *Tyrannus; or the MODE* (1661)

in Guy de la Bédoyère ed., *The Writings of John Evelyn* (Woodbridge, 1995), p. 166. The macaroni was similarly resplendent in a gown tied with rose-coloured ribbon, 'white dimity waistcoat . . . [and] slippers scarlet, with yellow heels', *Westminster Magazine*, 5 (1777), p. 577; on the popularity of red-heeled shoes see *Tatler* Nos. 26 and 113.

60. Marcia Pointon, *Hanging the Head. Portraiture and Social Formation in Eighteenth-Century England* (New Haven CT and London, 1993), p. 110.

61. Vanbrugh, *The Relapse; or, Virtue in Danger* (1696), ed. Michael Cordner (1989), I.iii, pp. 61–2.

62. George Stevens, *An Essay on Satirical Entertainments; to which is added Steven's New Lecture on Heads* (1772), p. 20.

63. John Bulwer, 'An appendix, exhibiting the pedigree of the English gallant', *Anthrometamorphosis; or, Man Transformed* (1656), pp. 530–1. Bulwer's satirical history of gallant fashions traces the hat to the 'Macrones of Pontus', a possible origin for the later term as applied in the 1760s and 1770s. Conversely, several eighteenth-century commentators suggested that the name derived either from the pasta eaten by these Italophilic young men or from 'macarone', defined as 'a coarse clownish man', Bailey *Universal Dictionary* (23rd edn, 1773).

64. Ellis, *Gentile Sinner*, pp. 24–5.

65. Etherege, *Man of Mode*, I.i. p. 59; III.ii. p. 90. In this sense, the fop had less in common with the gallant than with the 'huffing courtier', another early-seventeenth-century type whose 'occupation is to show his Cloaths' of which he was 'as tender . . . as a Coward is of his Flesh', Butler, *Characters*, pp. 36–7.

66. Etherege, *Man of Mode*, I.i. p. 59; III.ii. p. 90.

67. *Man Superior to Woman* (1739), p. 31. Less common was the association of vanity with childishness, although the idea of fops as overgrown children was used and served for many as a sign of effeminacy. Clement Ellis's 'true gentleman', for example, the antithesis of the vain gallant, 'could never since he was a child, play with a Feather . . . he leaves these *toyes* to those *silly Creatures* who are resolved to Continue for ever in their *Childhood* or *Infancy*', *Gentile Sinner*, p. 113.

68. Mary Evelyn, *Mundus Foppensis; or, The Fop Display'd* (1691), pp. 12–13. Alan Bray demonstrates how during the early seventeenth century kissing was an important display of masculine friendship and political power, but could also 'be read in a different and sodomitical light', 'Homosexuality and signs of male friendship in Elizabethan England', *History Workshop*, 29 (1990), p. 13. Mary Evelyn's association between men's kissing in public and subsequent sexual encounters was shared by later writers. Kissing between men did not feature in either theoretical or practical guides to polite male interaction and appears to have had no place in daily life. A century on from Evelyn, Johann von Archenholz noted Englishmen's refusal to kiss or even embrace;

continental visitors who did otherwise would 'in all possibility be insulted by the populace', *A Picture of England*, 2 vols. (1789), II, p. 103.

69. Ned Ward, *Adam and Eve Stript of their Furbelows* (2nd edn, 1710), p. 213; *Public Ledger* (4–6 Aug 1772), p. 1.

70. A similar argument is proposed in Alan Sinfield, *The Wilde Century: Effeminacy, Oscar Wilde and the Queer Moment* (1994), ch. 2.

71. *Character of a Town-Gallant*, pp. 2–3. 'What man', Dekker had asked in typically visceral fashion, 'would not gladly see a beautiful woman naked?' *Guls Hornbook*, p. 26; gallants too unattractive or inept for seduction responded by playing up their 'pretences to the pox' caught 'from a lady'. Butler, *Characters*, p. 226.

72. *The Spendthrift*, No. 14 (28 June 1766), p. 80; Staves, 'Few kind words for the fop'.

73. *Westminster Magazine*, I (1773), p. 30.

74. John Courtenay, *The Rape of Pomona* (1773), p. 13. The fop as cuckold was a relatively rare image which recalls a characterisation of male inadequacy more common during the sixteenth and seventeenth centuries. See Foyster, *Manhood*, esp. pp. 67–72, 104–17. Principally used to indicate deviant social performance, representations of fops were typically situated in public social arenas, not the bedroom.

75. 'The education of a fop', *Rambler*, No. 109 (2 Apr 1751), in Johnson, *Works*, IV, pp. 215–20. As befitted the broader type, Florentus's descent had been caused by a domineering mother and a pusillanimous father sunk into a 'submissiveness', merely content to '*appear* wise and manly' (217, my italics).

76. Baker, *Tunbridge-Walks*, III.i, p. 30; I.i, p. 8.

77. *Man Superior to Woman*, pp. 30–1.

78. *Oxford Magazine*, 10 (1773), p. 111.

79. No. 43 (21 Nov 1754), *The Connoisseur*, 3 vols. (1754–6), I, p. 226.

80. *Spectator*, No. 240 (5 Dec 1711), II, p. 434.

81. Vanbrugh, *Relapse*, II.i, p. 72.

82. Ward, *London Spy*, No. 9 (1703), p. 154; *Universal Magazine*, 55 (1774), p. 290.

83. Jonathan Swift had previously satirised modish men for 'the present polite Way of Writing . . . which consists in pronouncing the first Syllable in a Word that has many, and dismissing the rest', *Tatler*, No. 230 (28 Sept 1710), III, pp. 192–3.

84. *Ibid.*, No. 85 (25 Oct 1709), II, p. 40; John Gay, 'Trivia; or the Art of Walking the Streets of London' (1716) in Vinton A. Dearing ed., *John Gay: Poetry and Prose*, 2 vols. (Oxford, 1974), I, p. 145. On this practice see above, p. 78.

85. Lancaster, *The Pretty Gentleman*, p. 6. For Lancaster's alternative definition of 'manly' delicacy see above, p. 106.

86. *Ibid.*, pp. 8–9, 30. On fops and the French see Cohen, *Fashioning Masculinity*, pp. 38–41.

87. *Oxford Magazine*, 9 (1772), p. 177.

88. 'The character of a fop', in *Hell Upon Earth* (1729), p. 33. By contrast, drinking had formed an important part of many gallants' routine: Clement Ellis's character, for example, 'drinks out the day in a tavern' until inebriated, *Gentile Sinner*, p. 42.

89. *Female Tatler*, No. 9 (11–13 July 1709), p. 1; *Oxford Magazine*, 9 (1772), p. 177.

90. Fordyce, *Addresses to Young Men*, II, p. 160. Fops' dismissal of the vogue for sentimental manners was also captured in the fashionable ennui of the 'Insensibilists' club from Fanny Burney's novel *Cecilia* (1782).

91. Horace Walpole to Earl of Hertford, 6 Feb 1764 and to Viscount Nuneham, 27 July 1773, in *Correspondence*, XXXVIII, p. 306, XXXV, p. 458; Boswell, *Journal of a Tour to the Hebrides*, p. 201.

92. Bailey, *Universal Etymological Dictionary* (25th edn, 1783); Walpole cited in Paget Toynbee ed., *Satirical Poems of William Mason* (Oxford, 1926), p. 69.

93. Walter Lippmann, *Public Opinion* (1922, rpt 1965), p. 65.

94. Michael Echeruo, *The Conditional Imagination from Shakespeare to Conrad* (1978), pp. 13–14; Frank Felsenstein, *Anti-Semitic Stereotypes: A Paradigm of 'Otherness' in English Popular Culture, 1660–1830* (Baltimore MD and London, 1995), ch. 1 summarises the work of this and other theorists.

95. *Galateo of Manners; or Instructions to a Young Man How to Behave Himself in Conversation &c* (1703), preface.

96. No. 280 (21 Jan 1712), II, p. 591.

97. *Essays Relating to the Conduct of Life* (1717), p. 12.

98. Towle, *Private Tutor*, pp. 158–9.

99. 'Religion and macaronism are quite incompatible and differ as widely as light and shade', wrote one contributor to the *Sentimental Magazine* 2 (1774), pp. 503–4. Fops typically used churches for self-display and thus subverted eighteenth-century notions of polite behaviour as set out by the likes of Adam Petrie; Lord Foppington, for one, attended St James's, Piccadilly where he found 'much the best company', *Relapse*, II.i, p. 74.

Polite and impolite personalities

This book has so far examined eighteenth-century debates surrounding the merits of refinement, conduct writers' advice on the means to achieve this attribute and, most recently, the strategies by which men were warned of its effeminising excesses. But what did real-life individuals make of these issues? Chapter Five explores aspects of this question through the comments of three memoirists – the legal student Dudley Ryder, the Anglican clergyman John Penrose, and the author James Boswell – writing in the mid-1710s, mid-1760s and, in Boswell's case, during the last four decades of the century. As soon becomes clear, despite marked differences in personality and circumstance, each author paid considerable attention to the issue of refinement, and to their own and other men's performance in society.

To an extent, this focus on the social self is representative of changing patterns of diary and journal writing in which Ryder and Boswell engaged. By the eighteenth century the idea of record keeping as a tool for religious self-scrutiny had broadened to engage authors preoccupied with questions polite as well as pious. The keeping of diaries and journals was widely encouraged in eighteenth-century conduct literature as a means to detail, monitor and learn from one's performance as much within a temporal as a spiritual context.[1] Ryder and Boswell were exceptional practitioners of the genre, being both careful social observers and self-absorbed individuals who provided candid assessment of their reputation as gentlemen of the world. John Penrose's memoir, in the form of letters to his family, proved somewhat less self-analytical. However, the fact that Penrose described a stay in the fashionable spa-town of Bath ensures a similar interest in conduct at a resort that was for many the epitome of eighteenth-century polite society. The preoccupation of each author with polite self-fashioning makes these especially valuable testimonies for the purpose of this chapter. As we shall see, all three men comment on the principal themes we have considered in earlier chapters: the definition of politeness and sensibility, the steps necessary to acquire social polish, and the locations and company in which to develop this reputation. Each also examines their own and other men's relationship to women as agents of male refinement, and considers the implications of this association for standards of manhood, either via an assessment of individual men's standing in the community or, in Boswell's case, through a more overt discourse of manliness. Often these testimonies confirm the memoirists' successful pursuit of a gentlemanly identity. Yet their confessional tone also reveals when, and for what reasons, this did not occur. In addition, all three authors comment on episodes when polite standards were consciously subverted either to pursue alternative styles of manhood, or to escape from a society where success demanded strict self-assessment and engendered persistent self-doubt.

The remainder of this chapter is divided into three sections, each detailing a separate testimony. All three accounts exist as discrete commentaries from men who never met. A final section considers their contribution to our understanding of eighteenth-century polite society, the gentleman and manliness 'in action' and, lastly, some possible directions for future histories of eighteenth-century masculinity.

Dudley Ryder: conversation and confrontation

In June 1715 Dudley Ryder (1691–1756) began a daily record of his temper, reading patterns and 'acts as to their goodness or badness'. His aim was social improvement through self-scrutiny: to 'know myself better' and 'how the better to spend my time for the future'.[2] The son of a successful London linen draper, Ryder had been raised in a prosperous Whig, nonconformist household. Educated at Edinburgh and Leyden, he rejected the family business and studied law, entering the Middle Temple in 1713. Ryder's professional success – he became Lord Chief Justice in 1754 – testifies to his talent for law, and we have no reason to doubt that he was a conscientious legal student. Even so, it is striking how infrequently work features in the diary. Rather, Ryder's daily record focused far more on his acceptance and performance within a predominantly leisured world of coffee-houses, assemblies and household visits. The diary reveals Ryder as well versed in the language of politeness. Male and female acquaintances were frequently described as 'genteel', 'very polite' or 'complaisant', while less desirable associates were 'obscene', 'unmannerly' or 'affected'. Ryder also used such terms of himself, proudly noting times when he was complimented as 'a very pretty gentleman and very genteel' with 'delicate and tender sentiments of virtue'.[3]

Good speech and good sense

Ryder believed his reputation for polite sociability was chiefly dependent on a capacity for good conversation. The diary reveals a man who took every opportunity to ponder the requirements of this quality, and who from mid-1716 recorded his thoughts in a 'book of conversation'. Though the book is now lost, these views are still discernible from numerous diary entries. In early remarks, Ryder identified the need for conversation to be informal, imaginative and dynamic. Good dialogue was based on an exchange during which one's partner contributed a subject 'that leads me to say something . . . and continue the discourse', typically by discussing 'matters of speculation', not fact, so as to leave 'room for other people's thoughts'.[4]

Ryder was somewhat contradictory about the type of man best suited for such fluent exchanges. At times good speakers were thought born, not made, imaginative and inclusive discourse requiring a natural 'vivacity of spirit and temper'.[5] Yet his keeping of a book of conversation also suggests Ryder's faith in the acquisition of good practices. Some, such as the avoidance of vulgarity or pedantry, were very definitely the responsibility of the individual. Others were obtained less consciously through daily sociability. 'Being conversant in the world', as he put it late in 1715, 'raises the spirit of emulation' and encourages men to 'draw forth their talents'. It was for this reason that he dismissed the chances of finding worthwhile exchanges at home, where 'concern for one's reputation has no force or efficacy'.[6] Good conversation was therefore potentially competitive, though Ryder also criticised aggressive and combative speech which he thought suitable only for the classroom. Avoiding confrontation required self-regulation. On 25 September 1715, for example, he 'talked pretty well', on account of his having conducted himself with 'a kind of awe and restraint upon me'.[7] Self-control was also a necessary quality of the good listener. Silence was 'in general as necessary as . . . talkativeness', for it allowed others to speak, while generating respect for the listener. Failure 'to be silent', by comparison, 'insensibly weakens a man's credit with others'.[8]

How did Ryder fare in his own encounters? On occasions – especially during meetings with women, male social superiors or elders – he was conscious of a variety of errors. Displays of eagerness, for example, led him to 'resolve . . . to be more cautious . . . in what I assert'. At other times, he was prone to a bashfulness which 'takes off the gracefulness of speaking'.[9] In close male company, by contrast, Ryder believed himself a better communicator who, especially comfortable with edifying subjects such as politics and religion, spoke with confidence and at length. Not all meetings took this form, however. In contrast to the idealised image of free and easy chat, real-life encounters could be more stultifying. Breakfast with Mr Leeds, for example, was a tedious affair since, as a 'man of not much spirit', he proved 'unfit to keep up the spirit of conversation'.[10] Other men were more forthcoming, but lacked judgement, reserve or gravitas, as in the case of one Mr Gore who talked 'pretty well and smoothly' but with 'little of learning or deep judgement'.[11]

Among women, Mr Gore was thought a 'man of distinction', though Ryder believed his performance more that of a 'fine gentleman' – a term he used critically to denote men with an unbecoming preoccupation with trivialities such as fashion and society gossip.[12] Against these intemperate, inconsiderate or insubstantial speakers, Ryder set more suitable role models who epitomised appropriate male values such as intelligence, consideration and learned diversion. Thus Mr Porter was respected as 'a man of very good sense . . . [who] talks with an agreeable air'; Dr Hollier's 'witty turns' and 'pretty thoughts' made his 'very happy way of talking . . . [the] life and spirit of the company', while 'the pretty sort of man', Mr Utber, 'talks very well and pleasantly'.[13]

With conversation at its core, Ryder embellished his reputation for refined sociability with additional trappings of gentility. On the anniversary of George I's accession, for example, he dressed 'in best clothes and laced ruffles' for a promenade at St James's, where he met with 'company dressed very fine, scarce any without gold or silver trimmings to their clothes'.[14] Ryder later improved his appearance further with a better quality sword. 'I cannot but observe', he wrote the day after its purchase, 'how much I am myself touched with external show; having a new sword on I could not help looking at it several times with a peculiar kind of pleasure.'[15] Several weeks on, Ryder was again struck by his physical appearance. Catching sight of himself in a shop mirror, he was particularly pleased to see that he walked 'with a very genteel and becoming air'.[16]

Ryder's deportment had no doubt been improved by visits to his dancing-master, Mr Fernley. After conversation, skill at dancing was a prominent indice of a polite personality, being for Ryder both a statement on gracefulness and an activity through which he was likely to meet genteel company. Like John Locke, who had encouraged dancing as a sign of outer gracefulness and inner composure, Ryder saw his lessons as a means to develop his reputation as a well-rounded man in society.[17] Good dancers, like men of conversation, were, he thought, characterised by a self-composure and dignified elegance that was as revealing of character as was coffee-house dialogue. This at least was the theory. However, in December 1715

Ryder was unconvinced of his capacity for either quality after a lesson when he performed 'with too much gaiety'. It was, he believed, far more becoming for 'a gentleman to dance with ease and sobriety' than, as he had done, an 'abundance of odd unbecoming motions' indicating a 'light mind' given to 'extravagant flourishes'.[18] For all his strictures to do better, Ryder never fully mastered the art of dancing. Diary entries repeatedly wavered between self-congratulation at his relaxed composure and repudiation of his awkwardness. Such fortunes were often experienced in a single evening. Thus on 29 October 1715 he behaved 'pretty tolerably' and was not aware of 'any . . . unpolite manner', until the intricacies of a minuet 'made me think that everyone looked upon me as a clumsy dancer'.[19] Several weeks later Ryder fared rather better, beginning with a 'stiff air' before warming up to perform with 'a great deal of ease and freedom'.[20]

In self-confident mood Ryder could be as critical of awkwardness in others as he feared fellow dancers were of his deportment. Worse than clumsiness, however, were men's attempts to impress through overly showy or formal conduct. In July 1715 Ryder met a friend of his father who greeted him with a series of low and elaborate bows which he first took as a sign of the man's drunkenness, 'but it seems it is only his manner and was perfectly sober'.[21] Ryder found two faults with this greeting: first, the elaborate nature and frequency of the bow, and, second, the inappropriateness of this particular mode of display from an elder of presumably similar, or higher, social status.[22] From equals or superiors he clearly expected more informal conduct. Ryder himself appears to have greeted only men of a more elevated standing in this fashion. Two weeks later at St James's he met Charles Paulet, Lord of the Bedchamber to the Prince of Wales, and 'had the courage to bow to him . . . though I did it very awkwardly'. On this occasion, however, Ryder's spontaneous social error was overshadowed by Mr Haddon, an acquaintance who 'seems a little to affect the air of the courtier', though 'I don't think it much becomes him'.[23]

Alongside overly formal men were those who cultivated a reputation for nonchalance. Ryder encountered a number of these in the summer of 1715. The nineteen-year-old Samuel Powell, for example, was identified as one who 'affects the character of a genteel, careless, negligent gentleman', conducting himself 'with a strange kind of jaunty, unconcerned, merry laughing air'.[24] Mr Gould likewise 'affects very much an airy, unthinking brisk manner of behaviour', while Walter Crisp 'is a man that affects to be a polite gentleman and gives himself the air of talking a little loosely'.[25] In seeking this reputation for negligence, all three pursued a fashion 'much affected now and men think it genteel'.[26] Ryder, however, was more ambivalent towards a style which he thought rude and insulting. His anxiety over the popularity of negligent gentlemen recalls the concern of many eighteenth-century conduct writers regarding the challenge posed by rakes and libertines to new ideals of polite manhood. As we saw in Chapter Four, anti-civility was practised (and usually censured) less because it threatened to undermine manliness than because it offered an attractive alternative based on the subversion of politeness. However, other quests for refinement could and, in Ryder's opinion, did challenge acceptable standards of manhood. Walter Crisp's conversation, for example, was criticised not only for its being loose but, like Mr Gore's, also 'very trifling' in his bid to 'gain the character of a polite gentleman . . . to recommend him to the ladies'.[27]

Ryder also expressed frequent anxiety over the impact of polite living on his own character. By March 1716 his interest in dancing was having a detrimental effect on his legal studies. Preoccupied with questions of posture, Ryder had started to adopt dance positions while studying. Soon, however, deportment 'took up my thoughts that my reading was not with so good effect as it should have been'.[28] Elsewhere, he showed himself sensitive to enquiries about his future which he instinctively interpreted as criticism of his immature imbalance between professional responsibility and polite sociability. 'He takes me', Ryder wrote after such a discussion with Mr Whately, as 'one that am too gay and minds a genteel manner of behaviour and company of the ladies too much to make a great matter of the law'.[29]

Taken further, this pursuit challenged not only Ryder's professional prospects but also his broader reputation for intelligence, judgement and independence. Immediately after he met the affected Mr Gould in August 1715, Ryder's confidence had been boosted further by his participation in an erudite political discussion with another male friend. In the evening, however, he visited his Aunt Billio's house where he met a Mrs Loyd, to whom he was attracted, and now 'behaved myself but awkwardly'. What had so far been a successful day ended with recrimination: 'what a fool am I that I cannot be satisfied with the esteem of men of sense but must be uneasy if I am not esteemed by weak women too!'[30]

For Ryder, sense was a much considered and valued quality. It was, moreover, one that he identified as distinctly male, and of considerable importance for men's positive self-perception. 'Nothing', he wrote in late 1716, 'touches a man so . . . as what reflects upon his sense or understanding.'[31] In the figure of the man of conversation Ryder clearly believed it possible to combine sense with sociability and quality of expression. However, as his encounter at Aunt Billio's suggests, it was also possible to shatter this balance by paying too much attention to the impression rather than the quality of one's speech. Admirable 'men of judgement', as Ryder reminded himself, favoured 'good sense over good style'.[32] By abandoning intelligence, sobriety and discernment in his search for a polite reputation, Ryder knew that he risked substituting a commendable persona – the man of sense – for what in April 1716 he condemned as the 'trifling inconsiderable reputation' of a 'good tattler' or 'fine gentleman among the ladies'.[33]

In this and other instances of self-criticism, Ryder clearly equated the challenge to his manly identity with female society. Aside from relatives, women feature in three principal guises in the diary: as prostitutes – whom he visited on a handful of occasions – as potential lovers, and as partners in conversation. At a time when behavioural literature regularly stressed the reforming qualities of genteel female company, Ryder's criticisms provide a striking note of protest. Women's speech was for him categorised principally by its triviality and levity. 'We had a great deal of female conversation,' he wrote in July 1715, 'the great part of it turned upon scandal and stories of other people, especially their own sex.'[34] Early in the following year Ryder recorded another episode with 'tattling women' who raised 'stories without the least foundation', while at Mrs Hudson's female breakfast party he endured a discourse that 'turned entirely upon the manners, behaviour, way of living, clothes, dress &c., of their neighbours'.[35]

Ryder was seldom comfortable in women's company, thinking himself 'apt to look silly and a little uneasy' in their presence. At the same time he commented, often critically, on men who conducted themselves more successfully. One such individual was his cousin Joseph Billio who, in July 1715, entertained an assembled female audience by being 'perfectly free and familiar . . . saying whatever comes into his thoughts' with no consideration for, in Ryder's opinion, 'polite' propriety. Sitting 'silent and dumb' Ryder comforted himself with the belief that virtuous women actually determined their 'esteem of a man rather by the value that is put upon . . . by his own sex, though he does not make so gay and pleasant a figure in their company'.[36] In the following month, however, Ryder received evidence to the contrary when, with Mrs Loyd and a female cousin, he met a courteous army officer who entertained them during their visit to the military camp at Kensington. On leaving, the two women had ridiculed the soldier's dignified and learned manner since, as Ryder added, 'nothing but a free, very familiar pleasant kind of conversation is agreeable to them'.[37] Thus, far from cultivating refined speech within male society, polite female company confirmed what Ryder, ever mindful of the popular ladies' man Samuel Powell, saw as women's preference for the 'gay merry rattling conversation' of 'rakes and coxcombs' over the merits of men of 'virtue and good sense'.[38]

A polite reader

The experience of the showy Mr Powell, or of more laudable gentlemen such as Mr Porter, provided Ryder with two pictures of male behaviour –

one negative, one positive – on which he drew in his attempt to improve his own conduct. This he supplemented with a wide range of literary advice. A keen reader of classical and modern guides to conversation, essay periodicals and social satirical literature, Ryder showed a clear preference for studies from which he might gain insight into his own and others' social conduct.

Much of this advice came in the form of negative examples common to satires such as Alain Le Sage's *Devil upon Two Sticks* (1707) which he read in July 1715. In a notably bleak survey of human duplicity, Le Sage sketched a series of personality types – the stroppy coffee-house patron, the tiresome wit, the self-indulgent courtier – in which Ryder saw 'the different manners of men set in very clear and distinguishing light'. That he thought it 'very useful to be acquainted with books that treat of characters' probably prompted him to consult an English version of the genre, John Earle's *Micro-cosmographie* (1628). On the evening of 26 July 1716 Ryder read a selection of the sketches and, pleased by their 'wit and justness', vowed 'to examine them more narrowly'.[39] No further references to this particular work occur. However, even a single reading would have exposed him to a series of critical character studies – among them the gossipy, 'effeminate' 'gull citizen' or the overly formal 'affected man' – in which Ryder found representations of the traits he criticised in others and was keen to erase from his own conduct.[40]

Advice on affectation was also available in Joseph Addison and Richard Steele's *Spectator* periodical. Ryder was an assiduous reader of this publication which, along with the *Tatler* and *Guardian*, he consulted almost daily in the tavern, coffee-house and at home. He praised what he saw as Addison and Steele's understanding of the complexities of human nature and fully recognised the value of this information for his own development. Consultation of *Tatler* papers in June 1715 prompted his plan 'to read them often' to learn their authors' 'manner of observing upon the world and mankind'.[41] By October, Ryder had supplemented this with a complete survey of the *Spectator*, having now 'a design to read them all over again to improve my style and manner of thinking'.[42]

Ryder appears to have begun this second study soon after for, in the following week, he re-examined *Spectator* No. 38 on affectation. Steele's paper opened with a description of a foppish gentleman who abused his wit solely to flatter and win the affection of polite female company. This contortion of natural character had, wrote Steele, always been common in the 'dressing Part of our Sex' but was increasingly a feature of the 'wise Man [and] Man of Sense'. In these cases, Steele lamented the substitution of men's natural talents for a 'passion for praise' that undermined the authority of male dress, conversation and professional competence; such affectation was, he believed, especially prominent among pompous lawyers at court.[43]

For Dudley Ryder, legal student and would-be 'man of sense', Steele's warning had a particular force. 'Everything I read', he commented that evening, 'was designed against the fault that I find myself extremely guilty of . . . that is a too great desire and love of applause in things which are themselves the least commendable'.[44] The issue of affectation was certainly then in Ryder's mind, his reading coming a week after the purchase of his new sword. Initially a source of pride, its attraction soon troubled Ryder, who became 'vexed . . . that my mind is too apt to be affected with such trifles'.[45] Yet subsequent self-criticism, especially during his failed courtship of Sally Marshall in the spring of 1716, suggests that Steele's advice had a limited impact on Ryder's long-term conduct as memories of past indiscretions either faded or were side-lined during his bid to impress a companion. For Ryder, there was apparently no effective correlation between wise counsel, self-scrutiny and actual social practice. Rather, his comments highlight an on-going struggle to achieve personal development bolstered by frequent re-reading of what he continued to see as responsible and influential conduct advice.

Identification of poor behaviour was complemented by an understanding of more admirable modes of conduct. Here again, Ryder appreciated the importance of Addison and Steele's contribution to the content and tone of essential areas like conversation. As we saw in Chapter Two, much of this advice drew on aspects of classical, Renaissance Italian and seventeenth-century French traditions of male conduct literature. Diary entries also indicate Ryder's knowledge of these earlier guides, among them *De Officiis* (*On Duties*) by the Roman orator, Cicero. Ryder began reading *De Officiis* on 24 June 1715 and, assuming that he finished the work, would have received by now familiar advice on men's need for company, and the means to achieve this through seemliness and, in conversation, generosity, accommodation and tolerance.[46] Speech also featured prominently in another literary influence to which Ryder came near the end of his diary. Browsing in Moorfields in October 1716, he bought and began reading a first edition of Pierre d'Ortige de Vaumorière's 1691 *L'Art de Plaire dans la Conversation* (translated 1707 as *The Art of Pleasing in Conversation*). Like a number of late-seventeenth-century French authors, de Vaumorière encouraged men to adopt a less ceremonious and more relaxed, instructive style of conversation intended to entertain rather than to ingratiate. Yet his work also differed from many similar guides in its critical opinion of women's conversation, which de Vaumorière characterised as less cultivated and more indulgent than its male equivalent.[47] In view of his own thoughts on good male and expected female conversation, it is perhaps not surprising that Ryder looked favourably on his new book. A week after its purchase, he had reached Chapter Four, an examination of the limited benefits of men's mixing in female company. Ryder evidently agreed with what he read, remarking later that day on the book's 'very just and polite reflections with regard to conversation'.[48] It is a comment that reminds us of Ryder's use of advice literature not just as a model for future conduct but also as a means to confirm and validate existing opinions and practices.

Confrontation and feeling

Though eager, Ryder was not always a careful or consistent reader. We have already seen how his legal work suffered when he was preoccupied with dancing. Similarly, he appears to have been far from studious on 29 June 1715 when, in a 'drowsy careless posture', he flicked through the *Tatler* unable to 'fix to any one thing'.[49] At other times, Ryder's reading was determinedly selective rather than sloppy. In view of his interest in *Tatler* and *Spectator* papers dedicated to dicussions of refined living, it seems reasonable to suppose that Ryder knew of the *Spectator*'s disapproval of men who engaged in political disputes between supporters of the Whig and Tory parties. Recalling the destructiveness of civil war in the mid-seventeenth century, Addison had written of a 'furious Party Spirit' that threatened 'all the Seeds of Good-Nature, Humanity and Compassion', reducing the political speaker to 'an odious and despicable Figure'. In place of zealous party loyalty, Addison advocated an 'association' of men who valued the common ties of friendship, sociability and virtue over the divisions of political opinion.[50]

Regardless of Addison's advice, as a staunch Whig and nonconformist Ryder's selection of companions and conduct with strangers was clearly influenced by party affiliation and religious faith. Such views led Ryder into a number of encounters in which he not only broke Addison's embargo on political debate, but introduced contests to venues where politeness was expected to thrive. At the coffee-house, for example, he became involved in a dispute with a Tory clergyman which continued until Ryder 'got very much the better of him, [and] he was forced to go away'.[51] Defence of the new pro-Whig Hanoverian monarchy also led him to abandon the qualities he elsewhere identified as essential for men of conversation. Dinner at the Temple Chop-House in October 1715, for example, was curtailed by an argument with a Jacobite sympathiser with whom Ryder had not been 'very fit to talk seriously', being 'apt to be worked up into a kind of heat that makes me tremble . . . [and] speak with too much warmth and eagerness'.[52] Verbal attacks on religious nonconformity likewise caused him to lose the 'modesty and submission . . . as became me', and utter 'harsh terms that looked a little too ungenteel'.[53]

As this comment suggests, Ryder was certainly aware of his lack of refinement during political or religious debate. In this situation he practised one of two strategies. The first saw politeness relegated to an unimportant requirement at times of confrontation. We can see this, for example, in Ryder's discussion of certain church and chapel sermons which, like good conversation, he expected in theory to be performed with the same clarity and easiness he sought in the coffee-house. This said, such stipulations turned out to be less important when the content demanded a more dogmatic tone. Thus, while not 'very extraordinary polite', the bishop of Salisbury's sermon in June 1716 was judged 'good, honest' for its being 'full of abhorrence of the [Jacobite] rebellion and of popish principles'.[54] A second strategy saw Ryder maintain his own reputation for politeness by denying the same characteristic to those with whom he argued. On several occasions, he attributed Tory men's views to their lack of what he called 'polite learning' and defined as truthfulness and open-mindedness. Ryder's logic led him to criticise his dancing-master, whom he suspected of Tory sympathies, as a man with 'nothing of learning and politeness, very ignorant of the affairs of the nation'.[55] Oxford University, which he believed to be a Tory heartland, was likewise a place where 'learning or politeness has nothing to do', and students were 'bred . . . in the most narrow, confined and ungenerous principles'.[56]

On occasions, the attribute of politeness was also denied to the object of Ryder's affection, Sally Marshall. During an unsuccessful and often humilating courtship Marshall regularly mocked her suitor's declarations of love and intimacy. Ryder's family, who knew of his admiration for this imperious and often contemptuous woman, were in turn highly critical of her conduct in society. What Ryder saw as Sally Marshall's elegance, his cousin Robert Billio considered the 'clumsy rather than gentle' manners of a person whose lack of 'address and politeness' he attributed to 'her being the daughter of a tailor'. Perhaps irritated by Marshall's frequent rejections, Ryder appears to have enjoyed these particular slurs, which he rejected – but only, he told his cousin, 'in a style of raillery'.[57]

At other times, however, Ryder's response to Mrs Marshall was more distressed than dismissive. In the spring of 1716 he frequently described himself as being on the verge of tears when snubbed in favour of his rival, Samuel Powell. Yet Ryder also shows himself to have been alert to the unattractiveness of men's tears. Thus, though tempted to weep, he invariably held back for 'my reason tells me that it will never do'.[58] In March 1716, the one occasion when he could not 'prevent the tears gushing out', Ryder was forced to quit Mrs Marshall's company, though 'my eyes . . . betrayed what I had been doing'. Ryder's rival, Mr Powell, later confirmed the unacceptability of such actions, private or otherwise, when he expressed surprise over the incident, informing Ryder that he thought him 'almost mad'.[59]

Yet if men's weeping remained inappropriate, it is notable how in the same period Ryder also engaged confidently in early expressions of the physiology and culture of sensibility. In February 1716, for example, he attended the public execution of a Jacobite, which, notwithstanding his political views, he found 'very moving and affecting', despite his inability to put 'oneself into that form and temper of mind' of a condemned prisoner.[60] In March, Ryder attributed a bout of ill-health or 'vapours' to 'laxity of nerves'. This he treated by cold baths in London and at the fashionable spa resort of Bath, where he took the waters, wept for Sally Marshall and suffered Mr Powell's rebuke. Later thoughts of Mrs Marshall were said to have 'perfectly melted' him and 'introduced a softness and tenderness . . . that made me ready to dissolve', feelings that he found easier and presumably more acceptable to convey not by 'continued discourse' but 'dismal melancholy looks and broken sighs'.[61]

With his tears and sighs Dudley Ryder gives the impression of a man of feeling before his time. Yet, in contrast to later memoirists like James Boswell, Ryder did not perceive himself as a sentimental individual; even if he had it seems likely that he would have received scant praise from an indifferent Sally Marshall or an affectedly negligent Mr Powell. Rather, Ryder's diary reveals a man who evaluated social reputation principally in terms of dress, deportment and, above all, conversation. In optimistic mood, Ryder thought himself capable of a pleasing synthesis of external conduct and inner personality which, in conversation, found eloquence and informality based on an intelligence common to 'men of sense'. In his pursuit of this synthesis, Ryder consulted a range of advice manuals, periodicals and social satires from which he built a picture of desirable and undesirable male conduct. Yet the diary also shows how, in the flux of daily life, established notions of good conduct could be discarded or forgotten. An excessive interest in material trivialities like a new sword, confrontations over politics and religion, and errors committed in the company of Mrs Loyd or Sally Marshall offer instances of this neglect.

Concern at his loss of sense in female company also alerted Ryder to the potential tensions between polite and manly conduct. Ultimately, he was unwilling to compromise his position as a would-be man of conversation for what he saw as the gender and behavioural inadequacies of the 'fine gentleman'. In doing so, Ryder reveals his commitment (not always realised) to the advice of writers like Richard Steele in *Spectator* No. 38. However, Ryder's objection to 'fine gentlemanliness' was as much determined by his awkwardness in female company as it was by the wisdom of an Addison or a Steele. A confident Dudley Ryder criticised the fine or negligent

gentleman's affectation or showed himself gently complicit in mocking Sally
Marshall's deep-rooted vulgarity. But Ryder's confidence was often short
lived. Eager to become a respectable suitor but unable to perform with the
levity of his rivals, he proved unattractive to potential lovers and ridiculous
to his male competitors. Away from his textbooks, Ryder soon found that a
reputation for refinement and manhood owed as much to the opinions of
one's company as to the actions of oneself.

John Penrose: player in the polite world

In April 1766, fifty years after Dudley Ryder's visit, John Penrose (1713–
76), an Anglican clergyman from Cornwall, made his first trip to Bath with
his wife and daughter. The initial motive for the journey was medical.
Penrose, like many eighteenth-century middle- and upper-class men, suffered from gout, for which he now sought treatment with a course of Bath's
famous spa water. Penrose's letters, written daily to other family members,
were initially taken up with his poor but improving physical condition.
Better health enabled him to participate more actively in the fashionable
and genteel diversions with which eighteenth-century Bath had become
synonymous. In line with his changing experience of the town, Penrose's
correspondence develops into a detailed report of his own and others' involvement in this social world. Through his commentary during his 1766
visit, and a second trip in the following spring, Penrose provides a record of
one man's opinion of and activities within, to quote the Bath architect and
historian John Wood, 'this Theatre of the Polite World'.[62]

A genteel performance

First impressions of the resort went a long way to confirm the claims of
Wood and other apologists. On 11 April, two days after his arrival, Penrose
wrote of the family's reception of 'repeated Visits' from old acquaintances
and fellow residents in their lodgings. On the following day Penrose commented on the 'inconceivable' number of 'fine Ladies and Gentlemen' who
passed his window on their way to 'the most public Walks'. Nor was this
refinement a preserve of visitors. 'So polite the ordinary People in their
Dress', he wrote several days later, while a visit to the market revealed
tradesmen who 'in general speak so fine'. Exposure to such company clearly
had some impact on Penrose who, within a month of his arrival, claimed
that he too had 'grown vastly polite'.[63]

The driving force behind Bath's gentrification had been Richard 'Beau' Nash, master of ceremonies at the assembly rooms from 1704 until the late 1750s. Nash's vision transformed Bath from an aloof community into a more welcoming and relaxed environment renowned for what he, in common with early-eighteenth-century polite theorists, identified as a superior form of refined sociability. If anything, Nash saw his project superseding the limited refinements achievable in a sprawling and unruly metropolis. Like other eighteenth-century resort towns, including Tunbridge Wells and Scarborough, Bath's popularity rested on its image as the quintessence of polite living, where the rowdiness and aggression of London was subordinate to civilised leisure, entertainment and recuperation.[64] Promotional literature regularly described how provincial centres escaped, for example, the political disputes that had characterised Dudley Ryder's metropolitan encounters. Bath, as Lady Luxborough claimed in the 1750s, was a centre of 'good manners, and a coalition of parties and ranks'. Political and class tensions were further minimised by the presence of an acknowledged arbiter of social conduct. It was this role that Nash developed in Bath, his trademark white hat commanding, as Lady Luxborough put it, 'more respect and non-resistance than the crowns of some kings'.[65] The result, at least in theory, was a relaxed, tolerant and diverse social grouping maintained by its adherence to universally respected regulations applicable to members of a geographically and conceptually distinct polite society.[66]

How were new visitors expected to learn these modes of conduct? As Lady Luxborough's comment suggests, Nash's presence did much to maintain standards during the first half of the century. After his retirement, Nash's influence continued to be exercised through histories and guidebooks that informed subsequent visitors of his role in developing Bath as a uniquely refined environment. Like most new residents, John Penrose probably first encountered Nash's legacy, the patterns of daily life, and the more detailed requirements of good conduct through these guides. On his arrival Penrose found in his lodgings a copy of *The New Bath Guide* (1762) in which, in addition to the now obligatory sketch of Nash's achievement, he was exposed to general statements confirming the superiority of Bath manners, lists of the most popular venues and their opening times, and, more specifically, a summary of Nash's instructions for behaviour at the pump and assembly rooms. Similar information was available from two further publications, a 1750 map and the second volume of John Wood's *Description of Bath*, which Penrose also consulted regularly during his stay.

It would not have been difficult to piece together the expected daily pattern from these guides. In a self-consciously 'polite' resort, where class distinctions were of reduced significance, considerable emphasis was necessarily placed on time-keeping and gender relations as markers of good conduct. Respectable patrons were required to adhere to the strict hours kept at centres of social contact. A first visit to the pump room or baths took place between 7 and 10 am, and was followed by breakfast; mornings were spent visiting or church-going, before a noon promenade or carriage ride. After dinner at 2 pm came evening prayers and a second walk or trip to the pump room. Evenings culminated with visits, the theatre or a ball between 8 and 11 pm, after which, with no official provision for late-night drinking, male ball-goers were expected to return soberly to their lodgings.[67]

Many of the activities within this timetable were undertaken in mixed company, the principal exceptions being the breakfast hour – when men retired to coffee-houses while women returned to their lodgings – and possibly during promenades and visits, when men might gather for professional or learned conversation. In mixed social spaces, men and women were otherwise expected to mingle freely so as to benefit from the virtues of the opposite sex.

In line with Nash's broader concept of relaxed sociability through limited regulation, steps were also taken in certain venues to define a firmer, and hence politer, distinction between male and female conduct. One such site was the public bath. As John Wood pointed out, the seventeenth-century practice of men and women bathing together naked was now viewed as unacceptable and in need of polite regulation.[68] This interest in dress and undress also featured in Nash's rules concerning morning behaviour at the pump room; here men showed 'breeding and respect' by appearing before women not in their gowns and caps but fully dressed in wigs and coats. The propriety of complete dress was again emphasised at the evening assembly. Amended by Nash's successor, the stipulations during Penrose's stay required men dancing minuets to wear a 'full Dress' of 'French frock Suit' and 'Bag wig'; onlookers, though less closely regulated, were forbidden from attending in leather breeches, riding boots, spurs and swords.[69] While at the ball, men were also requested not to crowd the women, nor to take offence when prospective partners danced with others.[70]

Penrose's correspondence provides insight both into the character of polite Bath society and his personal experience and opinion of the resort. To an extent, his emerging daily pattern conformed closely with an expected routine of bathing, visiting, dining, church-going and promenading. Within a week of his arrival he had been prescribed a course of spa water to be drunk at 8 am and noon. Initially too infirm to leave his lodgings, by 25 April Penrose was able to attend the pump room. On that first visit he and his wife stayed for a hour, listening to music and the 'prating' of a 'great number of Gentlemen and Ladies'. Thereafter they attended the abbey; went shopping; took part in a second act of worship; and received evening visitors for conversation, cards and tea – Bath's principal social lubricant at evening and day-time meetings.[71]

Once he had ventured into public, Penrose's days were without exception busy and sociable. On 26 April, for example, he visited the abbey twice, the pump room three times, and walked on the parade with his wife. Earlier that day Penrose socialised alone, making 'two little Bath visits' to an old schoolfriend, Major Tucker, and a Mr Robinson. Both men appear frequently in the correspondence and were prominent members of Penrose's small but well-respected circle of male friends, many of whom he first encountered at the resort. Within this group Penrose appears to have paid little attention to the issue of social status; male socialising was conducted in an informal fashion and friends were visited without prior arrangement. Certain encounters were more demanding, however. A 'polite invitation' from Dr Stackhouse took Penrose to a formal breakfast for Cornish residents where he was 'elegantly regaled' by his host's generosity. A meeting with Penrose's patron, Lord Edgecumbe, was equally a 'grand Visit' undertaken on one afternoon while his wife was elsewhere entertained; both met later at the pump room before returning for tea with their landlady.[72]

Participation in resort life also advanced Penrose's knowledge of specific social practices as detailed in the town's promotional literature. By late April 1766, for example, he was aware of the need to dress appropriately before visiting the pump room, conscious that 'my fine flower'd Night-gown would make a despicable Figure'.[73] A visit to the bathing-pool showed a similar appreciation of the 'correct' dress, this time of others. Here mixed and public bathing was made acceptable, in Penrose's opinion, by each bather being clothed in 'a canvas Dress prepared for the Purpose'.[74] Finally, Penrose evidently appreciated and maintained the resort's time regulations regarding evening diversions, recording his latest night (home at just before 10 pm) on 26 May 1766.[75]

A critical review

Penrose's correspondence charts one man's steady acclimatisation and later active involvement in an apparently accessible and sociable community. It would, however, be wrong to see Penrose and his wife simply as leisured tourists. Comprehensive medical treatment meant that residents spent two to three months in lodgings that, as at home, had to be maintained and supplied. Part of each day was therefore taken up with the 'disagreeable subject' of 'Huswifery Affairs', which, as his comments imply, Penrose left mainly to his wife.[76] Nevertheless, Bath's high cost of living meant that financial management became a daily feature for male as well as female family members. 'Between the Dearness of the Meat and Dressing we shall be ruined', wrote an anxious Penrose in the second week of his visit.[77]

Subsequent letters provide details of joint shopping ventures in search of bargains, and Penrose's assiduous monitoring of price fluctuations. These, on occasions, preceded details of social encounters. 'Every thing is excessive dear', was an early impression on his return in April 1767. Thereafter Penrose quickly resumed his preoccupation with managing household expenditure: 'the principal News', he wrote on 17 June, 'is that Mutton is fallen one penny per pound'.[78]

Resort guides' descriptions of the gentlemanly itinerary made no comment on such prosaic matters. Thus, Penrose's detailed commentary reminds us of the pressures of daily life within a community where prudence was necessary for family well-being, while elegant consumption remained an indicator of taste and social refinement to one's guests.[79] Moreover, the time devoted to household management suggests some divergence between the image of polite, leisured gentlemen and real-life visitors, many of whom stayed in Bath on a limited budget. Penrose's usual decision to breakfast with his wife, not at the coffee-house, and his refusal to attend the ball, despite its popularity with other clergymen, provide further instances of his variation from the prescribed pattern.

To an extent, we should regard these differences as personal preference in a society where, as guides claimed, the range of possible activities prevented visitors from fully engaging in all available entertainments.[80] However, it is clear that Penrose was often ambivalent towards what he described elsewhere as Bath's 'insipid' and 'corrupting' culture of fashionable diversion. At best, Penrose believed that the resort offered a transitory encounter with a hyper-refined community, experience of which would be forgotten on his departure. Despite his claim to have 'grown vastly polite', therefore, he was certain that he would 'lose all my Politeness' on returning to Cornwall.[81] At first, this particular identification of 'politeness' as a peculiarity of Bath suggests his acceptance of the town's image as the epicentre of refined living. Yet other letters reveal that this association was not necessarily complimentary. Thus on several occasions Penrose pretended to chastise himself for his inability to perfect the 'polite' or 'fashionable' modes of speech as practised in circles restricted by the 'constraints of Politeness and Good-Breeding'.[82]

In addition to chafing at the curbs on speech, Penrose grew increasingly weary of the dress code demanded even of those who avoided the assembly room and ballroom. Required 'to be dressed in best Coat and best Wig' for a morning visit to the pump room, he wrote in late April 1766 of his desire to return to his lodgings, where 'I . . . have an opportunity of putting on my black Night-Gown'. It was, he bemoaned, 'a comfort I seldom enjoy'.[83] In the following week, Penrose began his evening's relaxation by choosing to 'unrig as soon as the Coast was clear: for 'tis very disagreeable to be all day dressed in form'.[84] Even at his lodgings, opportunities for changing into casual clothes were limited by the possibility of receiving visitors until as late as 9 pm. Penrose's letters convey the risks involved in relaxing unless one could guarantee that further guests would be intimate enough not to object to their host's informal appearance.

Close friends did indeed call on this occasion. Together they spent an evening 'cheap . . . with Respect to . . . Expence, but very expensive with Respect to Time'.[85] Throughout his stay, Penrose made regular comments about guests' intrusions. We should not from this assume that he was unsociable. A typical day saw Penrose converse at the pump room, take walks with friends and participate in a round of tea visits. His letters also reveal him as conscious and appreciative of the refined sociability of many fellow residents. Thus Lord Edgecumbe was praised for being 'extremely free' in his conversation, Mr Penneystone was 'one of the amiable and honestest of Men', and Mr Sleech 'very sociable and friendly'.[86] On numerous other occasions Penrose enjoyed the 'civility' and 'civilities' of fellow residents, characterised by their generosity, accommodation and thoughtfulness.

Yet despite his appreciation of refined conduct, Penrose clearly thought the expected level of socialising excessive. 'We have had no Respite', he wrote soon after his arrival, 'all is Hurry, Hurry'.[87] By mid-April his correspondence listed only new visitors since 'we are seldom free from Company, which sometimes greatly incommode me'.[88] Penrose highlighted several factors to account for his mounting frustration. First, guests prevented him from writing to his family, an activity he (in contrast to Dudley Ryder) consistently placed above the diversions of even close friends. Second, visits were often inconsequential. The habit was for quick engagements: callers 'bounce into the Room, and shew themselves, and away'.[89] Finally, an incessant round of visits also reduced the time spent reading either his family's correspondence or books other than the guides he found in his lodgings.[90]

Penrose's was perhaps the complaint of all bibliophilic holiday-makers who find good intentions replaced by leisured diversion. However, within what he satirised as Bath's demonstrably 'polite' environment this absence of scholarly activity was viewed with additional concern. Despite distancing himself from certain of the town's fashionable venues, Penrose was clearly troubled that his letters were increasingly devoted to the 'prittle prattle' of sociability, as if from the pen of a self-styled 'babler' or 'tatler'.[91] In these instances, Penrose thought himself increasingly distanced from the quality of 'sense' which, like Dudley Ryder, he valued as a commendable attribute of such welcome guests as Mr Grant, 'a very sensible man' who has 'read a great deal . . . I was well pleased with his Company'.[92]

The merit of a man of sense was all the more more apparent when set against some of the fashionable and, for Penrose, objectionable characters in Bath society. As a staunch Anglican, he was particularly concerned by the popularity of the town's Methodist community. Disregarding the notion that Bath should be a haven of polite tolerance, Penrose took every opportunity to condemn the emotional excesses of the Methodist preacher whom all 'sober . . . men of Sense in the Audience' believed 'affects the Orator'.[93] Anglican congregations behaved little better, however. On 5 May 1767 he was alarmed that a subscription for a clergyman at Bath abbey had raised only six guineas while a benefit ball for the current master of ceremonies, Samuel Derrick, provided £150. This injustice was compounded by what Penrose saw as the divergent qualities of the two men: the clergyman, 'a Gentleman of Sense, Virtue and many approved Qualities', and Derrick, 'an insignificant Puppy' whose popularity suggested a 'Gentry who . . . were Lovers of Pleasure more than Lovers of God'.[94]

Bath's role as a magnet for men of pleasure was a consistent theme in satires on the resort. Hedonists came in various guises, among them libertines, gamesters and hypochondriacs. Bath, as satirists pointed out, was also a popular haunt for fops who were attracted to a town dedicated to the art of display. As early as 1700 the satirist Ned Ward had claimed that the fops flocking west now outnumbered those in London. According to one anonymous observer, the mid-century town:

> . . . Lisbon-like *for ever will admit*
> *Those of all nations for her Benefit:*
> *Their gaudy Tinsel Streamer Beaus display,*
> *And in a Fleet their Course steer this Way.*[95]

Others saw the resort itself as instrumental in undermining established male values. Christopher Anstey's *The New Bath Guide*, the publishing success of 1766, told the story of Sim Blunderhead's trip to Bath in search of better health. In addition to being duped by quack physicians, Sim falls in with 'Sir Pye Macaroni' in whose company he emerges as a self-declared 'Beau Garçon'. Writing to his mother, Sim is relieved that 'my Face is':

> . . . *Not a little regarded at all Public Places;*
> *For I ride in a Chair with my Hands in a Muff,*
> *And have bought a Silk Coat and embroidered the Cuff;*
> . . . *My Manners so form'd, and my Wig so well curl'd*
> *I look like a* Man of the very first World.[96]

Penrose, like many others, read the *New Bath Guide* and found 'Some of it . . . very well', if too expensive at five shillings. Whether he approved of Anstey's mockery of Sim's over-refinement remains unclear. However, his earlier disapproval of the male fashion for parading in glasses – making men 'a mere Spectacle' – and his dismissal of the inconsequential and puppyish Mr Derrick does suggest an awareness of the consequences of modern manners for manhood, even if he did not characterise this relationship with overt reference to the popular fop type.[97]

Epilogue

Bath may have had a high percentage of genteel men of fashion, but it also witnessed bouts of less refined conduct. Nash's ban on swords had been prompted by a spate of fatal duels and, despite his initiative, similar encounters occurred throughout the century. Penrose himself experienced an aspect of this more aggressive culture in 1767 when, walking through the town's West Gate, he was assaulted by several drunken 'noisy Fellows' who took his stick and threatened to beat him.

Other men practised less conspicuous forms of impolite conduct. In the previous May, while walking to a tea engagement, Penrose had taken his family on a circuitous route to avoid Avon Street, a known centre of prostitution, described in his correspondence as a place 'of ill Fame'.[98] Just how Penrose learned of the street's reputation remains a matter for speculation: perhaps he was warned by residents already familiar with the area; equally, he may have read between the lines of John Wood's account of a street 'fallen into an Irregularity and Meanness not worth Describing'.[99] Unlike the other memoirists in this chapter, John Penrose was not attracted to the opportunities of Avon Street or its London equivalents. Moreover, in avoiding the street he appears to have responded to Wood's intention of warning readers from this area, thus further affirming the resort's association with refinement. Yet it seems reasonable to suggest that this information could be and probably was used by men seeking sexual adventure. Certainly Wood's advice does not appear to have undermined the trade in prostitution, for later commentators were forced to seek new ways to reconcile Avon Street's presence with neighbouring polite society. For Pierce Egan the issue in 1819 was less the existence of a 'frail sisterhood' than the assertion of its superiority over its London equivalent in terms of 'language, manners, and demeanour'.[100] In view of the trade's continuation, it seems safe to assume that a number of Penrose's contemporaries, along with other 'noisy Fellows', were willing and able to spend their stay moving between worlds of violence or paid sex, and gentlemanly propriety at the nearby assembly.

John Penrose came to Bath in search of better health, not refined company. However, once exposed to the patterns of its daily life he proved an active participant in many aspects of the resort's polite culture. His conversion was in part the result of an education in conformity. Times to visit, clothes to wear, places to walk (and avoid) were learned through a combination of guidebooks and word of mouth. Once established, Penrose was free to construct his own routine, ignoring activities and venues in which he had little interest. He emerges as a reasonably sociable man who, like Dudley Ryder, gave particular attention to the pleasures of good conversation but who, unlike Ryder, found this in female as well as male company. An apparently happily married man in his mid-fifties, Penrose experienced none of the tensions that female society brought to a lovelorn Dudley Ryder and which had soured his own opinion of the resort in May 1716.

Of course, Penrose was himself ambivalent towards Bath society. Often he resented the demands placed on his time and worried about the effects of too much socialising on his studies or relations with his family. This was not the complaint of a gouty misanthrope but of someone who detected a less admirable side to a resort where sober and moral sociability was abandoned for fashionable triviality. Penrose's assessment brings to mind the century-long debate over polite society's impact on gentlemanliness and manhood that we have traced in contemporary intellectual and popular literature. Respect for the tradesman's civilities or the gentility of the formal breakfast shows Penrose's appreciation of the merits of refinement. Yet this optimism was balanced by the ridiculousness of certain bespectacled gentlemen and their arbiter of fashion, Samuel Derrick. As in the literature of the day, Penrose's reaction to these foibles ranged from gentle satire to concern, notably when men like Derrick were thought to reflect a wider social malaise. In Penrose's correspondence, therefore, we see both sides of a debate between which he, and presumably others, wavered during their stay in this distinctive but, for its critics, disturbingly representative polite society.

James Boswell: civilisation and its malcontent

Our final case study looks at the testimony of one of the eighteenth century's most frank and self-indulgent memoirists. Born into a landed Scottish family, James Boswell (1740–95), like Dudley Ryder, studied in Edinburgh and the Netherlands before qualifying as a barrister. Boswell, however, failed to achieve prominence in the legal profession. From the mid-1770s, as law lost its appeal to him, he focused increasingly on a literary career which culminated in his monumental biography of Samuel Johnson (1791) drawn from an extensive journal.

Boswell began his journal in November 1762 on a trip to London. Over the next thirty-three years he assiduously fulfilled his early resolution to 'set down my various sentiments and my various conduct' in order that all men might 'with tolerable certainty judge "what manner of person he is"'.[101] The journal's interest rests to a large extent on Boswell's inability to discover lasting answers to this question, notwithstanding the rigorousness of his search. The breadth and candour of his self-scrutiny have made his memoir a valuable resource for historians interested in Boswell's personality and late-eighteenth-century concepts of self-identity, in addition to the social practices in which he engaged.[102]

A marked feature of Boswell's search, especially during the early to mid-1760s, was its characterisation as a quest for a manly reputation. The manliness of other respectable companions, coupled with Boswell's frequent strictures to himself to follow their example, suggests the importance of gender identity for his bid to develop an admirable, adult personality. His interest in manhood has received some comment from modern scholars, several of whom point to Boswell's preoccupation with his sexual performance. Boswell's appetite for sexual encounters is well known by anyone with even a cursory knowledge of the man. Second only to his celebrity as a biographer, Boswell's reputation as a fornicator has been firmly established by the likes of Lawrence Stone.[103] Drawing on this evidence, recent studies highlight the importance of Boswell's libido in fashioning a 'male character' which, as Felicity Nussbaum argues, rested 'precariously on the power to maintain dominance over women'.[104]

Polite Boswell

It is not my aim to question this interpretation, but to draw attention, first, to some of the other requirements Boswell thought necessary for manliness, and, second, to the centrality of politeness for this broader concept of manhood. We have already seen Boswell's appreciation of the value of the relationship between politeness and manliness in his praise of the 'manly' nature of Samuel Johnson's refinement in Scotland in October 1773.[105] By this date, Boswell had shown himself to be a careful student of politeness, an attribute which, from the early 1760s, he treated as a key means to effect his own progression from youth to adulthood, from boyhood to manhood. The importance of refined conduct becomes apparent when we consider the principal ways by which he sought to cultivate a reputation for manliness as confirmation of this progression.

For Boswell, becoming an adult man meant becoming a Londoner. His first visit to the capital in 1760 had ended in shame when, after falling into dissolute company, he had been recalled to Scotland by his disapproving father, Lord Auchinleck. Thereafter Boswell visited London for nine months in 1762–3, and from 1765 made lengthy annual visits before moving to the capital in 1786. Of course, throughout his life, London remained a prime location for Boswell's pre- and extra-marital sexual encounters. But as his journal also makes clear, these activities comprised only a small part of his urban experience, even as a rapacious young man in his early twenties. Boswell spent far more time seeking acceptance within a London of social and literary societies, parks, gardens and a network of less genteel but convivial chop- and coffee-houses.

Journal entries describing his London role models similarly suggest an attachment to adult sociability. In 1762, for example, he returned to the capital in 1762 not as a libertine, but with 'strong dispositions to be a Mr Addison'.[106] Boswell had first read the *Spectator* at the age of eight. Now that he was in London, the periodical proved a valuable guide as he sought to cultivate the responsible urbanity promoted by its authors. His journal for 1762–3 reveals him, like Dudley Ryder, to have been an assiduous reader of the *Spectator*, though, in contrast to Ryder, Boswell provides no analysis of individual papers. Without this commentary it is difficult to assess the precise role advice literature played in fashioning Boswell's notion of polite male conduct. Subsequent references to texts like Samuel Johnson's *Rambler* periodical and Adam Smith's *Theory of Moral Sentiments* certainly show his familiarity (and personal friendship) with influential theorists of personal and societal refinement. However, Boswell also appears to have placed more emphasis (as indeed many guides encouraged) on active participation within a metropolitan society where, he believed, 'men and manners may be seen to the best advantage'.[107]

Boswell's descriptions of the more admirable of these men invariably referred to their capacity for sociability and refinement. Early examples included Charles Douglas, duke of Queensbury, a man of the 'greatest politeness . . . Humanity and gentleness of manners'; and Norton Nicholls, who possessed an 'amiable disposition, a sweetness of manners, and an easy politeness that pleased me much'.[108] Among later instances were a 'genteel and lively' Mr Hall and the 'mightily delicate and polite' Mr Berenger, to whom we might also add Samuel Johnson and, from further afield, the Highlanders Boswell encountered during his 1773 tour of Scotland.[109] Alongside these accounts of admirable and polite men, Boswell gave careful consideration to his own reputation for manliness. Again, politeness was central to this identity. Thus, in London during 1762–3, he characterised himself as a mature adult distinct from the 'rattling uncultivated' youth of his first visit in 1760. In doing so, Boswell made much of his new-found 'composed genteel character' which enabled him to behave 'myself in a manly, & genteel manner'.[110]

What did this new persona mean in terms of day-to-day living? In certain circumstances, Boswell's search for polite manliness led him to adopt practices that were at odds with the generous sociability advocated by the likes of Joseph Addison. Eager to establish his London credentials, Boswell abandoned many of his former Edinburgh friends, whom he now thought rowdy and incivil. An invitation to Lady Betty Macfarlane's London house in early 1763, for example, went unanswered on three occasions 'as I wanted to have nothing but English ideas, and to be as manly as I possibly could'.[111] We can see a similarly self-absorbed approach in Boswell's slightly earlier encounter with a London sword-smith. Realising that he had come out without money, Boswell sought to present himself as a gentleman of sufficient standing to obtain a sword on credit. 'I determined', he wrote, 'to make a trial of the civility of my fellow creatures, and what effect my external appearance and address would have'. The exchange finds Boswell keen to test his refined London character, here composed of showy manners intended to ingratiate. In his journal Boswell recalled how, though initially unwilling, the shop-keeper had relented after his customer had paid him generous compliments and 'bowed genteely'.[112]

Boswell's desire for a new sword offers one instance of his general appreciation of the material trappings of breeding that found further expression in a penchant for fine and invariably 'genteel' suits befitting his status as a polite, or as he often put it, a 'pretty gentleman'. Boswell never lost this confidence in the role of dress in polite society. Yet subsequent comments also suggest an intriguing progression in, or at least another side to, this early and somewhat simplistic understanding of the relationship between appearance and refinement. Thus in a later essay, 'On luxury' (1778), Boswell provided an interpretation reminiscent of *Spectator* No. 631's account of the psychological impact of dress on sociability. 'Every one', he believed, 'has felt himself more disposed to decorum and propriety and courtesy . . . when genteely dressed', a relationship he attributed, as Addison had done, to the propensity for 'our faculties to assimilate themselves to that circumstance about us'.[113]

Evidence of this more mature understanding of sociability can also be found rather earlier in Boswell's appreciation of the value of conversation. From his initial encounters with London literary society, Boswell, like Dudley Ryder and John Penrose, soon became aware of the importance of good speech as a means to access and gain a reputation in this attractive adult world. At the centre of this society was Boswell's mentor, the 'stupendous

[Samuel] Johnson', a man whose 'vivacity with solid good sense' made for 'highly instructive and highly entertaining' conversation.[114] Boswell phrased his compliment with care, for in these concepts of instruction and entertainment we see two elements that were central to his understanding of good conversation and civilised sociability.

He was certainly pleased when he himself spoke confidently on edifying subjects such as politics or literature. In July 1763, for example, he discussed current affairs with the MP George Dempster. 'I behaved extremely well tonight', he wrote afterwards, 'I was attentive, cheerful and manly.' Dempster, by contrast, had practised 'sophistry' and was a 'feeble antagonist' and a 'very weak man'.[115] Boswell encountered a similarly poor speaker in 1764 in the figure of Monsieur des Essar, a member of a Utrecht debating society. Des Essar's speech failed on three counts: it was pedantic – as shown by his habit of publicly correcting Boswell's French – self-indulgent and dull. Again, Boswell depicted the effect as a loss of manliness in this 'fop in learning' who was 'vain . . . makes compliments . . . gets bored, and his misery makes the rest of us ashamed of ours'.[116]

In contrast to Monsieur des Essar, other men tried too hard to divert their audience. In 1765 Boswell suffered the company of a 'group of artificers' or 'professed wits' who put 'themselves to much pain in order to please', but who, in his opinion, would have been better company had they appeared 'as they naturally feel themselves'.[117] Though superior on this occasion, Boswell often considered himself guilty of the same intemperance. Having ignored the Spectatorial demand for self-control in conversation, he judged himself to have been overly jovial and 'too ridiculous' at a dinner in January 1763. This, he realised, would not qualify him as a man of sense or polite conversation, his fellow diners being likely to 'applaud a man for it in company, but behind his back hold him very cheap'.[118] Throughout his life Boswell contained but never mastered the impetuosity he deemed incompatible with commendable sociability. Later he identified his 'habit of telling everything' as the means by which 'a man . . . loses delicacy and dignity'.[119] Self-censure was, as ever, followed by private exhortations to perform with a greater degree of self-restraint by which he would achieve 'constant useful conversation, with mild and grave dignity'.[120]

This was not to say that conversation had to be 'useful' at the expense of all other qualities. Dr Johnson's habit of savaging his intellectual opponents, which at times Boswell admired, was more typically a source of discord. Perceptions of Johnson's often combative style were, Boswell realised, partly dependent on the audience. The 'remarkable elegance of his own manners', for example, made Lord Eglinton 'too delicately sensible of the roughness . . . in Johnson's behaviour'.[121] Elsewhere, Boswell, like Oliver Goldsmith, set Johnson's reputation for blunt behaviour against the sincerity of his inner feelings.[122] However, there were times when Boswell was unable to maintain this approach. As he wrote after one such confrontation in Scotland, 'I regretted that Mr Johnson did not practice the art of accommodating himself to different sorts of people. Had he been softer with this venerable old man, we might have had more conversation.'[123]

What Johnson lacked on this occasion was amiability or complaisance, another quality Boswell admired in male companions. Thus, Lord Mountstuart was 'warmly friendly', revealing 'an amiable affection not unworthy of a man'; the actor West Digges was 'a pretty man [with] . . . most amiable dispositions', while Adam Smith, the embodiment of Goldsmith's learned 'man of taste', blended scholarship with friendship and was 'really amiable', having 'nothing of that formal stiffness and pedantry which is too often found in professors'.[124] Smith's warmth meant that he avoided not only confrontation but also the formality associated with misguided notions of refined conduct. Such attributes were again prominent in Boswell's sense of his own position within polite society. Preparing for a trip to The Hague in 1763, for example, he wrote of his need to 'have no affectation' and to be 'an amiable pretty man'.[125]

Avoiding affectation required 'easiness'. Like conversation, this was a quality Boswell usually identified with his most respected, sober and confident companions, two of whom, Dr Johnson and Pasquale Paoli, met in 1766 'with a manly ease, mutually conscious of their own abilities and of the abilities one of each other'.[126] In moments of positive self-evaluation, Boswell likewise regularly drew attention to his being 'quite easy and comfortable', or having acted in an 'easy, genteel style'.[127] Relaxed and accommodating, a confident Boswell often measured easiness in terms of his ability to socialise with a broad range of people: 'I really can adapt myself to any company wonderfully well', he wrote on 10 August 1774 after an impromptu Edinburgh dinner party.[128] In Scotland, as on this occasion, much of Boswell's polite socialising took place over meals. In the same week, for example, he twice breakfasted with Lady Colville, dined with Lady Betty Cochrane and other 'good genteel company', spent another evening with Lord Pembroke 'with as much ease and genteelly as I could wish', and finally enjoyed 'a genteel supper' with Sandy Gordon.[129]

In England, Boswell likewise performed a considerable amount of his socialising around the breakfast and dinner table. This he supplemented with attendance at a broader range of polite venues, including York's 'very noble' assembly room, where he 'loved to see so many genteel people', while in London he added one-off attractions like Ranelagh Gardens and the Pantheon to the dozens of chop and coffee-houses he visited with friends and professional colleagues.[130] Though he often set out in familiar company, the breadth of his social circle meant Boswell regularly came across new acquaintances with whom he aimed to behave with the accommodation and confidence that marked Johnson and Paoli's first meeting. At other London venues, the number and mix of visitors increased the likelihood of chance encounters. Walking in St James's Park in September 1769, for example, Boswell had observed 'crowds of well-dressed people, without being known to one of them'. This is not to imply that Boswell was an avid seeker of new company. Like John Penrose, he at times took exception to the potential intrusions of polite society. Boswell never visited Bath, so we can only speculate as to what his opinion would have been of the streams of visitors that wearied the less gregarious Penrose. At least visitors at Bath tended to be established acquaintances. In Edinburgh, however, Boswell claimed that he and other refined pedestrians were subject to an insufferable degree of 'familiarity' and 'inquisitiveness' from unknown promenaders. This Boswell thought symptomatic of the city's 'very bad' manners, and a further distinguishing factor between incivil Lowland Scots and polite Londoners who, though sociable when introduced, otherwise exercised what he applauded as a pleasing and respectful reserve.[131]

With his attendance at coffee-houses, parks and the occasional assembly room, Boswell inhabited a world familiar to many eighteenth-century readers and historians of conduct and satirical literature. Yet, as the journals show, he also socialised in other, less elegant spaces that required just as much talent for easiness and conversation. Before settling in London in 1786, Boswell paid annual visits to the capital, to which he travelled by coach. Taking between four and six days to complete, these journeys from Edinburgh threw him into the close company of passengers from a variety of backgrounds. In August 1769, for example, he shared his carriage with a city lawyer and a country gentleman with whom he was 'very hearty'. On the following day he was joined by a woollen-draper, a gentlewoman and her daughter: 'we were exceedingly chatty', he wrote, 'how pleasant it is to live well with our fellow creatures and interchange civilities'.[132] Boswell was equally pleased with himself when, several trips later, he met a sea captain and sang patriotic shanties. This engagement was again interpreted as proof of his easy sociability: 'so soft and warm a composition am I that I adhere a little to almost all with whom I come into contact, unless they have qualities which repel me'.[133] Unfortunately, carriage travel also exposed him to such company. During the 1769 trip, for example, Boswell's party had been joined by a Northumbrian farmer 'very little removed from a brute' with 'the coarsest dress and manners'.[134] Even better company produced discomfort, caused to a large extent by Boswell's own, and by the mid-1770s increasing, sensitivity and readiness to take offence. Thus his 'nerves were hurt' when first faced with the sea captain's bluff good humour and, although recovering, he later fell back into 'gloom'. 'What misery', he wrote, beginning his 1776 journey, 'does a man of sensibility suffer!'[135]

Sentimental Boswell

Boswell's construction of his sentimental persona had been a gradual process. A student of Adam Smith at Glasgow in the late 1750s, his early journals show an appreciation of the language and signs of sensibility. Early in 1763, for example, he recorded how the Old Testament story of Joseph – a popular subject of sentimental advice literature – 'melted my heart and drew tears from my eyes'. Similar responses were derived from more contemporary sources: the *Spectator*'s promotion of the 'person of imagination and feeling' or the 'pathetic' father/son relationship in David Garrick's production of *Henry IV* which again 'drew tears from my eyes'.[136]

Reactions to the play were no doubt affected by Boswell's difficult relationship with his own father. Typically a distant, serious and censorious figure, Lord Auchinleck sometimes intruded directly upon his son's attempt to cultivate a refined and sociable personality. After a dinner with friends in July 1769, for example, Boswell wrote of how his father's 'manner awed and checked the freedom of conversation. This is really hard to bear.' Here Lord Auchinleck's humourless formality was at fault. Elsewhere, the problem was Boswell's superior refinement. March of that year had found them as friendly 'as my father's singular grave and steady temper will allow; for he has not that quick sensibility which animates me'.[137]

If father/son relations failed to engage Boswell's sensibility, then female company provided greater opportunity. This is not to say that his predominant attitude to women was sentimental. Boswell's appetite for sexual encounters is well known; moreover, the nature of these encounters, especially those with lower-class women, was often crude and exploitative. In addition, Boswell met a number of women to whom he was attracted by their evident, if not always welcome, intellectual superiority.

More typically, however, female company featured less as a source of mental stimulation than of social regulation and polish. It is worth remembering that it was Samuel Johnson's conversation with the duchess, not the duke, of Argyll that prompted Boswell to compliment him as 'fine gentlemen' in October 1773. Likewise, the week of genteel dining Boswell enjoyed in Edinburgh in August 1774 owed much to the fact that the men drank moderately and then took 'tea and coffee with the ladies'; several days later Boswell again 'drank socially' before the 'Ladies and gentlemen rose from table together. It was quite as I could wish.'[138]

Central to virtuous women's ability to refine was a capacity to feel. 'Figure to yourself', Boswell wrote of one romantic partner in the late 1760s, 'the finest creature . . . formed like a Grecian nymph with the sweetest countenance, full of sensibility'.[139] In his search for love we can see Boswell fully, and self-consciously, adopting the characteristics of the man of feeling. In May 1769, while pursuing another woman who 'melts my heart', Boswell spent time with his cousin (and future wife), Margaret Montgomerie. By June it was she who 'hung on my *heart*'. 'I read your letters with such feelings as I never before experienced', he wrote to her in July when, as a result of her company, 'my heart was softened'.[140] Once married, recollections of his family often prompted Boswell to openly sentimental expression. July 1786 found him in low spirits: 'When I got into the streets again I was so depressed that the tears ran down my cheeks. I thought of my wife and children with tender affection.' In the following year his wife's illness again prompted him to weep, whereupon he was comforted by his son 'like a man older than myself'. Finally, on news of her death in July 1789, Boswell wrote to his 'warm-hearted friend', William Temple, of his 'distress and tender painful regret' and again 'cried bitterly'.[141]

At such a tragic event it is unfair to imagine Boswell's as anything but a genuine and spontaneous expression of grief. Certainly on previous occasions he had complimented and sympathised with men who displayed similar emotions, an opinion that suggests Boswell's acceptance of male weeping both in private and with company. On other occasions, however, sensibility also served to indicate his distinctiveness from what he judged less refined company. Confronted by the spirited sea captain in March 1776, Boswell soon grew melancholic, his nerves 'hurt' by such boisterousness. In the previous month he suffered a similar experience on encountering a bluff huntsman: 'his animal spirits shocked my nervous sensibility', he wrote after meeting Sir Walter Montgomerie-Cunninghame complete with his recently killed quarry.[142] On both occasions, Boswell revealed an appreciation of his delicate nervous physiology and, in turn, an understanding of the link between feeling and a susceptibility to mental and physical ill-health that he claimed to share with what he termed other 'men of excellence'.[143]

Given that feeling was replete with positive connotation, fear of insensitivity loomed large in Boswell's middle to later years. In October 1769 he suffered a typical moment of self-doubt when, in Dr Johnson's presence, he became 'uneasy that I do not feel enough . . . in the keen manner that others say they do'.[144] Johnson's advice – that Boswell embellish his sensitivity by reading more melancholy literature – seems a typically facetious rebuke from someone critical of what he saw as the modern affectation for sensibility. Yet to an extent this image of a man cultivating and examining his capacity for feeling was precisely the course of action Boswell did take, although it was less bookshops than prisons and public executions that provided his principal testing ground.

Comments he made on his relationship to his best-known legal client, the convicted sheep-stealer John Reid, suggest Boswell to have been a man of abundant sensibility. In the weeks between Reid's sentence and execution in September 1774 Boswell made numerous appeals on the prisoner's behalf and paid him repeated visits. Events left Boswell gloomy in ways that evoked the work of moral philosopher David Hume, a friend with whom he had recently dined. Writing on 30 August 1774 he claimed 'by sympathy' to have 'sucked the dismal ideas of John Reid's situation'. Such suffering should surely have been sufficient. Yet a physically refined Boswell believed his experience more acute than Reid's, since 'spirits ... when transferred to another body of a more delicate nature, will have much more influence than on the body from which it is transferred'.[145] The nature of Boswell's response recalls that of Dudley Ryder sixty years earlier. For Ryder, the spectacle of a condemned prisoner, though moving, had demonstrated the impossibility of imagining other men's experience. By contrast, Boswell's appreciation of himself as a man of acute sensibility – 'a being very much consisting of feeling ... conducted by the forces of fancy and sensation' – enabled him not only to sympathise with, but to share in and even outstrip Reid's feelings in the days before his death.[146]

Boswell's preoccupation with sensibility invariably drew him to the public execution of former clients and other, unknown individuals. Here again the primary motive was to test his capacity for sympathy by imagining his own deportment on the gallows. What Ryder was unable to achieve, Boswell as man of feeling found a relatively straightforward state to attain and, again, to exceed. 'I never saw a man hanged but I thought I could behave better than he did', he wrote in March 1768. There were, however, exceptions – including James Gibson, whose execution Boswell had watched prior to this journal entry. Gibson had excelled by conducting himself with a degree of equanimity and 'steady resolution' that Boswell found impossible to imagine, and on which he regularly commented in his journal.[147] In 1774 John Reid was similarly praised for having behaved with 'great calmness and piety', while Peter Shaw met his death in 1785 with a 'steady but modest look'.[148]

In commending equanimity Boswell appears more in tune with the thinking of Adam Smith than of David Hume. As a student, Boswell had attended the lectures that formed the basis of Smith's *Theory of Moral Sentiments*; journal entries from 1764 and 1769 also reveal a detailed knowledge of his tutor's work in book form. Smith's line on conduct before execution was uncompromising. Displays of sorrow, he argued, would be regarded as self-indulgent by spectators from whom sympathy was only possible if prisoners controlled their emotions. In this sense, Boswell's ability to imagine others' feelings can be seen as directly related to this process of regulation, though in James Gibson's case it was the extent of his control which made sympathy difficult.

Smith's second reason for discipline focused on the maintenance of a man's reputation. In an argument that demonstrates Smith's attachment to stoicism, self-pity (a single tear was sufficient) was said to undermine a prisoner's claim to courage, regardless of his former bravery.[149] Though never adopting this line in full, Boswell clearly looked on men like Gibson as exemplars of an ideal male character capable of 'perfect calmness and manly resolution', or, in Peter Shaw's case, 'manly composure'.[150] Boswell's appreciation suggests the on-going importance of traditional styles of stoical and hardy manhood that, away from the gallows, he had previously sought in his bid to regulate youthful indulgence. 'To bear', he wrote in October 1763, 'is the noble power of man'.[151] Now, in later life, he saw self-command both as facilitating sympathetic exchange and as saving him and his nervous contemporaries from its excesses. Thus, while Boswell sympathised with his low-spirited friend William Temple, he also demanded that Temple manage his emotions. 'Read Epictetus. Read Johnson. Let a manly and firm philosophy brace your mind', he advised. Failure to do so, as the hypochondriacal Boswell well knew, left an individual 'hurt by everything' and 'renders him unmanly'.[152]

Impolite Boswell

Recent studies of Boswell's attitude to prisoners show how his sympathy extended only to those in whom he identified similar personality traits to his own. His rapport with John Reid has been attributed to his sharing a sense of injustice at Reid's sentence and to the kinship he felt with a fellow family man led to crime through heavy drinking, a vice in which Boswell indulged and by the mid-1770s was increasingly unable to control.[153] Yet for all this, Boswell clearly saw himself as Reid's superior, being both the son of a Scottish laird and a man of sensibility whose 'more delicate nature' accounted for his having 'suffered much more than John did'.[154] In this particular relationship Boswell's delicacy appears to have stimulated genuine fellow feeling. Elsewhere, however, such perceived gradations in refinement prompted more competitive, snobbish conduct, at odds with the social mixing envisaged by Addison and Hume as a feature of civilised urban living. Indeed, at times Boswell actively opposed this trend for easy sociability which he blamed for one of his principal bug-bears, the lack of good manners in Lowland Scotland. This he traced to the union with England in 1707. As we saw in Chapter One, the union had proved a significant event for advocates of social change who, like Hume, believed it to have provided a stimulus to Scottish modernisation. However, whereas Hume saw improvement, Boswell detected 'an abominable spirit of levelling', creating a society in which the decorum of hierarchy had been lost and all 'think themselves equally *gentlemen*'.[155]

At a personal level, Boswell's journal contains numerous criticisms of supposedly refined individuals who, in his view, were far from gentlemanly. By identifying these figures, Boswell gained opportunities to comment simultaneously on the nature of sub-standard politeness and on the sincerity and modernity of his own conduct. These were episodes of politeness not as sociability but as the competitive exercise of power or revenge. Thus, criticisms of Monsieur des Essar's vain conversation in 1764 followed the Frenchman's humiliation of Boswell at a Utrecht debating society. Count Gentili, an ostensibly elegant Corsican to whom he also took a personal dislike, had 'little true politeness, that is to say, little compliance or softness of manners', while the radical reformer, John Horne Tooke, was criticised in 1790 for speaking with 'smooth arrogance' against the Anglican Church in a way that 'showed him to be a man not in the habits of genteel company, where such abuse is now . . . impolite'.[156]

Criticism also provided Boswell with the chance to assert the manly tone of his own politeness when compared to that 'fop in learning', des Essar, and others. The 'prig . . . fop [and] idler' whom Boswell and William Temple encountered in 1763 was a man 'with manners very different from ours'; so too was Mr Miller, whose reported preoccupation with social trivialities put Boswell less in mind of a refined gentleman than a 'mere fribble'.[157]

In fact, like Dudley Ryder, Boswell was also often critical of his own shortcomings. His concern over his tendency for rowdiness, coupled with his calls for greater self-moderation, show the search for refinement as an ongoing struggle between personal urges and social pressures. Certain desires were particularly troublesome. In Chapter Two we saw how Boswell mediated during a debate between Sir Joshua Reynolds and Samuel Johnson over alcohol's contribution to male sociability. Throughout his life Boswell often echoed Reynolds's appreciation of moderate drinking as (as he phrased it in August 1774) 'the cement of the company'.[158] However, reports of less controlled sessions also suggest Boswell's acceptance of Johnson's belief in the incompatibility of alcohol and good conversation. 'Drinking never fails to make me ill-bred' he wrote after a typically heavy bout earlier that year.[159] The nature of this ill-breeding followed a familiar pattern: initial alcohol-induced loquaciousness, followed by a loss of propriety whereupon he became disputatious or crude. Immoderate drinking remained a male-only activity, often undertaken with professional colleagues. But once sober, Boswell typically recalled the distress his drunkenness had caused to his wife or other female company. Plans to reduce his drinking often concentrated on reintegrating himself in this society at alternative sites of mixed sociability such as the tea-table – a practice which a remorseful Boswell 'was determined . . . to revive' in April 1772.[160]

In addition to these episodes of lost control, we must finally consider Boswell's occasional, conscious abandonment of polite society. In certain circumstances this rejection was the act of a hypochondriacal man of feeling. The journal entry for 13 December 1783, for example, spoke of a desire to keep 'clear of society as disgusting', an agoraphobic tendency he thought 'in the family'.[161] At other times Boswell chose a more obnoxious course reminiscent of Dudley Ryder's 'negligent gentlemen', though in Boswell's case practised not as an alternative style but as a rejection of refinement. On these occasions, the incentive for his anti-social conduct was dependent on its location at the heart of polite society. Plans for a genteel supper with Lady Colville in July 1774 were ruined by Boswell's 'disagreeable humour, domineering and ill-bred', in which he persisted 'when I saw it was observed with dissatisfaction'.[162] Three years later, he wrote of his having 'for some time past . . . indulged [in] coarse raillery and abuse by far too much'. However, Boswell had evidently forgotten this self-criticism on the following day when, dining with his wife and a friend, he 'indulged bad temper . . . disregarding politeness'.[163]

Such poor behaviour indicates the pleasurableness of rule breaking in polite company from which, in view of Boswell's social standing and the tolerance of his wife and companions, he was scarcely in danger of being ostracised. As we have seen, his more sustained episodes of incivility took place away from polite society in the male-only environment of a tavern, where sober conversation easily degenerated from reserved sociability to drunken camaraderie. Meanwhile, for carnal rather than communal pleasures Boswell frequented an alternative sexual culture that went unmentioned at the mixed dinner or tea-table. Thus in April 1776, after behaving 'pretty decently' at a London society dinner, he descended into the seamier culture of the Charing Cross bagnio for sex. Shocked by the 'uncleanness' of his behaviour, Boswell returned the next day to find and speak with the prostitute in what he described as her 'blackguard lane'.[164]

Yet the sordidness that troubled the middle-aged Boswell had been an attraction in early manhood. To celebrate the king's birthday in 1762 Boswell had 'resolved to be a blackguard' by dressing in old dirty clothes, rampaging through the streets, and sexually abusing several prostitutes.[165] This was inversion on a grand scale: monarch's birthdays were traditionally occasions for elevated social behaviour. Then at Bath, Dudley Ryder had celebrated George I's birthday in 1716 at an assembly of 'very good company [with] good clothes', while John Penrose noted George III's 'very brilliant' well-wishers half a century later.[166] As a blackguard, of course, Boswell came closer to the 'noisy Fellows' who assaulted Penrose at Bath's West Gate. In choosing blackguard garb, Boswell cast off the qualities central not only to his refined persona but also to the associated manly identities – moderation, dignity, reserve – essential for this character. In its place came an alternative understanding of manhood defined in terms of boorishness as opposed to gentility, hardiness rather than delicacy, and sexual rapacity not sensibility.

James Boswell began his journal so that others would know 'what manner of person he is'. Readers are faced with a range of possibilities: libertine, drunk, blackguard, man of sense or feeling, polite or 'pretty gentleman'. This survey has shown how Boswell placed considerable emphasis on the latter identities in cultivating a manly reputation closely bound up with his life in London, a place where Boswell found men and manners displayed to their best advantage. Through reading and social observation 'polite Boswell' came to appreciate behaviour blending sober responsibility, entertainment, generosity and an easiness that enabled men of conversation (for Boswell, like Ryder and Penrose, a key expression of male sociability) to conduct themselves in a range of circumstances. The centrality of decorum, sense and self-control for good conversation made its practitioners worthy claimants of manhood against whom Boswell set the inadequacy of boys or 'effeminate' and 'foppish' men.

While never foregoing his appreciation of conversation, in later years Boswell sought a complementary reputation for sensibility. Unlike Dudley Ryder's inchoate selection of sentimental expressions, Boswell depicted himself as a fully formed man of feeling: a weeping, nervous, delicate and refined individual seemingly capable of remarkable acts of sympathetic exchange. In his appreciation of the value of sensibility, Boswell applied (or in Johnson's view affected) the attributes of the man of feeling with which he was familiar from the work both of scholarly theorists, like Hume and Smith, and a popularising melancholic literature mocked by Johnson. Compared to the other two men surveyed in this chapter, Boswell's understanding of polite society often proved conceptually ambitious, no doubt influenced by the enlightenment thinkers whom he studied and with whom he socialised. His 1778 discussion of good dress as a general agent of social harmony, or his appreciation of shared civilities between 'fellow creatures' in a carriage, reveal this more sophisticated appreciation of a modern community or (English) nation engaged in unprecedented levels of refined sociability.

At the same time, Boswell's love of society made him less discriminating than Ryder or Penrose when it came to the nature of this social contact. In contrast to the Spectatorial ideal in which politeness and sociability were synonymous, Boswell's evenings of hard drinking also reveal a more visceral form of human integration which he often carried over into genteel society. Invariably, he viewed these episodes after the event as a deviation from the refined ideal and as a source for recrimination. Like Dudley Ryder's diary, the journal reveals the effort required to achieve a polite reputation based on persistent self-scrutiny, doubt and censure. Equally, like Penrose's correspondence, it highlights the polite man's opportunity to absent himself in an alternative 'blackguard' world of sexual adventure which, if geographically close, remained enticingly distant from the polite patterns of daily life.[167]

The practice of polite manliness

The testimonies examined in this chapter offer insight into three personal encounters with eighteenth-century polite society. Each memoirist points to the complexity and contradiction of this society, both as a set of behavioural ideals and as a series of locations and venues, and reveals the consequences of their, and others', attempts to implement these codes in daily life. In previous chapters we have looked at eighteenth-century debates over the meaning of social refinement, and the implications of these for representations of the gentleman. As Anna Bryson argues for the early modern period, these debates, despite giving us 'little indication of the distance between . . . ideals and real behaviour', are valuable as 'a significant cultural fact', providing insight into the preoccupations and concerns of a particular society through its notions of good (and bad) social conduct.[168] In the testimonies studied here we are now presented with evidence of the relevance of this cultural fact for three eighteenth-century individuals.

Dudley Ryder, John Penrose and James Boswell each appreciated the value of polite society. In their commentaries on social performance all three show an effort to acquire, internalise, and then enact a range of social practices set out in advice guides or discernible from the conduct of their peers. In each, the personality of the early eighteenth-century polite gentleman, discussed in Chapter Two, features prominently. Nor is this surprising given the direct and enduring relevance of texts like Addison and Steele's *Spectator* for Ryder and Boswell's social education, or the impact of these theorists for later writing on polite gentlemanliness, and for models of polite living at resorts such as Bath.

The polite men studied here show a striking readiness to acknowledge the value of social conformity. Yet their concern was less with the intricacies of a specific social code than with a polite personality capable (in the manner encouraged by the guides) of combining self-control with easiness, reserve with accommodation and informality with intelligence. None of these writers was especially preoccupied with mastering an elaborate external show of manners. Ryder's interest in dancing was rooted in his desire to express inner virtue, and soon became a source of anxiety when it threatened his reputation as a serious legal student. Set against his general discussion of polite manhood, Boswell's show of external manners to a London sword-smith in 1763 comes across as a juvenile attempt to perform in a man's world. It is noteworthy that Boswell's principal guide to adult sociability was Samuel Johnson, whose attraction lay in his powers of conversation rather than the finer points of his dress or deportment. Boswell shared this high assessment of and concern to perfect his conversation with Ryder and Penrose, who likewise thought intelligent discourse the best means of con-veying personality in a polished and attractive form.

However, there were times when conversation was not enough. Dudley Ryder's description of his sighs and tender looks is striking, coming as it does in an account otherwise concerned with models of gentlemanliness associated with intelligence, moderation and self-control. Ryder's use of emotional signs in specific company reminds us that the culture of sensibility which matured in the third quarter of the century had early-eighteenth-century roots. Certainly, Dudley Ryder did not seek to make these senti-mental gestures integral to his daily conduct, and tears – their most extreme manifestation – attracted public criticism and remained a source of per-sonal humiliation to him. Such strictures do not appear to have prevented James Boswell from indulging more completely in displays of sensibility. During the 1770s, he adapted a range of medical and moral philosophical influences to become a nervous and refined man of feeling, reflecting a significant shift in mid- to late-century attitudes to social refinement, which saw men's tears recast as evidence of sympathetic feeling, and sighs and swoons as an indication of desirable romanticism, not ridiculous love-sickness. Equally, Boswell's movement between a polite and a sentimental persona reminds us of John Brewer's comment on the complex relation-ship between the two discourses, 'not least in the breast of many a refined person', while raising interesting questions about the reason for (and sincerity of) Boswell's choice between modes of refinement in different circumstances.[169]

If the influence of social ideals is apparent, the story of polite manhood in action remains rather less straightforward. Certainly, we can trace the ideals of conversation, ease and accommodation played out in the daily conduct of these often self-congratulatory individuals. Examples of the successful implementation of this personality remind us of the durability of traditional manly qualities – sense, moderation, self-control, independence

– that eighteenth-century behavioural authors and real-life practitioners considered central to fashioning the man of interesting, but not intrusive, conversation, the good listener or the sympathetic observer. All three writers argued the need for traditional values to avoid over-exposure to refined living that, at a certain level, all considered antithetical to manliness.

The memoirists' responses to affectation or excess took the form of self-censure for their own shortcomings, or the ridicule of other 'fine' or 'foppish' gentlemen deemed unable to mediate between refinement and effeminacy. In making these accusations, only James Penrose, interestingly, applied the term to strangers, guilty of the triviality that he clearly saw as integral to Bath polite society. For Ryder and Boswell, by contrast, the label 'fop' served as a device for personal revenge or rebuke. Ryder, jealous of other men's popularity with women, and Boswell, angered by Monsieur des Essar's vanity, were quick to label their enemies fine or foppish. To do so was both to link the person criticised with a range of traits associated with the type (regardless of his actual conduct), and to suggest the accuser's ability to participate in the very refined practices which, in others, precipitated foppish effeminacy. Ryder as a regular patron of the dancing-master, Penrose and Boswell as participants or advocates of the mixed tea-table, and all three as men sporting 'fine' clothing for special occasions, embodied a lifestyle that popular satires attributed to the fop, but which in the context of complex lives was more typically interpreted as evidence of true gentlemanliness. An appreciation of the complexities of character also redeemed other men from the taint of foppery. Based on what he knew of Mr Miller, for example, Boswell had expected to find a foppish 'fribble'; had they not met, he might well have continued to think of Miller in this way. However, face-to-face Boswell discovered him to be not an 'effeminate fop' but a 'tall, well-looking man, very elegantly dressed . . . and not so trivial as I imagined'.[170] The admirable dignity of Mr Miller's personality brought him down on the right side of the fine line between foppery and refined elegance, evident in all periods of male fashion.

The importance that each memoirist attached to his performance in polite society also demanded that he carefully observe both his own conduct and that of other, apparently more refined, individuals. In this, the testimonies suggest less success, revealing marked variations in the distance between 'ideal' and 'actual' behaviour. All three men failed to achieve a linear progression towards 'better' conduct. Boswell's on-going self-scrutiny of his credentials as a polite and sentimental individual – punctuated by moments of self-confidence or self-censure – provides the most vivid example of these fluctuating fortunes. However, a similar trend is evident in Penrose's quick appropriation of politeness, followed by his gradual, disillusioned association of this quality with triviality and tattle; and in Ryder's confident attack on affected gentlemen, followed by self-criticism for his own foolishness in female company. With Ryder, whose diary provides the clearest insight into the reading patterns of the would-be polite man, we also see how advice literature rallied him for better performance in the future, only for him to err and presumably to read again. Conduct literature emerges here as one half of a dialogue between ideal and actual behaviour, relevant precisely because of the difficulty in reconciling aims and practices.

The tensions involved in putting ideals into action were due in part to the multiple, often competing, notions of refinement existing at a single point in time. Sometimes, most notably in Dudley Ryder's case, competing forms of politeness could result in an individual's exclusion from a social circle to which he sought access. Alternatively, these rival modes and their practitioners were sometimes dismissed as outdated and unduly formal, at other times as too modern and overly negligent. In these contests, politeness became a source of competition, not sociability – witness the snobbery in which each of these polite men engaged when they withheld refinement from men of differing politics, religion, social status or nationality. Finally, the episodes of violence and sexual conquest experienced by Penrose or practised by James Boswell indicate the opportunities men had consciously to quit polite society for an alternative community, at one and the same time psychologically distant and geographically close and readily accessible. Here we see the gap between ideal and actual behaviour as intentionally exploited and enjoyed.

The source base for this chapter has necessarily been small and selective. There remains every opportunity to reconsider the interpretation offered here, as there is to explore the personal accounts of men aside from a Bath 'private gentleman' and the sons of a prosperous London tradesmen and a Scottish laird. What, for example, of others' experience from lower down the social scale, especially in a resort such as Bath founded on an ethos of 'polite' social inclusion and accommodation? Equally, what of men like Richard 'Beau' Nash, the resort's impresario, who themselves enjoyed a reputation of politeness or who – like Ryder's Mr Gore, Penrose's Samuel Derrick or Boswell's Monsieur des Essar – earned a reputation for fine or foppish conduct within polite society? Were these men aware of their reputation, and was it a commonly held view or the perception of a single individual?

Future studies of the relationship between manly ideals and practice face a number of obstacles, several of which have been evident in this chapter. As self-authored accounts of conduct, each testimony presents us with a personal interpretation of events as perceived, not as actual behaviour. There is much each of these writers does not record. It would be good to know whether Dudley Ryder finished the books he began; whether or to what extent John Penrose tailored his views on Bath to suit his audience; how far James Boswell affected his declarations of refined sensibility (as Dr Johnson supposed), and what on-lookers made of his habit of weeping in the street.

These limitations are not of course unique to men's testimonies, and have certainly not prevented the construction of a more comprehensive picture of eighteenth-century women's lives than that presented in contemporary conduct literature.[171] The purpose of building up this picture has been to reveal eighteenth-century women's integral place in economic, political, cultural and religious life. We do not need to study male testimonies to know this to be men's typical experience over time. Rather, the motive for future studies along the lines of this chapter, as for much of the new cultural history of manliness, is to acknowledge some of the difficulties men found in attaining these pre-eminent roles when in competition, not with women, but with other males. Becoming a polite man required hard work and rigorous self-analysis, and resulted in regular self-censure. This should not excuse the misogyny of a Dudley Ryder or the boorishness of a James Boswell, but it may go some way to understanding why they behaved as they did.

Notes and references

1. On this shift see Michael Mascuch, *The Origins of the Individualist Self: Autobiography and Self-Identity in England, 1591–1791* (Cambridge, 1997), ch. 4; Brewer, *Pleasures of the Imagination*, ch. 2.

2. *The Diary of Dudley Ryder, 1715–1716*, ed. William Matthews (1939), p. 29.

3. *Ibid.*, p. 346.

4. *Ibid.*, p. 36.

5. *Ibid.*, p. 282.

6. *Ibid.*, p. 143.

7. *Ibid.*, p. 106.

8. *Ibid.*, pp. 282, 146.

9. *Ibid.*, p. 65.

10. *Ibid.*, p. 130.

11. *Ibid.*, pp. 135, 146, 78.

12. Previously encountered in this book as a positive statement on admirable refinement, 'fine gentleman' had a parallel history as a label for an excess of these qualities, usually prompted by over-exposure to women's company. Richard Steele's *Guardian*, a periodical Ryder knew well, described the 'fine gentleman' in terms of his 'nimble Pair of Heels . . . laced Shirt, an embroidered Suit . . . fringed Gloves' and any similar 'Accomplishment . . . [that] ennobles a Man . . . in a Female Imagination'. By contrast, the 'true fine gentleman' was 'compleatly qualify'd . . . for the Service . . . as for the Ornament and Delight of Society'. No. 34 (20 Apr 1713), pp. 142–3.

13. *Diary*, pp. 114, 231–2, 345.

14. *Ibid.*, p. 66.

15. *Ibid.*, p. 119.

16. *Ibid.*, p. 131.

17. The diary contains frequent references to Ryder reading Locke, whom he admired, though no discussion exists of Locke's *Some Thoughts Concerning Education* (1693).

18. *Ibid.*, p. 151.

19. *Ibid.*, pp. 127–8.

20. *Ibid.*, p. 147.

21. *Ibid.*, p. 51.

22. Ryder was similarly critical of his brother wearing elaborate dress – here lace ruffles – in the company of a friend, Mr Swain; such dress, commendable at St James's, was on this occasion a 'vain foolish way of going' (151).

23. *Ibid.*, p. 62.

24. *Ibid.*, p. 74.

25. *Ibid.*, pp. 86, 114.

26. *Ibid.*, p. 74.

27. *Ibid.*, pp. 114–15.

28. *Ibid.*, p. 195.

29. *Ibid.*, p. 58. Ryder's anxiety was no doubt heightened by his decision not to enter the family business in which, as Margaret Hunt shows, a masculine work-ethic featured prominently, *The Middling Sort*, p. 222 for Ryder.

30. *Ibid.*, p. 87.

31. *Ibid.*, p. 359.

32. *Ibid.*, p. 50.

33. *Ibid.*, p. 228.

34. *Ibid.*, p. 45.

35. *Ibid.*, pp. 177, 135.

36. *Ibid.*, p. 51.

37. *Ibid.*, p. 73. On the military camp as a site of polite sociability see Gillian Russell, *The Theatres of War: Performance, Politics and Society, 1793–1815* (Oxford, 1995), pp. 33–41.

38. *Diary*, p. 270. Other encounters with women did little to reconfirm Ryder's manly identity: his romantic pursuit of Sally Marshall proved vexing and humiliating, while meetings with prostitutes produced feelings of shame and fears of 'hazarding my reputation' (292).

39. *Ibid.*, p. 285.

40. John Earle, *Micro-Cosmographie; or a peece of the world discovered; in essayes and characters* (1628, 9th edn, 1669), pp. 125–6, 157–60.

41. *Diary*, p. 38.

42. *Ibid.*, p. 117.

43. No. 38 (13 Apr 1711), I, pp. 159–61.

44. *Diary*, p. 121.

45. *Ibid.*, p. 119.

46. Cicero's advice on polite speech was considered in *Spectator* Nos. 104 and 259.

47. De Vaumorière, *The Art of Pleasing in Conversation* (1722 edn), pp. 71–92. John Wesley later criticised the guide as an example of the uncharitableness of early-eighteenth-century 'polite' literature. See above, p. 51 fn 89.

48. *Diary*, p. 354.

49. *Ibid.*, p. 45.

50. No. 125 (24 July 1711), I, p. 510; No. 57 (5 May 1711), I, p. 243. On Whig/Tory antagonisms see Geoffrey Holmes, *British Politics in the Age of Anne* (rev. edn, 1987).

51. *Diary*, p. 247.

52. *Ibid.*, p. 125.

53. *Ibid.*, p. 41.

54. *Ibid.*, p. 253.

55. *Ibid.*, p. 133.

56. *Ibid.*, p. 74.

57. *Ibid.*, p. 354.

58. *Ibid.*, p. 263.

59. *Ibid.*, p. 249.

60. *Ibid.*, p. 188.

61. *Ibid.*, pp. 347, 296.

62. John Wood, *An Essay Towards a Description of Bath*, 2 vols. (2nd edn, 1747), II, p. 446.

63. John Penrose, *Letters from Bath, 1766–1767*, eds. Brigitte Mitchell and Hubert Penrose (Gloucester, 1984), pp. 27–9, 36, 100.

64. On Bath's rise as the century's principal polite resort see R.S. Neale, *Bath 1650–1850: A Social History* (1981). Bath's reputation as a discrete polite society is examined in Peter Borsay, 'Image and counter-image in Georgian Bath', *British Journal of Eighteenth-Century Studies*, 17 (1994), pp. 165–79.

65. Quoted in Girouard, *English Town*, p. 78.

66. Oliver Goldsmith saw these regulations, or 'ceremonies', as a necessary contribution to the 'politeness, elegance and ease' of modern Bath, *Life of Nash*, in *Works*, III, p. 307; see above, p. 126.

67. Wood, *Description*, II, pp. 438–42.

68. *Ibid.*, p. 217.

69. Penrose, *Letters*, p. 136. The decision to ban swords had been made for several reasons: to prevent duelling between men, to encourage mixed company – swords were said to frighten women ball-goers – and, finally, to reform traditional images of gentlemanliness in which swords indicated superior social status.

70. Wood, *Description*, II, p. 29; in London Dudley Ryder had learned that the loss of a partner was an affront to a gentleman's honour; requests to dance were therefore to be made with discretion, *Diary*, p. 156.

71. *Letters*, p. 55.

72. *Ibid.*, pp. 57, 96, 45–6.

73. *Ibid.*, p. 68.

74. *Ibid.*, p. 55.

75. *Ibid.*, p. 146. Tighter controls on public entertainments produced conduct superior even to that of smaller provincial towns: 'good hours are kept here', he wrote in April 1766, and there 'are not such rakes, as . . . at Penryn Assembly' (57).

76. *Ibid.*, p. 42.

77. *Ibid.*, p. 37.

78. *Ibid.*, pp. 168, 203.

79. Penrose's correspondence included frequent reference to the 'genteel' nature of objects including cups, cutlery and furnishings.

80. Wood, *Description*, II, p. 446.

81. *Letters*, p. 100.

82. *Ibid.*, pp. 157, 36.

83. *Ibid.*, pp. 69–70.

84. *Ibid.*, p. 88.

85. *Ibid.*

86. *Ibid.*, pp. 45, 89, 116.

87. *Ibid.*, p. 27.

88. *Ibid.*, p. 46.

89. *Ibid.*, p. 88.

90. In his letter of 28 April 1766 Penrose noted the popular claim that serious study 'prevents the Efficacy of the Waters'; he had by this date 'read Scarce an Hundred Quarto Pages' (64).

91. *Ibid.*, pp. 54, 64, 112.

92. *Ibid.*, p. 80.

93. *Ibid.*, pp. 83, 125. For further criticisms see pp. 47, 85, 181.

94. *Ibid.*, p. 174.

95. *Bath, A Poem* (1748), pp. 5–6.

96. Christopher Anstey, *The New Bath Guide* (1766), pp. 68–9.

97. *Letters*, pp. 113, 75. Near-sightedness was 'quite the Fashion' for men in May 1766.

98. *Ibid.*, p. 103.

99. Wood, *Description*, II, p. 336.

100. Pierce Egan, *Walks Through Bath* (Bath, 1819), p. 172.

101. 15 Nov 1762, *Boswell's London Journal, 1762–1763*, ed. Frederick A. Pottle (1950), p. 39 (hereafter *BLJ*).

102. On the multiplicity of Boswell's identity see Susan Manning's 'Boswell's pleasure, the pleasures of Boswell', *British Journal of Eighteenth-Century Studies*, 20 (1997), pp. 17–32, and Felicity A. Nussbaum, *The Autobiographical Subject: Gender and Ideology in Eighteenth-Century England* (Baltimore MD, 1989), ch. 5.

103. Stone, *Family, Sex and Marriage*, pp. 572–99.

104. Nussbaum, *Autobiographical Subject*, p. 115; David M. Weed, 'Sexual positions: men of pleasure, economy and dignity in Boswell's *London Journal*', *Eighteenth-Century Studies*, 31 (1997/8), pp. 215–34.

105. See above, pp. 1–3.

106. *BLJ*, p. 62.

107. *Ibid.*, p. 68.

108. *Ibid.*, pp. 63, 257.

109. *Boswell in Search of a Wife, 1766–1769*, eds. Frank Brady and Frederick A. Pottle (1957), pp. 69, 291 (hereafter *BSW*).

110. *BLJ*, p. 47; *The Correspondence of James Boswell and William Johnson Temple, 1756–1795*, ed. Thomas Crawford, 2 vols. (Edinburgh and New Haven CT, 1997), I, p. 91.

111. *BLJ*, p. 145.

112. *Ibid.*, p. 60.

113. *London Magazine*, 57 (May 1778), in *Boswell's Column, 1777–1783*, ed. Margaret Bailey (1951), pp. 58–9.

114. *BLJ*, pp. 290–1.

115. *Ibid.*, p. 316.

116. *Boswell In Holland, 1763–1764*, ed. Frederick A. Pottle (1952), p. 198 (hereafter *BH*).

117. Quoted in Colby H. Kullman, 'James Boswell and the art of conversation', in Kevin L. Cope ed., *Compendious Conversations: The Method of Dialogue in the Early Enlightenment* (New York, 1992), pp. 83–4.

118. *BLJ*, p. 121.

119. *BSW*, p. 59.

120. *BH*, p. 165.

121. *BSW*, p. 189.

122. *Boswell: The Ominous Years, 1774–1776*, eds. Charles Ryskamp and Frederick A. Pottle (1963) (hereafter *BOY*). For Goldsmith's defence see above, p. 93.

123. *Journal of a Tour to the Hebrides*, p. 335.

124. *BOY*, p. 137; *BLJ*, p. 76; *Correspondence of James Boswell and John Johnstone of Grange*, ed. Ralph S. Walker (Edinburgh, 1966), p. 7.

125. *BH*, p. 37.

126. *BSW*, p. 334.

127. *Ibid.*, p. 41; *Boswell for the Defence, 1769–1774*, eds. William K. Wimsatt and Frederick A. Pottle (1960), p. 282 (hereafter *BD*).

128. *BD*, p. 276.

129. *Ibid.*, pp. 270–1, 279.

130. *BSW*, pp. 146–7.

131. *Ibid.*, p. 290.

132. *Ibid.*, pp. 282–3.

133. *BOY*, p. 253.

134. *BSW*, pp. 283–4.

135. *BOY*, pp. 250, 253. On the coach as a part public/part private space see Susan E. Whyman, *Sociability and Power in Late Stuart England. The Cultural World of the Verneys, 1660–1720* (Oxford, 1999), ch. 4.

136. *BLJ*, pp. 196, 68, 134.

137. *BSW*, pp. 258, 47.

138. *BD*, pp. 279, 282.

139. *BSW*, p. 191.

140. *Ibid.*, pp. 215, 234, 240.

141. *Boswell: The English Experiment, 1785–1789*, eds. Irma S. Lustig and Frederick A. Pottle (1986), pp. 79, 128, 286–7.

142. *BOY*, p. 241.

143. For Boswell, sensibility and hypochondria, see Mullan, *Sentiment and Sociability*, pp. 210–14.

144. *BSW*, p. 344.

145. *BD*, p. 300. See also Gordon Turnbull, 'Boswell and sympathy: the trial and execution of John Reid', in Greg Clingham ed., *New Light on Boswell* (Cambridge, 1991).

146. *BOY*, pp. 97–8.

147. *BSW*, pp. 150–1.

148. *BD*, p. 349; *Boswell: The Applause of the Jury, 1782–1785*, eds. Irma S. Lustig and Frederick A. Pottle (1981), p. 318 (hereafter *BAJ*).

149. Smith, *Theory of Moral Sentiments*, pp. 49–50.

150. *BSW*, p. 150; *BAJ*, p. 318.

151. *BH*, p. 377.

152. *BSW*, p. 193; *Boswell's Column*, p. 209.

153. V.A.C. Gatrell, *The Hanging Tree: Execution and the English People, 1770–1868* (Oxford, 1994), pp. 284–92; Turnbull, 'Boswell and sympathy'.

154. *BD*, p. 300.

155. *Ibid.*, pp. 148–9.

156. *Ibid.*, p. 96; *Boswell: The Great Biographer, 1789–1795*, eds. Marlies A. Danziger and Frank Brady (1989), p. 95.

157. *BH*, p. 198; *BLJ*, p. 240; *BOY*, p. 123. Fribble: 'an effeminate fop, name borrowed from Garrick', Francis Grose, *A Dictionary of the Vulgar Tongue* (1785).

158. *BD*, p. 291.

159. *Ibid.*, p. 242.

160. *Ibid.*, p. 134.

161. *BAJ*, p. 171; *BSW*, p. 62.

162. *Ibid.*, p. 239.

163. *BOY*, p. 177.

164. *Ibid.*, pp. 306–7.

165. *BLJ*, pp. 272–3.

166. *Diary*, p. 245; *Letters*, p. 198.

167. Boswell's 'blackguard' tour began in St James's Park and took in locations close to some of his chief venues for polite sociability: Child's coffee-house, the Spring Gardens and finally back to St James's. On the proximity of sites of prostitution and politeness see Tony Henderson, *Disorderly Women in Eighteenth-Century London. Prostitution and Control in the Metropolis, 1730–1830* (1999), ch. 2.

168. Bryson, *From Courtesy to Civility*, pp. 6, 279.

169. Brewer, *Pleasures of the Imagination*, p. 115.

170. *BOY*, p. 123.

171. Essays in Barker and Chalus eds., *Gender in Eighteenth-Century England* examine women's work and politics; for a vivid account of the stoicism required for childbearing and motherhood, see Vickery, *Gentleman's Daughter*, ch. 3.

CONCLUSION

Politeness is my Theme – To you I write,
Who are, what all would feign be thought Polite.
This is the Coxcomb's Av'rie, Courtier's Claim,
The Citt's Ambition, and the Soldier's Fame
. . . This forms, guides, checks, inspires, does all it can
To make man mild and sociable to Man.

(James Miller, Of Politeness. An Epistle *(1738))*

This book has examined the impact of eighteenth-century polite society on representations of the gentleman, on contemporary debates over the meaning and condition of manliness, and on the self-perception and conduct of real social actors. Each approach has revealed the importance of masculinity as a social category, created, maintained or undermined by men's social, not sexual, performance. Here we need to be careful not to caricature early modern concepts of gentlemanliness and manhood, in which issues of honour, self-command and reason were essential features of equally contested manly ideals. Nor should we discount the place of sexual activity as an eighteenth-century marker of male gender identity. As histories of manliness become more sophisticated, we are able to appreciate the coexistence of parallel, often competing, discourses of masculinity at a particular point in time. James Boswell's appreciation of the 'manly' blackguard and the 'manly' pretty gentleman reveal that such competitions occurred not just as literary types but as lived-out realities in the behaviour of individual men. None the less, while it is correct to recognise coexisting models, it is also possible to identify the presence of dominant discourses. This book has argued that to eighteenth-century male readers of conduct literature, periodical essays, magazine articles, sermons, novels and academic treatises, and to male participants in urban social spaces, this dominant ideal would have been understood – if not necessarily accepted – as centred on men's participation in polite society. Seen in this light, the prevailing eighteenth-century concept was of masculinity not just as a social but a sociable category in which gender identity was conferred, or denied, by men's capacity for gentlemanly social performance.

The standards by which manly sociability were measured passed through two key phases in the period 1660–1800, each reflecting broader ideological shifts in the meaning of polite society. The first saw the late-seventeenth- and early-eighteenth-century rise of the theme addressed by James Miller: politeness. To its proponents, politeness offered a new ethos of social interaction born of recent and, for these writers, largely welcome developments – an expanding commercial economy, urbanisation and the dissemination of latitudinarian religious thought – consolidated by the post-1688 political settlement. Politeness's appeal owed much to an understanding of refinement less as precise rules than as the act of being, in Miller's words, 'sociable to Man'. From its origins, politeness was understood by intellectually ambitious theorists as an instrument capable of easing and improving relations within society at large. In the hands of a later generation of Scottish academic analysts, refinement became a marker of the advanced state of social evolution in a polite or civil society broadly defined. These sociological or conjectural historical interpretations were not simply the preserve of an academic elite but also of optimistic readers, similar to Miller's ambitious 'citt', or town-dweller, for whom a sense of self-improvement was stimulated by participation in a literary and spatial public sphere that 'inspired' and made possible opportunities for politeness to a wide audience.

This sense of opportunity was further prompted by eighteenth-century images of the polite gentleman. Stripped of detailed rules or the privileges of birth, the modern man was distinguished from existing models, notably the courtier and the country gentleman, by his capacity for easy and sincere sociability – what James Miller later termed 'well-dressed humanity'. For many polite theorists it was the 'citt's ambition' rather than the outmoded 'courtier's claim' that would be best realised in an urban environment where polite sociability was a daily requirement of work and leisure. It was evidence of the importance of politeness as a moral and social code that proponents encouraged all men, including soldiers, to adopt its practices. Such calls were part of a wider attempt to rethink the application of traditional male values, such as intelligence, sense and self-control, which now became part of the process by which refined gentlemen 'formed', 'guided' and 'checked' their inner humanity and so became polite. Other male traits, such as violence or roughness, were simultaneously condemned as boorish and anachronistic. It was sufficient that these characteristics clashed with what was required of the new 'mild' gentleman. Yet calls for reform also stressed the advantages of men's proximity to virtuous female company within mixed social spheres.

This emphasis on mixed society required polite theorists to pay careful attention to refinement's impact on manliness as well as on notions of gentility. Commentators reminded readers that male/female socialising meant closer correspondence between the sexes, not a blurring of gender boundaries. In line with this they continued to assert the importance of established male values now set to work for sociable purposes. At the same time, politeness was expected to enhance and improve traditionally admired qualities. It was the achievement of theorists like David Hume and the aim of later periodical writers to demonstrate that the 'soldier's fame' was now attributable to both his refinement and his courage.

Miller's poetical epistle came too soon to capture the second key shift in eighteenth-century concepts of polite society and gentlemanliness: the mid- to late-century development of a culture of sensibility. This shift was never absolute and did not bring an end to established 'polite' vocabularies or practices as enacted in the coffee-house, pleasure garden or assembly room. Sensibility's appeal rested both on its claim to novelty and on its promise to restore the synthesis between humanity and social expression recently distorted by those who exploited polite codes for personal gain. To achieve this restoration, advocates encouraged increasingly spontaneous forms of conduct thought to reflect true feeling more closely. Popularisers of the culture drew on existing models of nervous physiology to explain the connection between inner sensitivity or sensibility and the expression of these feelings through a sociability based less on speech than on displays of sympathy. Sociable on account of this sympathy, and refined on account of his physical delicacy and fine feelings, the sentimental gentleman became an alternative, sometimes rival, performer within a polite society now conceived as much as a web of sympathy as a network of public venues dedicated to verbal exchange.

Potentially more sincere than the polite gentleman, the man of sensibility conveyed his sympathies via a series of physical gestures previously commonly associated with virtuous femininity. Establishing the manliness of feeling took various forms. In mixed society, sentimental men were distinguished by a readiness to act on their feelings (and to deploy their greater strength in doing so), whereas women limited themselves to displaying an appreciation of others' predicament. Among men, the manliness of sensibility was guaranteed by the on-going importance of self-regulation as a determinant of sympathetic exchange. During the culture's high point in the 1770s and 1780s, we can also detect efforts to redefine 'female' virtues, like weeping, as suitably male characteristics. Yet even then notions of tearful or intimate manliness continued to be conjoined with traditional male qualities in the multi-faceted figure of the responsible father, the courageous military hero or the manly Christ.

If James Miller's epistle preceded the vogue for sensibility, then it was certainly alert to another aspect of polite society considered in this book, namely that it had sceptics and detractors. Later in Miller's verse we discover a gallery of less admirable characters who distort the true moral origins of polite sociability to become sycophantic dupes or over-refined fops.[1] It was a commonly expressed concern that standards of modern living made foppery a likely outcome for sober-minded men exposed to fashion and triviality. The consequences of this decline were grave, for with refinement came effeminacy – like manliness a social category, described as the loss of physical strength, independence, judgement, courage, moderation and sense – which, cast as the scourge of modern men and the nation at large, shared the same breadth of application as did rival ideas of polite society. None the less, a growing confidence in the benefits of polite society also prompted a reconceptualisation of effeminacy's place in refined society. This is not to say that polite theorists discounted the threat of a loss of manhood. Effeminacy remained the antithesis of manhood, but was now seen as the effect of careless involvement in polite society, not involvement *per se*. Debates over effeminacy further remind us of the need to see eighteenth-century concepts of manliness (whether achieved or lost) as a nuanced contest over the relative weight of established male values at a particular point in time. As John Tosh argues, to appreciate the 'embeddedness and durability of certain aspects of early modern and modern gender identity' is not to suggest that a particular society failed to agonise over the character, condition and future prospects of these qualities.[2] It was because of their appreciation of the importance of such qualities that generations of pessimistic commentators warned of the imminent risk of individual and societal ruin. Equally, sponsors of politeness, like James Miller, aimed to deploy the effeminate fop character to steer truly polite gentlemen towards a suitable balance between modern sociability and other traditionally manly responsibilities.

As our study of diaries, journals and letters suggests, getting this balance right was an important requirement for those real-life men who, like Miller's quartet, would 'feign be thought Polite'. Implemented with care, refined sociability played an important part in the construction of adult manly identity. Accounts like James Boswell's further suggest the adaptability of later eighteenth-century models of sentimental manliness to broader shifts in the meaning of polite society, while all three memoirists castigated failed sociability as 'fine' or 'foppish'. Yet if the example of polite or sentimental or foppish gentlemen was clear in theory, the emulation (or avoidance) of their characteristics proved less straightforward. On the ground, refined gentlemanliness often became a source not only of easy confidence but also of self-doubt, not only of mild sociability but also of snobbish competition and ridicule. At the level of the individual social actor, the ideals of sociable manhood could prove elusive or contentious, or be abused and ignored. That they were, however, says much for the vibrancy of eighteenth-century debates surrounding men in polite society.

There is seldom a simple end point for histories of gender and social identity. Any proposed date raises questions about what is to happen next – in this case, in the nineteenth century. This is not the place to do more than sketch aspects of a recent historiography that suggests developments of sufficient significance to justify concluding this study in 1800, if only as a means of distinguishing the tone of an eighteenth-century debate from that of one on Victorian Britain. At the same time, however, we should be cautious of viewing later developments as original when similar themes can be shown to have been in place well before. Just as eighteenth-century proponents and critics of refined manhood worked traditional manly identities into new contexts, so nineteenth- and twentieth-century commentators have concerned themselves with seemingly 'topical' themes and 'original' debates that would have been pertinent to many Georgian gentlemen.

Change after 1800 owed much to what might be described as the breakdown of polite society, both as a network of venues and as a social ideal to be enacted therein. The motive force in each case was a desire to move away from random and accommodating to more exclusive and intimate forms of sociability. As Mark Girouard shows, this had implications for polite society's physical environment. Thus, during the early nineteenth century, purpose-built polite resorts such as Bath were transformed by moves to restrict access to the spa and assembly room; in other parts of the country, public venues either became members-only clubs or closed.[3] A similar fate befell two prime eighteenth-century sites, Ranelagh Gardens which went out of business in 1804, and Vauxhall which struggled on until 1859. In line with these changes, research on early-nineteenth-century courtship suggests that the men and women who had previously met at the assembly or public walk now socialised in the home, where the dining- and drawing-room became key locations for genteel contact.[4]

Such contact was now not only more private but also carried a stronger ethos of social exclusivity, a shift that owed much to the rise of an etiquette tradition. By the second decade of the nineteenth century, 'etiquette' had become the name for a new code of polite living. In contrast to eighteenth-century guides which tended to treat refinement as sociability, etiquette books focused more on the mode of social interaction via a series of precise dos and don'ts defining polite visiting, greeting and dining. A further important distinction was the use of these regulations to select, and exclude, those deemed worthy, or unworthy, of a genteel reputation. Of course, we should not be too quick to contrast eighteenth- and nineteenth-century codes. Earlier practitioners often used their refinement snobbishly as a source of power; likewise Lord Chesterfield's infamy had owed much to his promotion of manners for personal not communal advancement. Yet, as we have seen, Chesterfield's advice aroused hostility precisely because it contradicted an established ideal of sociability; moreover it did so while continuing to give the impression of a generous and accommodating spirit. Etiquette, by contrast, owed its popularity to a conscious emphasis on excluding (inferior) individuals who failed to understand and enact the detailed social rules by which breeding was now evaluated.[5]

Finally, it was clear that certain early-nineteenth-century commentators believed theirs to be a more violent and confrontational society than that of previous generations. Writing in 1829, the essayist William Hazlitt claimed that the 'term *blackguard*' was now 'peculiarly applicable' to men from the lowest criminal to the 'fine gentleman' who were said to share a tendency to 'violence and a contempt for the feelings of others'. Hazlitt here identified what he considered a deep-rooted national trait. Elsewhere, however, he pointed to a more discernible shift in social values between the 1780s and 1820s, fuelled by the emergence of belligerent nineteenth-century radical politics now shorn of what Hazlitt termed the 'external refinements of the old school'.[6]

The breakdown of an eighteenth-century polite society had implications for later representations of the acceptable and deviant gentleman, as well as for concepts of manliness. In an age of sober dressing and precise social codes, the colourful and showy fop gave way to the new figure of the dandy who, if continuing to err through his obsession with manners, did so in more meaningful ways than a predecessor who now passed from satirical tool to historical curiosity.[7] More positive images of nineteenth-century gentleman-liness took several forms. Historians of duelling have shown how this once criticised activity revived in the early 1800s. Drawing strength from a new preoccupation with refinement as precise rules, coupled with an interest in gentlemanly violence, the practice now found favour in guides like John Trusler's *System of Etiquette* (1804) complete with instructions on 'how to duel'. Alternatively, Hazlitt's emphasis on rough physicality was expressed in the image of the gentleman as sportsman, engaged in pursuits such as boxing which, like duelling, earlier conduct writers had judged as unbecoming in modern men. Male physicality was also evident in two more complex mid-nineteenth-century ideals: 'muscular Christianity', which saw bodily strength directed towards productive ends by religious faith; and 'neo-stoicism', in which physicality was combined with a less pious self-discipline to produce individuals characterised by decency, hardiness and, in contrast to the eighteenth-century man of conversation, dignified taciturnity.[8] As J.W. Burrow and others suggest, the distinguishing feature of these new ideals was an emphasis on the gentleman as a man of 'character' contrasted with an eighteenth-century ideal of the gentleman as social actor. Polished by social encounters, the eighteenth-century gentleman features in such accounts as someone fashioned in, and dependent on, society. His nineteenth-century equivalent, though not rejecting society, emerges as an independent individual whose sense of inner value ensured a consistent manly dignity and refinement, regardless of geographical location (important in an age of empire), or of whether he was in company or now, significantly, alone.[9]

There are certainly a number of original elements to this ideal. Yet it is also worth reflecting on some of the themes that nineteenth-century representations shared with earlier accounts in which, as this book has shown, issues of Christian morality and stoicism featured prominently in the construction and regulation of both a polite and a sentimental gentlemanly ideal. Among these similarities it is perhaps the eighteenth-century emphasis on the synthesis of external manners and inner 'character' that merits most attention. As we have seen, eighteenth-century commentators regularly identified this synthesis as the principal means by which the modern gentleman guaranteed his refinement and successfully adapted himself to a range of social situations. Nineteenth-century concepts of gentlemanliness may have given this ideal a new psychological complexity, but in so doing they developed rather than created a formula.

More recent accounts on politeness and gender identity further suggest the enduring relevance, and indeed the 'reinvention', of themes and contests familiar to an eighteenth-century debate. Though challenged by Victorian etiquette, earlier ideals of polite sociability have re-emerged in the work of the sociologists Georg Simmel (1858–1918) and Erving Goffman (1922–82). In the manner of early-eighteenth-century polite theorists, Simmel's 1910 essay 'On the sociology of sociability' emphasised the value and pleasurableness of convivial interaction between individuals enjoying equal status within the boundaries of a sociable group. Drawing on Simmel, Goffman's study of *Encounters* (1961) looks more closely at the formation of these groups as a response to broader social pressures that challenge pleasurable and egalitarian exchange.[10] Nor (just as in the eighteenth century) are these ideals held only by academic theorists. 'Politeness is out of fashion', claimed one nostalgic columnist in 1989, 'the prevailing ethos of British society is now confrontation rather than accommodation. Edge not ease.'[11]

For this commentator the modern threat to easy and accommodating sociability originates from within a tough (male) business and political culture. Attempts to humanise these forces see renewed emphasis on the benefits of men's closer social interaction with women, whom recent sociolinguistic studies claim to be capable of greater discretion, generosity and 'politeness'.[12] Shifting patterns of gender relations, especially within the workplace, have once again prompted male sympathisers to speak positively of the benefits of 'humanizing manliness . . . by allowing women to participate in it', while retaining the idea of enduring male values, such as heroism, 'since men find it easier to be courageous'.[13] Others, however, present a less optimistic picture in which manhood, now cast not as 'effeminised' but as 'betrayed', is falling victim either to this changing gender balance or to more profound shifts in social organisation among men. During the eighteenth century, the formation of a polite society of city-based, mixed-gender sociability prompted the development of new notions of refined gentlemanliness, and ensured a vigorous debate on standards of manhood. Three hundred years on, it is the *collapse* of these traditional forms of male association and community, and their replacement by internet anonymity, that is thought to threaten manly identity.[14] By contrast, promoters of change highlight the potential for better, quicker, easier sociability through technological 'progress' and associated cultural developments. Old debates reconfigured gain new momentum.

Notes and references

1. Miller's 'modern noble' becomes a 'Tyrant sat home, but Sycophant abroad/ A Slave at Court, but Rebel to your God'; while Sir John sits 'four Hours to hear an Op'ra sung . . . For 'tis not what they like, or what they know/But, as the *Fashion* drives the Fop must go' (*Of Politeness*, pp. 7, 14).

2. John Tosh, 'The old Adam and the new man: emerging themes in the history of English masculinities, 1750–1850', in Hitchcock and Cohen eds., *English Masculinities*, p. 238.

3. Girouard, *English Town*, p. 144.

4. Nenadic, 'Middle-ranking consumers and domestic culture'; Tosh, *A Man's Place*.

5. On etiquette as a force for social exclusion see Michael Curtin, 'A question of manners', and Morgan, *Manners, Morals and Class*.

6. William Hazlitt, 'English characteristics' (1829), in *Selected Writing*, ed. Jon Cook (Oxford, 1991), p. 157; 'The late Mr Horne Tooke', in *The Spirit of the Age* (1824), in P.P. Howe ed., *The Complete Works of William Hazlitt*, 21 vols. (1930–4), XI, p. 47.

7. Ellen Moers, *The Dandy: From Brummell to Beerbohm* (1960); John Harvey, *Men in Black* (1995). Citations in the *OED* show nineteenth-century references to 'fop' relating either to Restoration men of fashion, or reviving early modern notions of a fool, engaged in the 'fopperies' of a particular political or religious opinion.

8. On the rise of taciturnity see Cohen, *Fashioning Masculinity*; Norman Vance, *The Sinews of the Spirit: The Ideal of Christian Manliness in Victorian Literature and Religious Thought* (Cambridge, 1985); Mangan and Walvin eds., *Manliness and*

Morality; Paul Langford, *Englishness Identified. Manners and Character, 1650–1850* (Oxford, 2000), ch. 4.

9. J.W. Burrow, *Whigs and Liberals. Continuity and Change in English Political Thought* (Oxford, 1988), ch. 4; Stefan Collini, 'The idea of "character" in Victorian political thought', *Transactions of the Royal Historical Society*, 5th ser., 35 (1985), pp. 29–50. For a recent reinterpretation of the place of character in eighteenth-century literature see Paul Langford, 'Manners and the eighteenth-century state. The case of the unsociable Englishman', in John Brewer and Eckhart Hellmuth eds., *Rethinking Leviathan. The Eighteenth-Century State in Britain and Germany* (Oxford, 1999).

10. On the parallels between Simmel and Goffman's work and those of earlier writers, here Jean-Baptiste Bellegarde and Adam Smith, see Gordon, *Citizens Without Sovereignty*, pp. 94–8, and Dwyer, *Virtuous Discourse*, p. 54.

11. 'The pitfalls of rudeness', in *Times Higher Education Supplement* (24 Feb 1989). Also noteworthy is Theodore Dalrymple's subsequent equation of declining standards of British social conduct with a 'disappearance of the delicacy of feeling', *New Statesman* (20 Dec 1999–3 Jan 2000).

12. Janet Holmes, *Women, Men and Politeness* (1995).

13. Harvey Mansfield, 'The partial eclipse of manliness: what room is there for courage in a post-feminist world?', in *Times Literary Supplement* (17 July 1998).

14. Susan Faludi, *Stiffed. The Betrayal of the Modern Man* (1999).

The order of works listed in this select bibliography broadly follows the book's chapter sequence. Unless otherwise stated, the place of publication is London.

Theories of polite society

Two excellent starting points on the context and characteristics of polite society are Paul Langford's *A Polite and Commercial People. England, 1727–1783* (Oxford, 1989) and John Brewer, *The Pleasures of the Imagination: English Culture in the Eighteenth Century* (1997). Norbert Elias's *The Civilizing Process* (1939, trans. E. Jephcott, rpt Oxford, 1994) remains the classic account of the development of a concept of civility in early modern Europe. Elias's two studies within this title, 'The History of Manners' and 'State Formation and Civilization' provide both a survey of shifting styles of behaviour and a theoretical model of these changes. Elias's work on early modern civilising has since been developed and questioned by Anna Bryson, *From Courtesy to Civility. Changing Codes of Conduct in Early Modern England* (Oxford, 1998) and Daniel Gordon, *Citizens Without Sovereignty: Equality and Sociability in French Thought, 1670–1789* (Princeton NJ, 1994). Gordon offers a discussion of several French polite theorists influential in the dissemination of politeness in England, a theme likewise considered by Peter Burke, *The Art of Conversation* (Oxford, 1993) and Michèle Cohen, *Fashioning Masculinity: National Identity and Language in the Eighteenth Century* (1996).

Cohen also focuses on the impact of French guides on English concepts of refinement. In doing so she draws on the work of Lawrence E. Klein, especially his *Shaftesbury and the Culture of Politeness: Moral Discourse and Cultural Politics in Early Eighteenth-Century England* (Cambridge, 1994), which, like many modern studies on politeness, in turn owes much to essays in J.G.A. Pocock's *Virtue, Commerce and History* (Cambridge, 1985). Klein takes his discussion of politeness beyond the confines of Shaftesbury's lifetime and social milieu in two subsequent essays, 'Coffee-house civility, 1660–1714: an aspect of post-courtly culture in England', *Huntington Library Quarterly*, 59 (1997), 31–51, and 'Politeness for plebes: consumption and social identity in early eighteenth-century England', in John Brewer and Ann Bermingham eds., *The Culture of Consumption. Image, Object, Text* (1995); John Brewer's chapter, '"The most polite age and the most vicious": attitudes towards culture as commodity, 1660–1800', in the same collection offers a similarly broad sweep.

The material culture of polite society

Both Klein and Brewer regard the emergence of politeness as a consequence of the substitution of the city for the court as a principal locus of social refinement. Raised in Jürgen Habermas's *The Structural Transformation of the Public Sphere* (1962, Engl. trans. Cambridge MA, 1989), the concept of the urban public sphere has since been analysed as a historical model by John Brewer, 'This, that and the other: public, social and private in the seventeenth and eighteenth centuries', in Dario Castiglione and Lesley Sharpe eds., *Shifting the Boundaries: Transformations of the Languages of Public and Private in the Eighteenth Century* (Exeter, 1995).

Others writers concentrate on the physical components of the public sphere: Roy Porter's *London. A Social History* (1994) and Peter Borsay's *The English Urban Renaissance: Culture and Society in the Provincial Town, 1660–1770* (Oxford, 1989) provide detailed overviews on the development of metropolitan and non-metropolitan urban cultures. Both studies also offer much information on specific sites of polite sociability, as do Aytoun Ellis, *The Penny Universities: A History of the Coffee Houses* (1956), and Stephen Pincus, '"Coffee politicians does create": coffee-houses and Restoration political culture', *Journal of Modern History*, 67 (1995), pp. 807–34. David H. Solkin's *Painting for Money. The Visual Arts and the Public Sphere in Eighteenth-Century England* (New Haven CT and London, 1992) details the rise of London pleasure gardens, while Mark Girouard's *The English Town* (New Haven CT and London, 1990) examines life in the assembly room and on the promenade, as well as surveying the personnel and scope of 'polite society'. The impact of these venues on would-be members of this society, male and female, in north-west England is examined by Amanda Vickery, *The Gentleman's Daughter: Women's Lives in Georgian England* (New Haven CT and London, 1998).

J.A. Downie and Thomas Corns eds., *Telling the People What to Think: Early Eighteenth-Century Periodicals from* The Review *to* The Rambler (1993) surveys aspects of the literary public sphere, and includes chapters on the century's most influential essay periodical, *The Spectator* (1711–14), ed. Donald F. Bond,

5 vols. (Oxford, 1965). Many of the general histories of politeness examine Addison and Steele's publication; more specific studies on the *Spectator's* cultural message are Lawrence E. Klein, 'Property and politeness in the early eighteenth-century Whig moralists. The case of *The Spectator*', in John Brewer and Susan Staves eds., *Early Modern Conceptions of Property* (1995), and Erin Mackie's introduction to her *The Commerce of Everyday Life* (New York, 1998), the most recent selection of *Spectator* and *Tatler* papers.

Sensibility and men of feeling

Two studies, Kathryn Shevelow's *Women and Print Culture: The Construction of Femininity in the Early Periodical* (1989) and Shawn Lisa Maurer, '"As sacred as friendship, as pleasurable as love": father–son relations in *The Tatler* and *The Spectator*', in Beth Fowkes Tobin ed., *History, Gender and Eighteenth-Century Literature* (Athens GA, 1994), examine the contribution of both titles to the development of new styles of 'sentimental' parenting. There is now an extensive literature on the emergence of the culture of sensibility, the diversity of which reveals its nebulous character. Janet Todd's *Sensibility. An Introduction* (1986) places sensibility within the context of European intellectual history, while John Mullan's *Sentiment and Sociability: The Language of Feeling in the Eighteenth Century* (Oxford, 1988) and G.J. Barker-Benfield's *The Culture of Sensibility: Sex and Society in Eighteenth-Century Britain* (Chicago IL and London, 1992) provide excellent and wide-ranging surveys. These, together with G.S. Rousseau's 'Towards a semiotics of the nerve: the social history of language in a new key', in Peter Burke and Roy Porter eds., *Language, Self, and Society. A Social History of Language* (Cambridge, 1991), highlight the relationship between sensibility and new medical theories of the nervous body; Markman Ellis's *The Politics of Sensibility: Race, Gender and Commerce in the Sentimental Novel* (Cambridge, 1996) provides another helpful summary of these themes while broadening the debate to include the application of sentimental discourse in later eighteenth-century politics.

The prominent role of Scottish writers in developing this particular strand of social refinement is revealed in John Dwyer's *Virtuous Discourse: Sentiment and Community in Late Eighteenth-Century Scotland* (Edinburgh, 1987); his 'Enlightened spectators and classical moralists: sympathetic relations in eighteenth-century Scotland', in Dwyer and Richard B. Sher eds., *Sociability and Society in Eighteenth-Century Scotland* (Edinburgh, 1993) also demonstrates the complex relationship of reason and emotion, and the durability of stoicism in eighteenth-century theories of sensibility, notably in Adam Smith's *The Theory of Moral Sentiments* (1759), eds. D.D. Raphael and A.L. Macfie

(Oxford, 1976). David Hume's contribution to the history of civilised society is examined in Nicholas Phillipson's *Hume* (1989); Phillipson also looks at Hume's relationship to models of English politeness in 'Politics, politeness and the Anglicisation of early eighteenth-century Scottish culture', in Roger Mason ed., *Scotland and England, 1286–1815* (Edinburgh, 1987). Some of Hume's own thoughts on these subjects are found in his *Essays Moral, Political and Literary* (1742/1752), ed. Eugene F. Miller (Indianapolis IN, 1985) and in *Selected Essays* (Oxford, 1993), with an introduction by Stephen Copley and Andrew Edgar. In *Virtuous Discourse* John Dwyer also considers the impact of sensibility on representations of idealised manliness in Scottish essay periodicals. Others, including Barker-Benfield and Mullan, 'Sentimental novels', in John Richetti ed., *The Eighteenth-Century Novel* (Cambridge, 1996), investigate the subject from the perspective of Henry Mackenzie's 1771 novel *The Man of Feeling*, ed. Brian Vickers (Oxford, 1987). David Solkin's *Painting for Money* and John Barrell's, 'Sad stories: Louis XVI, George III, and the language of sentiment', in Kevin Sharpe and Steven N. Zwicker eds., *Refiguring Revolutions. Aesthetics and Politics from the English Revolution to the Romantic Revolution* (Berkeley CA, 1998) provide excellent accounts of the depiction of real-life sentimental heroes.

Histories of men and manhood

Given the considerable scholarly interest in representations of femininity and women's lives in polite society, it is perhaps surprising that little has been written about polite men and manliness. In part this gap is due to the, as yet, relatively under-developed state of histories of masculinity. Natalie Zemon Davis's groundbreaking call for histories of gender to incorporate men, '"Women's history" in transition: the European case', *Feminist Studies*, 3 (1975/6), pp. 83–103, has stimulated essays by Susan Dwyer Amussen, '"The part of a Christian man": the cultural politics of manhood in early modern England', in Amussen and Mark A. Kishlansky eds., *Political Culture and Cultural Politics in Early Modern England* (Manchester, 1995) and Alan Bray, 'To be a man in early modern society. The curious case of Michael Wrigglesworth', *History Workshop Journal*, 41 (1996), pp. 155–65. The work of John Tosh has been central to developing our understanding of nineteenth-century men's lives, notably within the domestic sphere. In addition to *A Man's Place. Masculinity and the Middle-Class Home in Victorian England* (New Haven CT and London, 1999), Michael Roper's and his 'Introduction' to their edited volume, *Manful Assertions: Masculinities in Britain since 1800* (1991) provides a valuable insight into the intellectual and methodological problems of writing a 'gendered history of men'. Alongside Tosh's work, Norman Vance's *The Sinews of the Spirit: The Ideal of Christian Manliness in Victorian Literature and Religious Thought* (Cambridge, 1985), and James Mangan and James Walvin eds., *Manliness and Morality: Middle-Class Masculinity in Britain and America, 1800–1940* (Manchester, 1987) examine the nineteenth-century themes of muscular Christianity and neo-stoicism.

The absence of specific studies of late-seventeenth- and eighteenth-century masculinity has recently been redressed by Elizabeth A. Foyster, *Manhood in Early Modern England: Honour, Sex and Marriage* (1999); Robert B. Shoemaker, *Gender in English Society, 1650–1850: The Emergence of Separate Spheres?* (1998); and essays in Tim Hitchcock and Michèle Cohen eds., *English Masculinities, 1660–1800* (1999). The impact of social refinement on eighteenth-century attitudes to manliness is considered in Anthony Fletcher's *Gender, Sex and Subordination in England, 1500–1800* (New Haven CT and London, 1995), Barker-Benfield's *Culture of Sensibility* and Cohen's *Fashioning Masculinity*, which also asks pertinent questions about the period's frequent application of the term 'effeminacy'.

Effeminacy and foppery

Cohen, like Alan Sinfield's *The Wilde Century: Effeminacy, Oscar Wilde and the Queer Moment* (1994), sees constructions of manliness as contingent less on relations with women than with other 'manly' and 'effeminate' men. In addition she seeks to problematise the definition of effeminacy as both a marker of men's social as well as sexual failings. The broader intellectual context for late-seventeenth- and eighteenth-century debates over standards of manliness is examined in essays in Istvan Hont and Michael Ignatieff eds., *Wealth and Virtue. The Shaping of Political Economy in the Scottish Enlightenment* (Cambridge, 1983) and Christopher J. Berry, *The Idea of Luxury. A Conceptual and Historical Investigation* (Cambridge, 1994). Eighteenth-century meanings of effeminacy are also considered in Philip Carter, 'An "effeminate" or "efficient" nation? Masculinity in eighteenth-century social documentary', *Textual Practice*, 11 (1997), pp. 429–43, which questions Randolph Trumbach's equation of effeminacy and effeminate stereotypes, such as the fop, with male homosexuality as set out in his two essays, 'The birth of the queen: sodomy and the emergence of gender equality in modern culture, 1660–1750', in Martin B. Duberman *et al.* eds., *Hidden from History: Reclaiming the Gay and Lesbian Past* (1991) and 'Sex, gender and sexual identity in modern culture: male sodomy and female prostitution in enlightenment England', in John C. Fout ed., *Forbidden History: The State, Society and the Regulation of Sexuality in Modern Europe* (Chicago IL and London, 1992).

The characteristics of the fop type are discussed in Robert B. Heilman, 'Some fops and some versions of foppery', *English Literary History*, 49 (1982), pp. 363–95, and J.L. Styan, *Restoration Comedy in Performance* (Cambridge, 1986); while Valerie Steele's 'The social and political significance of macaroni fashions', *Costume*, 19 (1985), pp. 94–109, and Miles Ogborn's 'Locating the macaroni: luxury, sexuality and vision in Vauxhall gardens', *Textual Practice*, 11 (1997), pp. 445–62, consider modifications to the type during the 1770s. The place of the fop type in debates concerning family relations is considered in Susan Staves, 'A few kind words for the fop', *Studies in English Literature, 1500–1900*, 22 (1982), pp. 413–28, while Philip Carter, 'Men about town: representations of foppery and masculinity in early eighteenth-century urban society', in Hannah Barker and Elaine Chalus eds., *Gender in Eighteenth-Century England: Roles, Representations and Responsibilities* (1997) explores its role in discussions of polite society. The links and differences between the eighteenth-century fop and early nineteenth-century dandy are set out by Ellen Moers in *The Dandy: From Brummell to Beerbohm* (1960) and Aileen Ribeiro's *The Art of Dress. Fashion in England and France, 1750–1820* (New Haven CT and London, 1995). Frank Felsenstein's *Anti-Semitic Stereotypes: A Paradigm of 'Otherness' in English Popular Culture, 1660–1830* (Baltimore MD and London, 1995), provides a helpful overview of modern theories of social stereotyping.

Polite and impolite personalities

Of the three individuals considered in Chapter Five, James Boswell has received the fullest treatment, with a two-volume biography by Frank A. Pottle, *James Boswell: The Earlier Years, 1740–1769* (1966) and Frank Brady, *James Boswell: The Later Years, 1769–1795* (1984). In the wake of the bicentenary of Boswell's *Life of Johnson* (1791), ed. Pat Rogers (Oxford, 1980), studies including Greg Clingham ed., *New Light on Boswell* (Cambridge, 1991) have brought the biographer out from Samuel Johnson's shadow. Much of this new work has concentrated on Boswell's self-fashioning as recounted in his journal, which is examined by Felicity A. Nussbaum, *The Autobiographical Subject: Gender and Ideology in Eighteenth-Century England* (Baltimore MD, 1989). Susan Manning focuses on hedonism and retribution in 'Boswell's pleasure, the pleasures of Boswell', *British Journal of Eighteenth-Century Studies*, 20 (1997), pp. 17–32, while Colby H. Kullman, examines self-presentation through speech in 'James Boswell and the art of conversation', in Kevin L. Cope ed., *Compendious Conversations: The Method of Dialogue in the Early Enlightenment* (New York, 1992). The formation of a personal gender identity is considered in David M. Weed's 'Sexual positions: men of pleasure, economy and dignity in Boswell's *London Journal*', *Eighteenth-Century Studies*, 31 (1997/8), pp. 215–34, and Philip Carter, 'James Boswell's manliness', in Hitchcock and Cohen eds., *English Masculinities*.

Of the two other memoirists, William Matthews provides a brief biography of Dudley Ryder in the introduction to *The Diary of Dudley Ryder, 1715–1716* (1932); material from Ryder's diary also appears in Margaret R. Hunt's *The Middling Sort: Commerce, Gender and the Family in England, 1680–1780* (Berkeley CA, 1996). Details on John Penrose's life are sketched in the introduction to his *Letters from Bath, 1766–1767*, eds. Brigitte Mitchell and Hubert Penrose (Gloucester, 1984). Penrose's comments also feature in Borsay's *English Urban Renaissance*, while his 'Image and counter-image in Georgian Bath', *British Journal of Eighteenth-Century Studies*, 17 (1994), pp. 165–79 and Girouard's *English Town* provide excellent surveys of the development of Bath as a polite resort.

Debating polite society

Biographical details of leading figures within the Moderate Church of Scotland are provided by Dwyer's *Virtuous Discourse* and Richard B. Sher's *Church and University in the Scottish Enlightenment: The Moderate Literati of Edinburgh* (Edinburgh, 1985). James Fordyce's brand of sentimental moralising comes in for brief, but sharp, criticism in Janet Todd's *The Sign of Angelica: Women, Writing and Fiction* (1989), while Knox is discussed more sympathetically in Robert W. Uphaus, 'Vicesimus Knox and the canon of eighteenth-century literature', in Paul Korshin ed., *The Age of Johnson*, 4 (1991), pp. 345–61. The bitter relationship of these and other writers with Lord Chesterfield is discussed in Roger Coxon, *Chesterfield and his Critics* (1925). Several recent studies, notably Michael Curtin, 'A question of manners: status and gender in etiquette and courtesy', *Journal of Modern History*, 57 (1985), pp. 395–423, and Paul Langford's *Public Life and the Propertied Englishman, 1689–1798* (Oxford, 1991), consider the ramifications of Chesterfield's *Letters to His Son* (1774) ed. David Roberts (Oxford, 1992) for popular images of aristocratic gentlemanliness in the late eighteenth century. A similarly critical exchange between Edmund Burke and Mary Wollstonecraft, again over the duplicity of refinement, is examined in Virginia Sapiro, *A Vindication of Political Virtue. The Political Theory of Mary Wollstonecraft* (1992); Susan Khin Zaw, ' "Appealing to head *and* heart": Wollstonecraft and Burke on taste, morals and human nature', in Gill Perry and Michael Rossington eds., *Femininity and Masculinity in Eighteenth-Century Art and Culture* (Manchester, 1994); and Claudia L. Johnson,

Equivocal Beings. Politics, Gender and Sentimentality in the 1790s (Chicago IL and London, 1995). Wollstonecraft herself also provided a résumé and critique of the work of Fordyce and Chesterfield in *A Vindication of the Rights of Woman* (1792), in *Political Writings*, ed. Janet Todd (Oxford, 1994).

Chesterfield's *Letters* are commonly identified as one of the final examples of the courtesy book genre which receives a detailed examination in John E. Mason, *Gentlefolk in the Making: Studies in the History of English Courtesy Literature and Related Topics from 1531 to 1774* (Philadelphia PA, 1935) and George C. Brauer, *The Education of a Gentleman: Theories of Gentlemanly Education in England, 1660–1775* (New York, 1959). In the wake of new research it appears that throughout the period, writers of courtesy literature were also required to compete with contributors to a more egalitarian and morally vigorous conduct book tradition. Discussions of this latter genre can be found in, among others, Shoemaker, *Gender in English Society*; Hunt, *The Middling Sort*; Nancy Armstrong, 'The rise of the domestic woman', in her and Leonard Tennenhouse eds., *The Ideology of Conduct* (1987); and Marjorie Morgan, *Manners, Morals and Class in England, 1774–1858* (Basingstoke, 1994). Morgan argues for an early-nineteenth-century reaction to the morality of conduct literature in the shape of the etiquette guide which provided a new readership with detailed advice on the negotiation of 'society', a subject also considered by Michael Curtin, 'A question of manners'. Two final titles, *How to Be a Perfect Gentleman: A Handbook of Etiquette and Guide to Polite Society* (1989), a work of social education; and Janet Holmes's *Women, Men and Politeness* (1995), a study in sociolinguistics, reveal the continuing interest in issues of social behaviour and gender formation at the close of the twentieth century.

INDEX

Achilles, 108
Addison, Joseph, 24, 34, 36, 57, 58–68, 102, 126, 170–1, 185, 186, 193
affectation, 126–8, 167–8, 170–1
alcohol, 65–6, 83 fn39, 194
Allestree, Richard, 32, 44, 60
Amussen, Susan, 71
Angiers, Samuel, 42
Anstey, Christopher, 181
Armstrong, Nancy, 33

Bath, 15, 18, 19, 38, 138, 175–83
  prostitution at, 182
  reputation for effeminacy, 181–2
  reputation for politeness, 175–6
  routines/dress at, 176–7
  see also Nash, Richard 'Beau'; Penrose, John
Barker-Benfield, G.J., 8, 24–5
Barrell, John, 131
bathing, 177–8
Bellegarde, Jean-Baptiste, 17–18, 21, 25–6, 62, 68, 69, 75
Bentinck, John, 110
blackguards, 135–7, 195–6, 214
  see also fops; gallants; macaronis
Blackstone, William, 17
Blair, Hugh, 28–9, 44, 92–3, 96, 107, 108
Blakeney, William, 110
Borsay, Peter, 38
Boswell, James, 40, 58, 65–6, 183–201, 209
  background and education, 183
  and conversation, 186–8
  describes Samuel Johnson, 1, 18, 93, 152, 187–8
  and dress, 186, 195–6
  and 'easiness', 188–9
  on English politeness, 185–6, 189
  on London, 185, 189
  in Lowland Scotland, 186, 189, 193–4

  and manliness, 184, 187, 188, 193, 195–6
  on polite society, 17
  and politeness, 184–90
  at public executions, 192–3
  reading habits of, 185, 190
  relations with father, 185, 190
  relations with women, 190–1, 195
  rudeness of, 193–7
  on Scottish Highlands, 1, 3–4
  and self-criticism, 187, 191, 194–5
  and sensibility, 190–3, 195
  and *The Spectator*, 185, 190
  and stoicism/self-control, 187, 192–3
  and weeping, 190, 191
Boswell, Margaret Montgomerie, 191
Boyer, Abel, 20, 22, 57, 59, 65, 79, 154
boys, advice on social conduct, 54–5, 56, 63, 95
Braithwait, Richard, 60
Bray, Alan, 160 fn68
Brewer, John, 28, 34, 52 fn97, 198
Brutus, 104, 109, 120 fn57
Bryson, Anna, 7, 11, 22, 34–5, 55, 127, 197
Burke, Edmund, 111–14, 123 fn101, 126, 128
  Reflections on the Revolution in France (1790), 111–14
Burke, Peter, 62
Burney, Fanny, 88–9
Burrow, J.W., 214
Butler, Samuel, 140, 154

Casa, Giovanni della, 33, 56
  Il Galateo (1558), 33, 50 fn64, 56, 132
Castiglione, Baldassare, 63, 67, 127
  Il libro del Cortegiano (1528), 33, 55–6, 58
Caulfield, John, 137
ceremony, 62, 125–6, 167
  see also affectation; politeness